W9-COS-574

The Russian Research Center

The Russian Research Center of Harvard University is supported by a grant from the Carnegie Corporation. The Center carries out interdisciplinary study of Russian institutions and behavior.

Russian Research Center Studies

1. *Public Opinion in Soviet Russia: A Study in Mass Persuasion*, by Alex Inkeles
2. *Soviet Politics — The Dilemma of Power: The Role of Ideas in Social Change*, by Barrington Moore, Jr.
3. *Justice in Russia: An Interpretation of Soviet Law*, by Harold J. Berman
4. *Chinese Communism and the Rise of Mao*, by Benjamin I. Schwartz
5. *Titoism and the Cominform*, by Adam Ulam
6. *Documentary History of Chinese Communism*, by Conrad Brandt, Benjamin Schwartz, and John K. Fairbank
7. *The New Man in Soviet Psychology*, by Raymond A. Bauer
8. *Soviet Opposition to Stalin: A Case Study in World War II*, by George Fischer
9. *Minerals: A Key to Soviet Power*, by Demitri B. Shimkin
10. *Soviet Law in Action: The Recollected Cases of a Soviet Lawyer*, by Harold J. Berman and Boris A. Konstantinovsky
11. *How Russia Is Ruled*, by Merle Fainsod
12. *Terror and Progress USSR: Some Sources of Change and Stability in the Soviet Dictatorship*, by Barrington Moore, Jr.
13. *The Formation of the Soviet Union: Communism and Nationalism, 1917–1923*, Richard E. Pipes
14. *Marxism: The Unity of Theory and Practice*, Alfred G. Meyer
15. *Soviet Industrial Production, 1928–1951*, Donald R. Hodgman

Soviet Industrial Production

1928–1951

DONALD R. HODGMAN

Harvard University Press · Cambridge

1954

Distributed in Great Britain by
Geoffrey Cumberlege
Oxford University Press, London

This volume was prepared under a grant from the Carnegie Corporation of New York. That Corporation is not, however, the author, owner, publisher, or proprietor of this publication and is not to be understood as approving by virtue of its grant any of the statements made or views expressed therein.

Grateful acknowledgment is made to Naum Jasny and Stanford University Press for permission to quote from The Soviet Price System, *copyright 1951 by the Board of Trustees of Leland Stanford Junior University.*

Library of Congress Catalog Card Number 54–3629
Printed in the United States of America

to

Naomi

Preface

This book by Professor Donald Hodgman is the first in a series of studies on the Soviet economy undertaken at the Russian Research Center at Harvard. It is hoped that within a year five or six additional books in this series will be in print. Thus a long gestation period which began some six years ago is coming to an end. The present moment, therefore, seems propitious for restating briefly some of the principles that have in the past guided the direction of these studies.

The economic work at the Center did not start from a *tabula rasa.* Quite the contrary. At the end of the last war the appropriate shelves at the Widener Library, to say nothing of the Library of Congress, contained, along with Soviet publications, long ranks of books on the Soviet economy produced by Western writers. A very large body of literature dealing with all or nearly all branches of the Soviet economy had been created. Unfortunately, the quantity of that material was more impressive than its quality. It seems fair to say that *with a few very notable exceptions*, the level of economic and statistical analysis was rather low. It is true that many useful facts had been patiently assembled. But it is equally true that very often the potentially most important facts were disregarded because in the absence of an analytical framework their significance was not properly recognized. The truth of the matter was that, for long years, Western professional economists and statisticians had failed to pay much attention to the problems of the Soviet economy. To repeat, there were most significant exceptions, but they seemed to prove rather than to disprove the rule.

It is this situation that essentially determined the first basic decision with regard to the economic work at the Center. That work was to be done by people who, preferably as students at American universities, had received a thorough training in economics and statistics. They had to be first of all professional economists. The task of the Center was then to induce such men to acquire in addition the special skills and knowledge which would transform them into experts on the Soviet economy. This was a serious decision. It implied that a long time of preparation and growth would elapse before fruition could be expected. It would have been easy, and it was tempting, to follow another course, and to see every year a number of "quickies" added to the existing literature. But the temptation was resisted and now, in retrospect, there seems to be little reason to regret the fact.

The second basic decision related to the *type* of economic study to be prepared at the Center. Conceivably, one might have aimed at a comprehensive coverage of postwar economic developments in Soviet Russia. This would have required organizing a group of people united in close teamwork. If successful, such an approach, after a number of years, might have resulted in the appearance of a periodical publication designed to serve as an information bulletin on the Soviet economy. There would have been some merit to such a decision. On the other hand, so to arrange the Center's economic effort would have tended to duplicate the work carried on in various government agencies in Washington. In addition, and no less important was the fact that such a program of group research might have failed to attract to the Center men of keen and creative minds, that is to say, self-reliant individuals who, although benefiting from informal association with the other members of a loose group, work best when left free from the trammels of teamwork.

Finally, it had to be considered that gaps in our knowledge of Soviet economic developments called, above all, for patient basic research, particularly on the period of the 'thirties when the flow of Soviet economic data had been most abundant or rather least restricted. Only on the basis of thorough investigations of this and earlier periods was it possible to gain firm footholds for approaching present-day Soviet economy.

The sum total of these considerations resulted in the adoption of the principle that each of the economists at the Center should engage in the preparation of an independent monographic study. The theme of each of these studies should be one of broad significance for the understanding of Soviet economic processes but at the same time it should be sufficiently confined to allow a good deal of penetration into the depths of the available material. That, perforce, meant primary reliance on the decade of the 1930's. Naturally, the Center undertook to guide the individuals concerned in the selection of the subjects of study, but it remained clearly understood that no member of the group should choose a topic unless he felt that it genuinely excited his instinct of scholarly inquiry.

It must be left to the readers of this series to judge the extent to which the studies that have been prepared provide a sufficient justification for the general principles just described. But it may be in order to suggest that the present study by Donald Hodgman supplies, perhaps, the clearest illustration for the application of those principles.

The construction of an independent index of Soviet industrial output was precisely one of the badly neglected tasks in the field of research on the Soviet economy. It had been recognized for some time, thanks to the work of Prokopovicz, Jasny and others, that the official Soviet index of industrial output at 1926–27 prices contained a gross upward bias which made it a very unreliable gauge of Soviet industrial growth. But to criticize the Soviet index effectively was one thing, — to provide a substitute measure of industrial growth quite another. Clearly the latter was an enterprise that would require an enormous effort. One of the distinctive features of the present study is the fact that its author remained undeterred by the stupendous magnitude of the task which simply could not have been completed without unswerving devotion and persistence. To be sure, Mr. Hodgman might have been provided with a staff of helpers who would have collected figures and made computations for him. That could easily have been arranged. Yet, apart from some assistance in checking references and computations, the study now presented to the reader is one man's job. And that is how it should be. Only in this way, by maintaining at all times immediate contact with his raw material, can an author in the Soviet economic field properly appraise the importance and the limitations of his results. Only in this way can he present his conclusions with confidence and conviction. The Russian Research Center has made this study possible. But it was most important at the same time to resist the temptations which are present in organized research. Creative and responsible research cannot be done in groups except in rare cases and most of the time at some cost to the quality of the product. This principle has been followed throughout in the studies of the present series.

However great was the author's enthusiasm for the self-chosen task and the industry applied in carrying it through to successful termination, these qualities alone would never have sufficed. What was needed was a creative idea. It was a happy moment when it occurred to Mr. Hodgman that an independent index of Soviet industrial output could be constructed by using as weights Soviet data on wage pay rolls in the individual industrial branches. This was a simple solution to the problem, but ingenious innovations once formulated usually appear to be simple indeed.

It is in this sense that Mr. Hodgman's study provides, at least to this writer's mind, an encouraging corroboration of the validity of the general principles sketched out in the foregoing. The statistical data which Mr. Hodgman decided to use as the basis for the construction of his index had been known for a long time. But it required the penetrating eye of a trained economist and statistician to breathe life into the figures and put them to constructive use. The Soviet officials who had included a tabulation of these figures in their statistical handbook hardly had any inkling of what imaginative research could do with them. If they had suspected that, with the help of these data, an index would be prepared which would be free from the exaggerations inherent in the official Soviet index, they might have thought twice before permitting publication of these figures.

What we have now as a result of Donald Hodgman's work is a picture of the speed of Soviet industrialization in the crucial period of the 'thirties, which probably is as reliable a measurement as can be made of the rate of growth of an economy in the process of rapid economic change. It is a particular advantage of this method that indigenous magnitudes have been used as weights. By avoiding the use of weights pertaining to some non-Russian economy (such as dollar prices and so on) Mr. Hodgman succeeded in creating a relatively firm base for viewing the rate of industrial growth in Russia in terms of its own development. The importance of such a study cannot be over-rated. It elucidates a most important period of Soviet economic history. It shows that what remains after exaggerations and distortions are removed is an annual rate of industrial growth in the 'thirties of some 14 per cent, which is, of course, a very high rate by any standard. But, transcending its historical significance, is the fact that without Mr. Hodgman's study we should be unable to deal at all with such a grave question as that which confronts us now. When we view the present development of Soviet industry, the question uppermost in our minds is whether or not some signs of retardation in that process have become evident. Does Soviet industry still grow at the same rate as it did in the fourth decade of the century or has that growth been foreslowed? This is obviously a question of the greatest possible moment. Mr. Hodgman's study has provided a basis of comparison which makes it possible for us to essay an answer.*

Perhaps one more comment is in order. The field of Soviet economic research is an eminently controversial one. In addition, Soviet data are frequently so incomplete and so misleading that the greatest care must be exercised in processing and interpretation. More than in any other field of research, the rule of the scholar in Soviet economic research must be to give the reader as full an opportunity as is humanly possible to follow the writer's use of the original data. This perforce involves publication of extensive appendices. While the reader may resent being burdened with masses of statistical detail, he should consider that without such documentation he would neither be able to form an independent judgment of the validity of the conclusions nor even be in a position to appreciate the methods used.

The progress that has been achieved over the past decade in the American study of the Soviet economy is remarkable indeed. Professor Abram Bergson's studies on Soviet national income, following his earlier study of Soviet wages, Mr. Naum Jasny's *magnum opus* on Soviet agriculture and his computation of Soviet price indices, the various studies prepared by economists at the Rand Corporation in California — all these, along with others, have greatly advanced our knowledge and understanding of the Soviet economy. Perhaps it does not seem presumptuous to express the hope that the Russian Research Center series of economic studies, beginning with the present book, will come to be regarded as a significant contribution to the growing body of serious literature on the Soviet economy.

Alexander Gerschenkron

Harvard University

* It is true that thanks to Mr. Jasny's important contributions a rate of growth for Russian industry in terms of the 1926–27 prices is now available. It would seem, however, that because of the remote base period used by Mr. Jasny, the main merit of his computations was to provide for the first time a quantitative expression for the degree of distortion in the official Soviet index.

Acknowledgments

This study was conceived and the broad outlines of its development were established during my tenure for three years of a fellowship from the Russian Research Center, Harvard University. It has been completed at the University of California, where my appointment as research associate in the Institute of Slavic Studies has relieved me from a portion of my teaching duties in the Department of Economics. It is a pleasure to acknowledge the generous assistance of both organizations.

I owe a special debt of gratitude to Professor Alexander Gerschenkron, who has been a kindly guide and critic of both author and study for the past five years. His stimulating criticism and generous encouragement have been of major assistance in seeing the task through to completion.

Many colleagues have given me much help from their specialized knowledge of various aspects of the Russian economy and have more than once rescued me from my own defects and enthusiasms. To Drs. Joseph Berliner, Alexander Erlich, Walter Galenson, Gregory Grossman, Franklyn Holzman, and Demitri Shimkin go my sincere thanks and appreciation.

Professor Clyde Kluckhohn, Director of the Russian Research Center, and Mrs. Helen Parsons, Administrative Assistant to the Director, consistently gave sympathetic attention to special administrative problems encountered on the way and to my requests for clerical and computational assistance. At the University of California I have had the expert clerical assistance of the staff of the Bureau of Business and Economic Research.

Helen Constantine skillfully typed the appendix tables from my original work sheets, and Jean LeCorbeiller performed a large number of the computations set forth in the appendix with a stern eye to the number of significant places to which I was entitled.

Grateful acknowledgment is made to Row, Peterson and Company, Evanston, Illinois, for use of excerpts from articles by James Blackman and Walter Galenson, and for extensive use of my own article on industrial output in *Soviet Economic Growth*, edited by Abram Bergson; to Naum Jasny and the Stanford University Press for permission to quote from *The Soviet Price System*; to The Rand Corporation for use of Alexander Gerschenkron, *A Dollar Index of Soviet Machinery Output, 1927–28 to 1937*, and of Warren Eason, *Trends and Prospects of the Soviet Population and Labor Force*; to the author, Macmillan & Company Ltd., and St. Martin's Press, Inc., for permission to quote from Colin Clark, *Conditions of Economic Progress*, 2d edition; to *The American Slavic and East European Review* for use of my review article, "Soviet Machinery Output," which appeared in February 1953; and to Harvard University Press for permission to quote from D. B. Shimkin, *Minerals — A Key to Soviet Power*, from Abram Bergson, *The Structure of Soviet Wages*, and for extensive use of my article, "A New Production Index for Soviet Industry," which appeared in *The Review of Economics and Statistics* for November 1950.

My wife, Naomi Hodgman, has been an unfailing source of support and encouragement and has contributed much to the successful completion of the study by her cheerful acceptance of an increasing share of our common responsibilities as the study's demands on my time increased.

Donald R. Hodgman

Berkeley, California
June 1953

Contents

Charts

Tables

IN ADDENDUM

IN APPENDICES

IN TABULAR SECTION

1

Official Measures of Soviet Industrial Production

The volume of industrial output is one of the most significant general measures of the strength of an economy, and its change over time, especially when related to the change in other economic magnitudes, such as the size of the population or the industrial labor force, provides an important indication of the effectiveness of an economic system. For this reason Soviet industrial growth has become in recent years the object of keen interest and careful scrutiny. Soviet industrial production is of interest not only as a gauge of the economic and potential military-industrial strength of one of the world's great powers, but also as part of the evidence to be considered in weighing the relative merits of planned versus free-enterprise economic systems. Many of the economically underdeveloped areas of the world are impressed by the Soviet achievement of rapid industrial development, and are considering the applicability of the Soviet model of industrialization to their own economic development. These are some of the issues which make desirable a careful appraisal of Soviet industrial growth.

Proper evaluation of the record of Soviet industrial production is complicated by known technical deficiencies in the over-all value statistics for industrial production which have been published by the Soviet government and by the increasing paucity of the more detailed physical production data which the Soviet government has seen fit to release for publication. Interest has centered primarily on the value aggregates as measures broadly descriptive of the total volume of industrial production and the trends in its development over the years. The balance of this chapter is devoted to a discussion and critique of the official measures of the value of Soviet industrial output.

Soviet Indices of Industrial Production

There are four principal published value series for Soviet industrial output (Table 1). The most comprehensive of these includes the output of *all industry* (state, coöperative, and private). It is the only index published since 1938. Prior to 1938, however, this index was not regularly reproduced in Soviet publications. Values for selected years prior to 1938 were brought to light by Naum Jasny only after careful examination of Soviet source materials.

TABLE 1
Official Measures of the Value of Soviet Industrial Production, 1928–1938 (billion 1926–27 rubles)

Year	All industry	State and coöperative industry	Large-scale industry	Census industry
1928	21.8	18.0	16.9	15.8
1929	25.7	23.0	21.2	19.9
1930	—	—	27.7	25.8
1931	—	38.6	34.2	32.3
1932	43.5	43.3	38.8	36.9
1933	45.7	—	42.0	39.9
1934	—	—	50.5	48.2
1935	67.9	—	62.1	59.5
1936	85.6	—	80.9	78.0
1937	95.4	—	90.2	87.0
1938	106.1	—	100.4	—

SOURCES — All industry: N. Jasny, *The Soviet Price System* (Stanford University Press, 1951), p. 172; State and Coöperative Industry: TsUNKhU, *Sotsialisticheskoe stroitel'stvo SSSR* (Socialist Construction USSR; Moscow, 1934), p. 24; Large-scale Industry: N. Jasny, *The Soviet Price System*, p. 172; Census Industry: 1928–1934, TsUNKhU, *Sotsialistischeskoe stroitel'stvo SSSR* (Socialist Construction USSR; Moscow, 1936), pp. xxii–xxiii; 1935–1937 computed by applying percentage increases from 1934 as given in Ia. A. Ioffe, *SSSR i kapitalisticheskie strany* (USSR and the Capitalist Countries; Gosplanizdat; Moscow, 1939), p. 127.

The next most comprehensive of the official indices is that for the output of all *state and coöperative industry* published apparently only during the First Five Year Plan years. The omission of the output of private industry from this index exaggerates the increase in industrial production from 1928 to later years, since private industry was being absorbed rapidly by state and coöperative industry. Most private industry had been absorbed by 1932. One Soviet source places the share of private industry in the value of total industrial output at 1926–27 prices at 10.5 per cent in 1929 and at 0.5 per cent in 1932 and later years.[1]

A similar criticism applies to the output series for *large-scale industry* available for the years 1928–1938.[2] This series omits not only private industry but small-scale state and coöperative industry as well. Large-scale industry expanded rapidly after 1928, partly by absorbing small-scale industry, while the output of small-scale industry declined in absolute terms. Thus the index for large-scale industry creates an exaggerated impression of total industrial expansion.

The coverage of a fourth series, so-called *census industry*, is similar to that for large-scale industry save for the omission of fisheries, lumbering, and railway repair shops. The census industry series was computed for purposes of comparison with industrial output in Imperial Russia in 1913 and apparently has not been published since 1937.

All of the official historical series for Soviet industrial production represent gross output rather than net output or value-added. A gross measure of industrial output depends not only on changes in the physical volume of production but also on changes in the organizational structure of industry. As the degree of combination or integration of industrial units increases, the number of independent accounting units decreases, and with it there occurs a relative decline in the gross value of industrial output. A reverse trend in the organization of industry, a greater splitting-up of industrial units, produces an artificial increase in the value of gross output. These considerations are of special significance in the case of Russian industry.

The entire course of industrial development in the Soviet Union has been an extremely turbulent one. The reconstruction of industry during the period of the New Economic Policy of the years 1921–1927 was followed by the extremely rapid industrialization drive of the first three five year plans, and this in turn by the conversion of the economy to war and then the reconversion to peace during the 1940's. Under such conditions the amount of reorganization of industrial enterprises which took place was considerable. Organizational changes occurred both under the impact of technological change, which proceeded at a rate without precedent, and for reasons of administrative efficiency.

The tractor industry provides one such example.[3] In the fiscal year 1926–27 the fully integrated tractor factory "Krasnyi Putilovets" produced 700 tractors. These were included in the gross output of industry at their full wholesale price. By 1931 the production of tractors by the same plant had increased to several tens of thousands. The full value of these tractors was likewise included in the gross output of industry. Between 1926–27 and 1931, however, the production of tractors in the "Krasnyi Putilovets" plant had ceased to be a fully integrated operation and, in fact, the main plant was receiving subassemblies from 16 subplants whose output was likewise included in the total gross output for that industry. The Soviet writer does not indicate the degree of exaggeration thus introduced into the gross output measure of the tractor industry.

There were, of course, instances of an opposite nature. The same Soviet writer indicates, for example, that the electrical industry became much more highly integrated under the Soviet system than it had been prior to World War I.[4]

No quantitative estimates of the net effect of these organizational changes are available. Soviet industrial administration has been characterized by strong pressure of rewards and punishments on plant managers and higher officials in the pyramid of industrial administration to fulfill and surpass ambitious production goals. In these circumstances the use of a gross measure of industrial output may have introduced a systematic bias in favor of splitting rather than integrating industrial establishments whenever there was room for choice.

Accounting reorganization may have been of even greater importance in introducing bias, since an increase in the number of independent reporting units served the purpose of inflating output totals as well as physical reorganization and was much more readily accomplished. Thus the following complaint appeared in a Soviet planning journal in late 1934.

> The current practice of several branches of industry is to show separately in the plan for gross output at prices of 1926–27 the production of a number of shops which are not independent enterprises [for example, the refractory material shops of a steel mill]. The procedure has been preserved even until 1935. The list of shops the production of which should be included in gross output should be established by the commissariats in their instructions to the branches of industry and should be worked out on the basis of current regulations and in conformity with Gosplan.[5]

While no quantitative estimates of the distortions introduced into gross output measures of Soviet industrial production by organizational changes in production and accounting are available, it is likely that these are much less important sources of bias than distortions arising from the methods of valuation of industrial output adopted in Soviet statistical practice.

Valuation of Soviet Industrial Output[6]

All products entering the gross value of Soviet industrial production are valued, theoretically, at average wholesale prices of the fiscal year 1926–27. Uniform lists of 1926–27 commodity prices were not prepared, however, until the year 1936. Thus, during the years prior to 1936, separate industries and even separate enterprises had their own individual lists of 1926–27 prices at which they valued their output. As a result, identical commodities entered the production index at different values. Thus, with changes in the relative share of different plants from different regions in the total output of a particular commodity, the value measure of gross output also changed, but without any necessary accompanying change in total physical quantity of the commodity.

More important in its effect on the official indices than the lack of uniformity in prices of identical goods was the problem of pricing goods which, for various reasons, had no real 1926–27 price. This problem was encountered, both in pricing commodities which had not been produced at all in the year 1926–27 and in pricing semi-fabricated and unfinished goods which, though produced in 1926–27, had not been sold on the market in that year.

To meet this problem the Central Statistical Administration of the Soviet government issued instructions with regard to approved methods of calculating substitute 1926–27 prices. *Finished goods* for which no actual 1926–27 prices were available were to be valued at the average price f.o.b. factory of the first three months during which they were in production or, alternatively, at the price which prevailed at the time the new products entered mass production.[7] *Semi-fabricated and unfinished goods* for which no 1926–27 prices were available were to be valued at cost in terms of wholesale prices f.o.b. factory of the current year. Thus, "1926–27 prices" for new products and for semi-fabricated and unfinished goods were actually current year prices. Whether or not this introduced a bias into the official statistics for value of industrial output, and in what direction, depended upon prices and productivity of the factors of production in the current year relative to 1926–27. Increased factor costs not offset by increased productivity resulted in artificial inflation of the official value aggregates and vice versa. Some indirect evidence on this problem is examined below.

Finally, until 1936 or 1937, attempts to compute the value of output at 1926–27 prices were confined largely to enterprises under the administrative supervision of the industrial commissariats. A number of organizations such as the industrial coöperatives and some government departments including the People's Commissariats for Water Transportation and for Communications reported output, either in prices of the year 1932 or in current prices. Some of this output apparently was omitted from total gross output, but the bulk was included after conversion to 1926–27 prices by means of general price coefficients.[8]

1936 Reform in Valuation Procedures

To correct these defects the Central Statistical Administration, in coöperation with the industrial commissariats and government administrative departments, undertook in 1935 a general review of 1926–27 prices and in 1936 issued uniform, country-wide lists of these prices for established products, publishing new instructions for calculating substitute prices for new products, semi-fabricates, and repair work. In revising the 1926–27 prices greater allowance was made for differences in style and quality of different goods; prices of finished goods were brought into line with prices of their component materials or parts, and prices of identical goods were made uniform in all producing regions.

Prices for *new products* and *new models* were to be set by the enterprises themselves according to instructions specific to each branch of industry. Constant prices for new goods were to be based on current prices converted to 1926–27 prices by use of coefficients presented in the price handbooks. In the absence of special instructions, new goods were to be valued at current wholesale supply prices, and these values were then converted to values of the year 1926–27 according to the relation of current to constant prices for similar commodities as given in the price handbooks. New prices calculated in this way by the individual enterprises were to be submitted on June first of each year to the respective commissariats which, in turn, submitted them to the Central Statistical Administration (at this time called the Central Administration of National-Economic Accounting) which then compiled and published an approved, official, and uniform list of new prices for the guidance of all enterprises.

The valuation of repair work at 1926–27 prices presented formidable problems. Since repair work does not result in finished goods for sale, there were no market prices for it in 1926–27. To the extent that repair work can be resolved into standard, constituent operations, it might have been possible for Soviet statisticians to work out 1926–27 costs for these operations from accounting records. Alternatively, the 1926–27 cost data might have served as the basis for computing coefficients by which current costs could have been converted to 1926–27 levels. Soviet authorities apparently judged both of these alternatives to be impractical. Instead, enterprises were directed to value repair work at its *planned* costs of production for the current year.

Semi-fabricated and unfinished goods for which no 1926–27 prices were available were to be valued at cost in terms of wholesale prices f.o.b. factory of the current year and then converted to 1926–27 values by one of the following methods. If 1926–27 prices were available for subsidiary parts of the unfinished goods, physical units established by inventory were to be valued at these prices. Or, coefficients to convert current costs to 1926–27 prices were to be calculated by comparing the value of appropriate finished goods produced during the last three months and valued at current costs with the value of the same finished goods in 1926–27 prices. Conversion coefficients might be calculated for individual articles, groups of articles, or the output of entire industries, depending on the technical conditions of production and the availability of the necessary cost, price, and production data. When a physical inventory of production of unfinished goods was not feasible, bookkeeping records were to be used to obtain a measure of unfinished goods production at current costs. This value was then to be converted to 1926–27 prices by means of a conversion coefficient calculated from the price and cost relationship of finished goods.

Effects of 1936 Reform

While the 1936 reform of valuation procedures may have represented an improvement on theoretical grounds, the resulting improvement in practice was attenuated by shortcomings in application. It had been foreseen, for example, that the revised system of 1926–27 prices would call for revision of the production totals for previous years to make them comparable to the totals for 1936.[9] This revision was to be made not by recalculation of the earlier totals but by applying a general correction coefficient to the over-all totals. The coefficient was to be based on a comparison of output totals for 1936 calculated in revised 1926–27 prices and in the unrevised 1926–27 prices used in composing the plan for 1935. The annual plan for 1936 is calculated in the revised 1926–27 prices, but carries completely unrevised output totals for earlier years. To the best of the writer's knowledge no revised output figures for these earlier years have ever been published.

Moreover, the revised system of 1926–27 prices preserved one of the major defects of the unrevised 1926–27 prices. The revised 1926–27 prices for most of those finished goods which had not actually been produced in 1926–27 were taken from that later year when the goods first entered production. Thus even after the 1936 reform the official "1926–27 prices" for many finished goods were, in fact, the prices of years later than 1926–27.[10] Since current-constant price relatives for established products served as the basis for converting current costs or prices of new products, semi-fabricated goods, and unfinished goods to "1926–27" levels, in effect this procedure frequently converted current prices of these products to price levels of other years than 1926–27. Thus the 1936 reform failed to secure the desired temporal homogeneity of 1926–27 prices.

There were other practical difficulties. Standard conversion coefficients calculated from 1935 to 1926–27 price relatives became obsolete within a year but frequently were applied without change in later years as well. Finally, in practice, the instructions of the Central Statistical Administration often were disregarded.[11] Products for which actual 1926–27 prices were not available, especially unfinished goods and semi-fabricates, simply were valued at the annual average price of the year when they first were produced, with no attempt to convert these values to correspond with the price level of the year 1926–27.

Bias in the Official Production Statistics

The extent and direction of the bias introduced into the official production statistics by these defects in valuation procedure depend on the proportion of total output valued in current prices as opposed to actual 1926–27 prices and the relation of current to constant prices.

(*a*) *Output valued at current rather than constant prices.* Some quantitative evidence as to the proportion of total output valued at current prices is supplied by A. I. Rotshtein, a Soviet economist. Table 2 taken from

Rotshtein's book, *Problemy promyshlennoi statistiki SSSR* (Problems of Industrial Statistics of the USSR), shows the gross output of the industry of four industrial commissariats in the Leningrad *oblast* in the years 1932 and 1934, both at prices of the current year and at constant prices of the

TABLE 2

Value of Gross Output of Selected Industries of the Leningrad Region at Current and Constant Prices

Year	Value at current prices (millions of rubles)	Value at constant prices (millions of rubles)	Ratio of value at constant prices to value at current prices (per cent)
1932	4,567.6	4,522.0	99.00
1934	5,067.4	5,065.0	99.95

SOURCE — A. I. Rotshtein, *Problemy promyshlennoi statistiki SSSR,* I, 246.

year 1926–27. The column of percentages at the extreme right of the table is calculated by dividing the value of output in constant prices by the value of output in current prices. The difference between the two measures of gross output of industry does not exceed 1 per cent in either year! Rotshtein provides a simple explanation for the virtual identity of the two measures:

> Both in 1932 and in 1933 there was a significant change in the nomenclature and assortment of the products of Leningrad industry. For this reason a significant part of total production expressed in constant prices consisted of new products which, therefore, were valued in prices of the current or preceding year. As a result the relationship of constant and current prices was so close to unity that those which deviated from this relationship might be successfully and completely ignored.[12]

In short, the constant and current prices for new products were one and the same, and new products predominated in the output of the Leningrad region.

How typical of all industrial production in the Soviet Union was the experience of Leningrad industry? The value of output at constant prices of 1926–27 of the industry of the four industrial commissariats in the Leningrad region in 1934 was exactly 10 per cent of the total output of all large-scale industry in that year and 11.6 per cent in 1932.[13] Some idea of the representativeness of this sample may be obtained from the data for 1935.[14] The share of Leningrad industry in total industrial output in 1935 was most important in the production of electrical power by regional stations, peat, oil shale, metalworking (including machinery), paper, leather footwear, and fishing. Unfortunately, the composition of the *value* of industrial output in the Leningrad oblast in 1935 cannot be determined from the quoted table, since data are in physical units for all industries except metalworking.

In the machinery industry the introduction of new products occurred at a more intensive rate than in any other branch of Soviet industry. In 1932 the value of output of the Leningrad metalworking industry (mainly machinery) was 1,930.7 million rubles,[15] or about 43 per cent of the value of output of the four industrial commissariats in that year. Value of metalworking production in the Leningrad oblast is not available for 1934. In 1935, the metalworking industry of the Leningrad oblast produced output valued at 2,785.0 million rubles. If an interpolated figure of 2,358.0 million rubles is taken as an approximation to the value of metalworking production in 1934, metalworking in that year accounted for about 46 per cent of the value of industrial production of the four industrial commissariats. The share of the metalworking industry in the value at 1926–27 prices of total output for all large-scale industry in the Soviet Union in 1934 was 27 per cent. Since metalworking was proportionally more important in industry of the Leningrad oblast than in Soviet industry as a whole, the amount of new product bias in country-wide production totals may be presumed to have been less than in those for the Leningrad oblast.

From the proportions of metalworking output to total output in the Leningrad oblast in 1932 and 1934 and the identity of value aggregates of production in both current and constant prices, it is clear that the identity of current and constant prices must have been pronounced in other lines of production as well as in metalworking, that is, the metalworking industry was not the only source of new product bias. It would be rash, however, to generalize from the evidence afforded by the Leningrad oblast to the conclusion that a similar identity in current and constant prices prevailed throughout all industry. Special conditions of product change and development must have held in the Leningrad oblast. Nevertheless, the evidence afforded by the comparisons of the values of output at current and constant prices of industry of the Leningrad oblast indicates clearly that a quantitatively important portion of industrial output was in fact valued at current prices.

The extent of this practice has been appraised by a Soviet economist writing in 1948:

> It is necessary to recognize that constant prices are largely conventional. For, to give an example, the relative weight of new production in the machinery producing industry is extremely high and as the machinery prices are computed on the basis of projected or budgetary cost of output of the given year, these prices, despite the use of correction coefficients, differ little in the majority of cases from prices of current years.[16]

This point may be illustrated further by evidence taken from the *State Plan for Economic Development of the USSR in 1941*. This document, which was intended only for restricted internal circulation in the Soviet Union, is unique among published sources for its presentation of the value of industrial production in both current prices and "constant 1926–27 prices" as well as at current costs of production. These materials have already been reproduced and commented on by Gerschenkron and Jasny, so that it will suffice to summarize findings and conclusions.[17]

Aggregate value of the planned output of machinery and military products at costs of production was only 1.5 per cent above the value at "constant 1926–27 prices," while for fourteen other major branches of industry the difference between the two values was 127 per cent. Machinery and military production accounted for 43 per cent of total production of these branches of industry at "constant 1926–27 prices" but only 25.2 per cent at costs of production.

The close resemblance of constant prices to current costs of production is most clearly discernible for machinery and military products because of the great predominance of new products in these lines. The phenomenon, however, is not limited to machinery and military products but occurs to some degree with all new products. Therefore, the 127 per cent difference between value at cost and at constant prices of the production of the fourteen other main branches of industry must not be interpreted as a gauge of developments in the general level of industrial costs or prices from 1926–27 to 1941.

(*b*) *Price movements from 1926–27*. Whether the substitution of current for constant prices for a considerable portion of the products of Soviet industry introduced any systematic bias into Soviet statistics of industrial production depends on the relation of current to constant prices. If current prices were higher than constant prices, their use had an inflationary effect on output totals and vice versa. A comparison of current prices with actual 1926–27 prices is impossible for any entirely new product. A comparison of costs of the factors of production may serve as a substitute standard in such cases.

Review of price movements in the Soviet economy since 1926–27 is complicated by the fact that the Soviet government has published no price indices for years later than 1931. Official indices available for wholesale and retail prices of industrial goods for years prior to 1931 indicate a moderate decline in prices of industrial goods from the fiscal year 1926–27 to the fiscal year 1927–28, followed by a gradual rise in 1928–29 and a further rise in 1929–30.[18]

Fortunately, our knowledge of price trends in the Soviet economy is not limited to these meager official indices. Naum Jasny has recently published a study of prices of industrial products in the Soviet Union for the period 1926–27 to 1949.[19] The study is based on compilations of prices from official sources. From these prices he has computed price indices for selected years.

Jasny faced grave obstacles in obtaining prices for identical products in different years, securing representative product coverage, and finding appropriate weights to combine individual price relatives into a general index. Limitations in the data with which Jasny worked made it impossible to resolve all of these difficulties satisfactorily. It may be questioned whether product coverage is sufficiently broad to be representative of over-all price developments in an industry like machinery. Further, Jasny indicates that "Prices on which the indexes are based are partly estimated; weights estimated throughout except for building materials." [20] The estimated weights are nowhere made explicit.

Despite these reservations as to the accuracy of Jasny's price indices for any particular year, there can be no question as to the validity of the generally upward trend in industrial prices revealed by his price indices. Jasny finds that the general level of prices of all industrial goods on a tax-free basis was slightly below the 1926–27 level in 1930, was two and one-half to three times the 1926–27 level in the late 1930's, and had risen to five or six times or more the level of 1926–27 by 1949.[21] With such an upward trend in the general price level the use of current prices in lieu of 1926–27 prices in computing the Soviet official indices of industrial output must have introduced an inflationary bias.

It has sometimes been argued, however, that increased productivity of labor and industrial subsidies may have held down costs of production and prices of new products after 1926–27, even in the face of general price increases.[22] It is undoubtedly true that improved techniques and increased productivity of labor resulted in reductions in the costs of many new products. It is doubtful, however, whether such cost reductions brought the constant prices of new products into line with the 1926–27 cost-price level. The effect of cost reductions on the values at which new products entered the production index was greatly attenuated by the practice referred to earlier of assigning constant prices to new products on the basis of costs during the first year or even the first few months of production. Most cost reductions may be presumed to have occurred over a longer period of time as experience in producing the new product increased. Cost reductions subsequent to the establishment of constant prices, of course, had no effect on these prices.

The effect of valuing new products at the high unit costs of their first year in production was reinforced by a general cost inflation beginning in 1930. Industrial costs were forced up by more rapid increases in industrial wages than in labor productivity and by increases in prices of agricultural raw materials. Comparison of the official index of average annual wages in large-scale industry with the official index of the productivity of labor in large-scale industry for the years 1928–1935 (see Table 3) points to slight declines in unit wage costs in 1929 and 1930, followed by a slight increase in 1931 and a much larger increase in 1932. By 1935 the index of unit wage costs so calculated stands at 143 per cent of 1928. Since the index of the productivity of labor is subject to whatever inflationary bias may exist in the production index, the rise in the index of unit wage costs so derived may be taken as an absolute minimum and quite probably a considerable understatement.

The effect of cost inflation on Soviet industrial prices in these years undoubtedly was counteracted in part by subsidies from the state budget. It is not likely, however, that higher costs of production for new products were entirely offset by budget subsidies. The most important of the industries which received budget subsidies were cement, ferrous and nonferrous metals, chemicals, machinery, timber, coal, peat, and iron mining.

TABLE 3

Labor Productivity, Wages, and Unit Wage Costs in Soviet Large-Scale Industry, 1928–1935 (per cent of 1928)

Year	Productivity of labor	Average annual wages	Unit wage costs (ratio of average annual wages to labor productivity)
1928	100.0	100.0	100.0
1929	112.9	110.0	97.4
1930	123.9	119.0	96.0
1931	133.3	136.1	102.1
1932	136.7	169.3	123.8
1933	148.6	191.0	128.5
1934	164.5	221.5	134.7
1935	191.1	273.0	142.9

SOURCES — Official index of labor productivity 1928–1934 from *Socialist Construction in the USSR* (Moscow, 1936), p. 25; 1935 from *SSSR i kapitalisticheskie strany* (Moscow: Gosplanizdat, 1939), p. 75; Official index of average annual wages in large-scale industry from *Sotsialisticheskoe stroitel'stvo SSSR* (Moscow, 1936), pp. 512–13.

The production of new products by the mining and timber industries can scarcely have been important, so that subsidies paid to these industries were intended largely to keep down the prices of established products and thus could have had only an indirect influence on the costs of production in industries with a high ratio of new products, such as machinery and chemicals.

Moreover, in the logic of the situation, it is not likely that subsidies paid to offset the high costs of new products were intended to reduce the price of these products to a hypothetical 1926–27 level. Confronted by a general cost inflation, planners might conceivably have set current prices for new products below current costs in anticipation of lowered costs when production reached its expected maximum efficiency. They would have done so, however, with some reference to the level of costs and prices, especially labor costs, of the current year. They are not likely in this situation to have attempted to establish current prices for new products at the long-run normal level which would have prevailed had the general price level of 1926–27 been maintained. Unless this unlikely course was followed, however, new products entered the official index of industrial production at higher levels of costs and prices than those of the year 1926–27.

Soviet economists and planners were uncomfortably aware of distortions in the official production measures arising from the practice of "pricing-in" new products at current prices. In a defensive article entitled "Why Plan Production in the Constant Prices of 1926–27?" published in 1935, Sh. Turetskii, a prominent Soviet economist and member of the State Planning Commission, wrote:

> The immense growth and increase in the proportion of new products poses the question of principles governing the establishment of constant prices for these products. In this connection recent years have witnessed a well-known arbitrariness, when products have been valued at comparatively high prices or at costs of production of the output period. A similar method in the valuation of new products cannot fail to influence a number of general indicators in the national economic plan.[23]

Turetskii had prescribed the correct principle for setting constant prices for new products in an article published in 1934.

> To the extent that prices on old-established products correspond to conditions of full mastering of the productive process, it is natural that for new products the point of departure for setting constant prices should be *the full costs of production of the new product when its production is fully mastered* (projected estimates of the costs of production) *with the established percentage mark-up* depending on the degree of profitability of the particular branch of industry.[24]

This second quotation is of interest for its emphasis on full costs of production plus percentage mark-up as the basis for constant prices of new products, as well as for its emphasis on costs of the full-scale production period.

Prior to World War II Soviet writers apparently felt compelled to exercise great circumspection in discussing the effects of including new products at current prices in Soviet production measures at constant prices. Their criticisms usually were couched in purely theoretical terms with the hedge that whether the actual effect of current price valuations for new products was inflationary or deflationary depended on relative price movements of different commodities, their importance in the total production picture, and so on. Only in one case which has come to the attention of the writer has this discretion been laid aside, and a clear assessment of the effect of pricing-in new products at current prices been offered.

In a review of a book on Soviet national income, A. Kurskii, a prominent Soviet economist, comments as follows on the question of valuation of net product and services:

At the present time national income as well as the gross output of industry and agriculture are planned in constant prices of 1926–27. This system of prices does not reflect the actual interrelationships of separate branches of the economy at the present time. Thus, for example, the proportion of new products in the gross output of industry is increasing, and the valuation of new types of industrial products in prices of 1926–27 is nearer to current prices. *This magnifies the value of industrial products in comparison to agricultural products, in the composition of which the proportion of new products is not as high.*[25]

The final sentence carries the clear implication that current prices are higher than prices of the year 1926–27 and that, as a consequence, their use introduces an inflationary bias into Soviet measures of change in the physical volume of industrial output.

There can be no doubt that the Russians themselves were handicapped in the planning and administration of the economy and in the work of economic analysis by the inadequacy of their production statistics valued at 1926–27 prices. Presumably the administrative and economic chaos accompanying the war delayed the abandonment of 1926–27 prices. Finally, however, in 1948 the Soviet government replaced 1926–27 prices with current wholesale prices in all their important uses.

The decision was contained in Decree No. 2783 of the Council of Ministers published on July 28, 1948.[26] According to this decree the production of finished and unfinished goods alike was to be calculated in current wholesale prices. When wholesale prices were unobtainable, current costs of production were to be used in conjunction with a coefficient to convert costs to wholesale prices.

Since January 1, 1949 the gross value of Soviet industrial output has been calculated both in current wholesale prices (net of the turnover tax) and in constant prices. Values in current prices are used in a variety of enterprise accounting records and reports. Values in constant prices serve as gauges of plan fulfillment and measure changes in the physical volume of industrial output. According to a recent Soviet text on industrial statistics the constant prices in use until January 1, 1951 were 1926–27 prices.[27] During the year 1951 output was valued in the wholesale prices in effect on January 1, 1951. Comparison of output in 1951 with monthly totals and the annual total for 1950 was accomplished by converting 1950 output totals in current prices into values at 1951 price levels by means of price indices. The official constant prices for the period of the Fifth Five Year Plan (1951–1955) are stated to be the wholesale prices which became effective on January 1, 1952. During the first three months of 1952 all enterprises were required to convert annual and monthly production totals for 1950 and 1951 into the newly-adopted constant prices of January 1, 1952 by means of price indices to facilitate intertemporal comparisons over the five years of the plan period.

There is some extenuation for the shortcomings of official Soviet production statistics in the circumstances surrounding their birth. Soviet statisticians were faced with the problem of computing and keeping current a comprehensive index of industrial output during a period characterized by an extremely rapid change in the volume and composition of industrial output. More important, the same production statistics were employed operationally in planning, recording, and coördinating the work of thousands of individual industrial enterprises. It was clearly impractical to require the personnel of these enterprises to follow intricately devised statistical methods in calculating constant prices for new products. Nevertheless, the 1936 reform of pricing procedure was a step in this direction.

Recognition of the genuinely intractable problems with which Soviet authorities had to grapple does not excuse their failure to publish a revised index for the years prior to 1936 at the time of the 1936 reform in pricing procedures. Nor does it explain why no official index has ever been published based on some year later than 1926–27. The shift to current wholesale prices for planning purposes in 1949 afforded a second occasion for the publication of revised indices for earlier years, but this opportunity was also ignored.

Presumably such an index based on a later year could avoid many of the technical defects of the official index. It may also be presumed that such an index would present to the world a somewhat different picture of Soviet industrial growth than does the index supposedly based on 1926–27 prices. The chapters which follow are devoted to the construction of a revised index of Soviet industrial production, utilizing Soviet value relationships of the year 1934 and Soviet physical production data. This revised index is constructed on the net value-added principle.

2

Value-Added Weights for Soviet Industry

Both conceptual and statistical hazards confront any attempt to improve on the defective official Soviet measures of industrial production. The conceptual problem is to devise, if possible, a method which will satisfy the economic rationale underlying production index methodology when the data are those of a controlled rather than a market economy. In this study, the problem arises in the selection of an appropriate measure of the relative importance of the numerous physical products which must be aggregated to obtain a general measure of Soviet industrial production. The question is whether customary weighting procedures are acceptable within the framework of Soviet economic organization and practice.

Statistically the challenge is to implement the chosen method, working only with *published* Soviet industrial statistics. The statistical problem is made difficult mainly because of statistical sins of omission on the part of the Soviet government. Certain important economic statistics are available only for a limited number of years; others appear only at odd intervals or in fragmentary form, if at all. Their interpretation frequently is complicated by the casual attitude of both official agencies and individual authors toward proper definition and explanation of statistical concepts and measurements. Accordingly, more than the usual number of obvious difficulties and hidden pitfalls are encountered.

The purpose of this chapter is to discuss the considerations which underlie the method adopted in this study to assign relative importance to physical products in computing aggregate output. Some problems which arise in the statistical implementation of the method are described in Chapter 3. In subsequent chapters the revised production index is presented and discussed and then employed to shed some light on other aspects of Soviet industrial growth such as changes in labor productivity and the per capita supply of consumers' goods.

The general problem of aggregation of unlike physical units is common to all production indices. No completely rational or intellectually satisfying solution to this problem exists. In established production index methodology, products which are incommensurable in their physical dimensions are assumed to be comparable in terms of value. The comparability of value units rests on the implied identification of equal value units with equal amounts of consumer satisfaction, the latter assumed to be homogeneous and subject (at least ideally) to cardinal measurement. Value-added customarily is preferred to gross value because of the consumption as well as the creation of products in the productive process.

In practice the dictates of even such shaky theoretical underpinnings as these are not customarily fulfilled. Prices (gross value) substitute for value-added. When value-added is used, its statistical measure corresponds only approximately to the theoretical concept. The obstacles to devising adequate weights become truly formidable when, to these general inadequacies of industrial statistics in all countries, is added the policy of the Soviet government of withholding important current economic statistics. Thus, the Soviet government has made no systematic presentation of price data in public sources since the mid-twenties.

Recent investigations by Western economists have brought to light a greater quantity of price data for the years since 1930 than were previously thought to exist.[1] For the most part these prices are contained in price lists published by various industrial ministries in the USSR. They deal primarily with prices of producers' goods and are specialized by branch of industry or type of product. There are important omissions, especially among consumers' goods. At the present writing it is not clear whether there are prices for a sufficient number of products for any single year to permit their application as weights to physical output data in computing an index of Soviet industrial output. Certainly the possibility is an interesting one.

An alternative approach to the problem is to construct a new index on the basis of the Russian physical product series and appropriate world market prices. A variant of this approach is to use the prices of some other economy, say, that of the United States.[2] Such an approach makes possible the direct comparison of absolute levels of output between the countries concerned. There are offsetting disadvantages. Separation of the national pattern of production from the national pattern of prices breaks with the accepted rationale of production indices.[3] Moreover, this method does not offer a solution to the problem of obtaining an index constructed on the value-added rather than the gross value principle. Whatever the usefulness of this approach, it is clearly not a substitute for an index of Soviet industrial output in which quantity series, taken from official Soviet statistics, are given a weight in the general index according to the structure of value-added in Soviet industry.

The problem, then, is to devise a measure of value-added in Soviet industry or, at least, a reasonable approximation to such a measure. The present study uses salaries and wages (including pay-roll taxes) to represent value-added weights for a given industry. This procedure raises two questions: (1) What is the relation of weights based on salaries and wages to weights based on net value-added? and (2) Do value weights based on planned prices, in an economy where consumer sovereignty has been suspended, satisfy the underlying rationale of index number construction?

The Concept of "Net Value-Added"

The measure of value-added, customarily used in constructing indices of the physical volume of manufacturing output for the United States, is that published in the *Census of Manufactures*.[4] Value-added as computed by the Census is the difference between value of product (i.e. the selling value f.o.b. factory) and costs of materials, fuel and purchased electric energy consumed, costs of containers, and freight and haulage costs. "Census value-added," as has been pointed out by Solomon Fabricant, contains elements such as depreciation, maintenance and repairs, taxes, etc. which should be deducted along with costs of materials, fuel, purchased electric energy and the like to obtain a more accurate measure of "net value-added."[5] Commenting on this improved measure of net value-added Dr. Fabricant writes: "The net value-added in an industry as defined here is of course identical with the proportion of the national income produced in the industry."[6]

The United States Department of Commerce, the main source of national income statistics for the United States, likewise identifies net income originating with net value-added in an industry.[7] The composition of net value-added in an industry defined to equal net income originating in an industry differs, however, depending on the concept of national income which is taken as the criterion. Thus if national income is regarded as the sum of the *values of final products at market price* (Kuznet's criterion) net value-added in any industry equals the sum of wages and salaries, entrepreneurial withdrawals, interest, dividends, rent, and corporate savings. Business taxes, with the exception of pay-roll taxes, are regarded as payments by business to government for services consumed in the productive process and are excluded. If the *factor cost* concept of national income (that adopted by the Department of Commerce) is taken as a criterion, net value-added in an industry equals the sum of the above items plus income and profits taxes on business. Indirect taxes on business, such as the sales tax, are still excluded. The rationale for this distinction in treatment of taxes advanced by the Department of Commerce is as follows:

> Since national income is designed to measure output in terms of the costs or incomes of the factors of production it should change only if either the volume of factor services or their unit remuneration changes, and not because of a mere change in tax rates. If it is assumed that corporation profits taxes are not shifted and indirect business taxes are generally shifted forward, inclusion of corporate income taxes in national income and exclusion of indirect business taxes from it are clearly indicated, since on these assumptions mere changes in tax rates will not cause changes in an income total so defined.[8]

The present study accepts the factor cost concept of national income as the criterion for identifying net income originating or net value-added in Soviet industry. This decision rests on considerations arising from the absence of consumers' sovereignty (as distinguished from consumers' choice) in the Soviet economy. Use of value weights to assign relative importance to different products implies commensurability of values. The comparability of value units is based on the assumption that prices have been formed in a system of interlinked markets within which the location and use of the factors of production and their relative prices have been determined in response to users' preferences. To the extent that there are obstacles to factor mobility and accompanying price changes in response to demand, the rationale for the comparability of value units is attenuated.

In the Soviet economy, the market for consumers' goods is in a certain sense isolated administratively from the market for factors of production. The bill of goods produced by industry in any given period is determined by planners' preferences rather than consumers' preferences. While planners may consider consumers' preferences in regard to the composition of the bill of consumers' goods to be produced, the aggregate amount of productive resources devoted to consumers' goods is determined by the planners' decision as to the division of the gross national product between consumption and gross investment.

Thus, while the system of planners' preferences operates across the entire range of producers' and consumers' goods in the Soviet economy and determines the quantities produced and thus the relative scarcities of productive factors, consumers' preferences operate only within the consumers' goods market and even there influence the pattern of production only within restricted limits. There is, of course, no guarantee that the relative evaluation of different consumers' goods by planners and consumers will be the same. More important, since consumers' goods in general are in short supply, Soviet authorities customarily have set consumers' goods prices well above costs of production to equate aggregate supply and demand in the consumers' goods market, to absorb purchasing power, and to keep savings within bounds which will not affect work incentives. Therefore, the evaluation of national income originating in the consumers' goods industries will differ markedly, both absolutely and relative to producers' goods industries, depending on the choice between factor cost and market price as the basis for national income valuation.

Use of factor cost is preferred to market price on the grounds that factor prices are determined in a system of interlinked factor markets common to producers' goods and consumers' goods industries alike and therefore are comparable among different industries. Market prices, on the other hand, are formed in administratively isolated markets, and are much higher in relation to costs of production in the market for consumers' goods than in the market for producers' goods. Factor costs, therefore, provide a much more consistent basis for inter-industry value comparisons than do market prices.

Net Value-Added in Soviet Industry

In Soviet accounting procedure wholesale supply prices of Soviet industrial products are composed of three major elements: costs of production, profits, and the turnover (or sales) tax. Costs of production, in turn, consist of pay rolls, value of raw materials and semi-fabricated inputs, fuel and electric power, amortization charges, and clerical and administrative expenses. Thus, when the material costs of production (including amortization) are deducted from the selling value of output f.o.b. factory for Soviet industry, the resulting remainder includes salaries and wages, pay-roll taxes, retained profits, the profits and turnover taxes, and a miscellaneous accounting category — "other money outlays." The items in this remainder which represent factor costs constitute net income originating in a given industry and, therefore, are the net value-added weights for the production of that industry. The question as to which items do represent factor costs must be considered in relation to the actual organization of the Soviet economic system.

Salaries and wages are conceptually similar in Soviet and American usage and present no special difficulty. Salaries and wages have been less important, however, in determining the standard of living of the Soviet worker than that of the American worker for two reasons. One is that in the Soviet system, benefits provided by the state are of greater relative importance in terms of a worker's real income than in the American system.[9] The other reason (associated with an emergency measure rather than with a permanent feature of the Soviet system) is that in the Soviet Union during periods of rationing a worker's privilege to buy in a restricted store at special prices frequently had a greater determining effect on his real standard of living than the actual ruble income which he earned. Nevertheless, wages remain, as will become clear, the most important part of net income produced and, therefore, of net value-added in Soviet industry.

Pay-roll taxes in Soviet industry differ from those in American industry in that, at least during the 1930's, receipts from this source were used not only to provide social insurance benefits but also to provide funds for training and education of workers, to furnish stipends for the local committees of the trade unions, to finance a number of union-administered personal services, and even to provide housing for workers. Nevertheless, as Bergson has pointed out:

> Logically regarded the Soviet social insurance payments represent a redistribution of earnings over time undertaken by the state, rather than addition to earnings. The premium paid, it is true, is called a payroll tax, and is listed

in the enterprise's books as a cost item *separate* from wages. But since the tax is a percentage of the payroll, the distinction is purely formal so far as the cost of hiring labor is concerned. From the point of view of the insured persons the correspondence of the benefits to the premium paid is assured by the fact that the benefits also are proportionate to earnings. Properly calculated, the money wages of the U.S.S.R. accordingly should include the premium of pay-roll tax.[10]

Therefore pay-roll taxes should be included in the net income originating in a given Soviet industry and thus in the net value-added weight for that industry.

Entrepreneurial withdrawals do not constitute an independent category of income payments in the Soviet economy, since private ownership and operation of business has been abolished in the Soviet Union. In so far as entrepreneurial withdrawals may be considered a return for unusual personal ability in the form of wages and salaries, they are reflected in the latter category in Soviet accounting practice. To the extent that entrepreneurial withdrawals represent a share in profits arising from innovations or cost reductions, they are included in Soviet accounting practice partly in profits retained by the enterprise and partly in the profits tax. Although it is theoretically desirable to include entrepreneurial-type profits in net income produced in an industry, the statistics which are available do not permit their identification so that they must be omitted. Entrepreneurial-type profits are to be distinguished from the more general categoy of profits in Soviet industry discussed below. The omission of entrepreneurial-type profits from the net value-added weights may result in the relative underweighting of the lumber and woodworking industry and of one or two consumers' goods industries (fur, leather footwear, liquor, macaroni products) in which such profits in the 1930's may have been considerably above the average.[11] In general, however, these profits were quite small relative to wages and salaries, so that omitting them does not affect appreciably the relative weights of most industries which are included in the index.

Since the means of production are owned by the state, in the Soviet system *rent, interest, and profits* have vanished as personal income categories in the Soviet Union.[12] Moreover, although Soviet industry pays interest on short term credit, and an element of rent may theoretically be identified in the turnover tax, neither interest (other than on short-term credit) nor rent generally appears as a specific factor cost in industrial accounting. Thus, although it is theoretically desirable to include interest and rent payments in net income produced in a given industry, it is quite impossible to do so, since they cannot be disentangled from the profits and turnover tax of which they are a part.

Profits and the turnover tax. As has been indicated above it is theoretically desirable to include entrepreneurial-type profits in net income produced in an industry, but, since they cannot be isolated statistically, there is no choice but to omit them. Entrepreneurial-type profits, however, do not account for the entire profit category in Soviet industrial accounting. Analytically, a large part of industrial profits do not differ essentially from the turnover tax. The distinction between the turnover and profits tax made by Soviet authorities in practice is justified for administrative purposes.[13]

The turnover tax, the major source of income of the state budget, is set in relation to the volume of goods sold by an enterprise, usually as a certain percentage of the planned wholesale price per unit. The turnover tax is independent of the profitability of the enterprise and depends only on the volume of sales. The profits tax is set as a percentage of actual profits which are determined by the difference between costs of production and sales less the turnover tax. Profits and thus the budget income from the profits tax depend on the productive efficiency of the enterprise and its ability to meet or exceed planned cost reductions. The turnover tax is collected currently as sales are made, while the profits tax is collected twice monthly and is subject to adjustment when the final audit of the firm's books has been made each quarter and annually.[14] Budget income from the turnover tax is thus more certain than from the profits tax, and presumably this is one reason for two separate types of taxes rather than a single tax. There is another reason, however, which is probably more important.

The investment and related pricing policies of the Soviet government have as a matter of course resulted in wide planned gaps between costs and income for some firms and exceedingly narrow gaps or losses for other firms. Large surplus funds which would otherwise collect in certain industries are taxed into the budget by the turnover tax lest managerial incentives become blunted by too large profit margins and lest too large funds in the hands of management loosen central control of the productive process.

Nevertheless, while there are these practical justifications for a distinction between profits and the turnover tax, the line which divides them is arbitrary with respect to their analytical significance. Both are a part of the common magnitude defined by the difference between costs and price, and the incidence of both is on the final consumer (since there is no entrepreneurial or rentier class in Soviet society). Therefore neither profits of this type nor the turnover tax can be regarded as measures of factor cost to an enterprise or industry.[15]

There is a further reason for excluding profits and turnover tax from the net value-added weights for a specific industry. As has been mentioned, selling prices for the output of Soviet industry are established by central economic authorities within the framework of general political and economic policy and need bear no special relation to costs of production in a given industry. Thus the selling prices of producers' goods may or may not be set to cover costs. The selling prices of consumers' goods, in contrast, are ordinarily set not only to cover costs but high enough to equate supply and demand in a consumer market in which goods have been constantly in short supply as a result of a high rate of net investment in the economy. The net result of this price policy is that the major part of profits and turnover tax in Soviet industry accumulates in the consumers' goods industries and is then siphoned off into the state budget. To include these profits and the turnover tax in the value-added in the consumers' goods industries would distort the relative importance of consumers' goods in the economy judged by the criterion of resource use (factor costs). Therefore, for both the foregoing reasons, net value-added in a specific industry is best represented by factor costs net of profits and the turnover tax.

The accounting category "other money outlays" consists of a miscellaneous collection of cost items which do not belong under any of the other cost categories but which are more in the nature of overhead costs. It includes such items as telegraph and postal expenses, expenses of certain business trips not classified with wages, purchases of technical literature, contributions toward the publication of a factory newspaper, outlays on the training of workers, interest on short-term credit, some minor unspecified taxes, services of the research and development organizations, payments to marketing organizations, and other miscellaneous expenditures. These "other money outlays" have been excluded in their entirety from the net value-added weights for the given industry. Those items which represent purchases of services from other organizations (for example, telegraph and postal expenses, payments to marketing organizations, and travel expenses) or purchases of materials (for example, technical literature) cannot be considered as net income produced in the industry which consumes them. That part of the costs of training workers and of services of research and development organizations within the enterprises which represents wages and salaries, along with interest on short-term debt should be included in net income produced in an industry. Since the actual composition of "other money outlays" is not given in published statistics, these items cannot be separated from those which should be excluded.[16] Treatment of the newspaper costs and of unspecified taxes is more or less arbitrary. Therefore, the decision is to exclude the entire category from the weights.

To sum up, salaries and wages, pay-roll taxes, interest, rent, profits, the turnover tax, and the miscellaneous accounting category — "other money outlays" have been considered as possible elements of net income originating and thus of value-added in Soviet industry judged by the criterion of factor cost. Salaries and wages and pay-roll taxes have been accepted as appropriate value-added weights for the output of a given industry. Profits, other than those of the entrepreneurial type, and the turnover tax are excluded from value-added in a specific industry since their nature is that of an indirect tax, and they do not represent factor costs to the industry. Although it is theoretically desirable to include entrepreneurial-type profits, rent, interest, and the wage elements included in "other money outlays" in value-added by a given industry, these elements have been omitted, since both conceptual differences in the Soviet economic system and lack of data make it impossible to estimate them by industries. The omission of these theoretically desirable elements probably has no significant effect on the relative weights for the different industries, since these elements are small relative to salaries and wages and pay-roll taxes.

Value Weights and Planned Prices

Whether value weights based on planned prices (in this case the price of labor) in an economy where consumer sovereignty has been suspended satisfy the underlying rationale of index number construction remains to be considered. The pertinent criterion in deciding this question is whether or not the planned prices reflect the relative scarcity of resources employed in the production of the final bill of goods produced by Soviet industry in a given period. The composition of the final bill of goods produced by Soviet industry in any period is determined by decisions of the central economic authorities rather than by the play of consumers' demand, so that this criterion substitutes planners' preferences for consumers' preferences in the role of final demand. This does not alter the conclusion that prices must reflect resource scarcity relative to demand, however determined, if prices are to serve as guides to achieving maximum economic efficiency.

Assume that Soviet economic authorities have decided on the finished bill of goods to be produced, say, in one year. A limited amount of resources is available for use in the production of this bill of goods. If these factors of production are to be used efficiently, the price established for each factor must reflect its scarcity relative to the demand for it in the production of the planned bill of goods. The prices so established may be conceived as making up the basic price structure for the given period. Such a price structure must be the basis of any cost accounting and analysis which is to be *economically* significant. It is to be noted that the composition of the final bill of goods and consequently the price structure reflects planners' preferences and not consumers' preferences; yet, up to this point, it does not involve subsidy or turnover tax.

The introduction of either a subsidy or turnover tax (accepting the concept of an underlying, economically significant price structure) represents a modification of price relationships on noneconomic grounds. The presence of either in an industry indicates a disparity between actual production costs as determined by factor prices and production techniques and the planned sale price of the product of the given industry. The turnover tax is used to drain off excess profits which would otherwise accrue to an industry whose products are priced high relative to costs of production in order to equate market supply and demand. The subsidy is used to support industries which are operating at a deficit, usually because current sale prices for their products have been set in relation to their anticipated rather than their attained production efficiency and costs. Use of the turnover tax and the subsidy permits the Soviet economic authorities to pursue a differential price policy when so desired. In practice, this has meant favoring producers' goods industries at the expense of consumers' goods industries. Why do the Soviet authorities choose to use a system of differential prices or price discrimination rather than to establish new planned prices set to serve planned goals?

When consumers' sovereignty has been suspended but consumers are still paid in money rather than in kind, some such device as the turnover tax is essential. The subsidy could in fact be discarded if prices on all producers' goods were set to cover costs, but this would simply inflate the entire price structure and shift the whole burden of equating consumers' supply and demand to the turnover tax. Until 1936 Soviet economic authorities apparently preferred to avoid such severe price adjustments, possibly in the hope that costs could eventually be lowered. In 1936, however, subsidies were sharply reduced, and the prices of many industrial products were raised in an attempt to place the previously subsidized enterprises and industries on a self-supporting basis.

It is perfectly true, of course, that the turnover tax and the subsidy are instruments which could be used to modify a faulty, underlying price structure in the direction of becoming more representative of actual scarcities relative to production demands. In such a case prices gross of subsidies and the turnover tax would be better guides to the efficient use of productive factors than prices net of them. In the Soviet case, however, the major use of the turnover tax is not to correct for partial disequilibria among individual industries but to redress the general disequilibrium in the economy produced by the clash of planners' and consumers' preferences regarding the division of the national income between consumption and net investment.[17] Subsidies, on the other hand, were necessary because prices had been set with an eye to future (perhaps, long-run normal) rather than present cost-price relationships. Thus both turnover tax and subsidy have been more in the nature of distorting rather than corrective influences on the basic price structure. From this it may be concluded that prices of both consumers' goods and producers' goods taken net of the effect of subsidies and the turnover tax are more representative of actual scarcity relationships in the economy than prices gross of these magnitudes.

It is of particular interest, then, that the value weights for the new index of Soviet industrial production presented in this study are salaries and wages including the pay-roll tax. Obviously, pay rolls are the one element of costs of production and of price which are free of the specific distortions caused by subsidies and taxes. The effect of rationing on workers' real income, however, may not be unlike subsidies to labor when, as was the case in the Soviet Union, ration privileges are different for different industries and for different grades of workers. It is unfortunate, therefore, that 1934, the base-weight year for the new production index, was a year during which rationing was still important in the Soviet economy. In the presence of widespread, discriminatory rationing, money wage differentials are less accurate indices of differences in real wages than would otherwise be the case. Nevertheless, money wage incentives and rationing incentives are not likely to have been set at odds with each other by Soviet planners. Therefore, it seems likely that money wage differentials can be taken as fairly meaningful guides to differences in the Soviet system's evaluation of the services of different types and grades of labor. For pay rolls to be accepted as meaningful approximations to net value-added weights, however, it is necessary to show that the price of labor in Soviet industry evidently is set so as to reflect the relative scarcity of grades of labor of varying productivities.

Under abstract assumptions this condition is satisfied if labor is employed in a productive activity up to the point at which its cost to the enterprise, that is, its wage or salary plus the pay-roll tax, equals its marginal revenue product. To the extent that social insurance costs of using labor vary in different industries, the pattern of wage relatives calculated net of social insurance taxes will differ from the pattern of wage relatives calculated gross of these taxes, that is, the pattern based on differences in marginal revenue productivity. It would be desirable, therefore, in testing wage relatives for their approximation to productivity relatives to conduct the test in terms of wages gross of the pay-roll tax. In fact, however, the statistical evidence which can be presented on this question is based on wages net of pay-roll taxes.

The evidence which can be adduced is taken from Abram Bergson's careful study of Soviet wage statistics, *The Structure of Soviet Wages.*[18] As a result of his study Bergson finds strong support for the hypothesis "that the principles of relative wages in the Soviet Union are also capitalist principles." There are two main props to this argument; one is statistical, the other, institutional.

The statistical argument rests on an industry-by-industry comparison of Soviet and American earnings frequency distributions. Distribution of earnings frequencies depends not only on the structure of wage differentials in an industry but also on the number of workers employed in the different occupations in that industry. The occupational-skill pattern of an industry may be largely determined by technical considerations. Therefore, in an attempt to reduce differences in levels of industrial technique, Soviet data used in the comparison are for the year 1928, while American data are taken from the year 1904. To whatever extent the proportions of workers of different skills are stable in the comparisons of wage variation, the resulting measures of inequality in earnings frequency distributions must reflect directly differences in wage differentials.

Bergson found that:

> In an industry-by-industry comparison . . . the inequality of wages among the bulk of the wage earners is nearly the same in the Soviet Union in 1928 and in the U.S. in 1904. Scattered statistics suggest that Soviet and American wage variations are proximate in more recent periods.[19]

Bergson observed further that the ***general level*** of wage variations in different industries in the Soviet Union in 1928 and in the United States in 1904 is closely proximate. This means that the relative inequality in earnings frequencies in a given industry is about the same in both economies and that the rank ordering of industries on a scale from greater to less inequality is also proximate.

These results suggest that within individual industries employing similar techniques of production and thus having similar occupational-skill patterns of demand for workers, the principles of wage determination in the Soviet Union and the United States must strongly resemble each other. It may well be that the wage structure in individual industries reflects marginal productivity and marginal disutility considerations on the part of management and marginal workers. Our knowledge of Soviet institutional practices affecting wage rates lends credence to this possibility. Bergson states:

> Support for the application of capitalist principles to Soviet wages is to be found, finally, in the administrative techniques used in the Soviet Union to determine relative wages. From the widespread use of the piece system, in particular, it may be concluded that, at least among industrial workers employed at the same stage in production, differences in earnings in the Soviet Union approximate differences in productivity.[20]

Both of the exhibits, which thus far have been admitted as evidence that the price of Soviet industrial labor evidently is set so as to reflect the relative scarcity of grades of labor of varying productivities, are subject to a common defect. They relate only to individual industries. The comparisons of Soviet and American earnings frequencies distributions are industry-by-industry comparisons; piece-work wages are oriented to physical productivity permitting interpersonal comparisons of productivity only within "the same stage of production."

What is the likelihood that interindustry discrepancies in relative marginal productivities and wage rates were compensated by a flow of workers from less well paid to better paid occupations and industries? This question can be answered only indirectly. Statistics on labor turnover in the early 1930's indicate hirings and departures equal to or in excess of the average number employed in large-scale industry.[21] There was, therefore, very considerable labor mobility in these years. Whether the flow was in the direction of the economic optimum cannot be definitely stated, but some rough correspondence does not seem unlikely.

Finally, Bergson concludes from a study of wage administration practices in Soviet industry, that in economizing money costs of production and in allocating labor efficiently among competing uses, employers are prompted to distribute workers among different employments so that their relative productivity corresponds to their relative money wages.[22] Taken together with the previous conclusions, this suggests that "the forces of supply and demand which operate in a capitalist labor market are also active in the Soviet labor market."[23]

The assembled evidence appears to indicate that salaries and wages in the Soviet Union are meaningful prices in terms of measuring the scarcity of labor of different types and grades relative to the demand for labor in the production of the final bill of goods produced by Soviet industry. Thus, both theoretical considerations and empirical evidence suggest that, within the limitations of the available data, salaries and wages, including pay-roll taxes, are the most suitable approximation to value-added weights for an index of Soviet industrial output.

3

Statistical Procedures in Constructing the Production Index

Comments of Western observers of the Soviet economy in the past few years have stressed the paucity of published Soviet economic statistics and the doubtful reliability of those data which have been released for publication. The reader will wonder how these obstacles have been overcome in the present study.

It must be noted that empirical research on the Soviet economy has no monopoly on problems posed by shortcomings in available statistical materials. Any comprehensive statistical study may be expected to require the exercise of judgment and some compromise in the course of applying statistical materials to theoretical categories. Moreover, the recent emphasis on the inadequacy of current Soviet statistics, while completely justified, has misled the general reader with respect to the availability of statistics for earlier years. For the period 1928–1937 in particular, there is a wealth of Soviet statistical material which justifies and supports careful economic analysis.

The present study seeks to erect as strong a foundation as possible from the much more abundant statistics of the 1930's, and, then, to build a more fragile superstructure for the 1940's from such materials as are available. Nevertheless, even the more abundant statistics of the 1930's have gaps and pitfalls which raise special problems. These problems have made necessary the adoption of a somewhat more complicated statistical procedure than is common in the construction of production indices. It is the purpose of this chapter to blueprint the statistical procedures used in constructing the revised index of Soviet industrial output. Readers wishing to descend into the engine room for a closer look at the machinery are invited to inspect the appendices.

The total weight of an industry or industrial group in the production index is proportional to its share of the total annual industrial pay roll for 1934. The over-all weight for an industry is subdivided among the available quantity series for products produced in that industry according to the actual or estimated share of these individual products in the total labor cost of the industry. The total weight for a given industry is assigned to the available product series regardless of whether or not all products produced by the industry are represented. Thus weights are assigned on an imputed rather than on an earned basis.[1] This procedure assumes that the missing series move with the weighted average of the available series. The final index is a weighted mean of quantity relatives with 1934 serving as both the base year and the year from which the weighting system is derived. Thus the index is theoretically equivalent to an index of the aggregative type with actual quantities (rather than quantity relatives) for the various products being multiplied by 1934 unit value-added weights.

Since 1934 is the base-weight year, it is of interest to get some perspective on the general economic situation in that year before turning to a detailed consideration of the statistical procedures used in constructing the production index. The year 1934 was the second year of the Second Five Year Plan. According to official statistics, by 1934, 99.6 per cent of the total gross output of industry was produced by socialized industry; 71 per cent of peasant farmsteads had been collectivized as of July 1, and 86.4 per cent of the total gross output of agriculture was produced by collectivized agriculture.[2] Like most of the years of the five year plan period, 1934 was a year of rapid economic expansion. Official figures for national income in "1926–27 prices" indicate an increase in 1934 of 15 per cent over 1933, in gross industrial output of 20 per cent, in agricultural output of 4 per cent, and in the industrial labor force of 5 per cent. Rationing of consumer goods which was to be suspended in 1935 was still widespread and of great importance in 1934. With the exception of forced labor for civil and political criminals and some requirements regarding the obligations of persons given technical training at state expense, the labor market, at least among industrial workers, was generally a free market, as witness official figures on labor turnover in large-scale industry. In 1934 new employment was 101 per cent and departures 97 per cent of the average monthly number of wage earners employed in large-scale industry.[3]

In choosing the base-weight year or period for a production index, it is customary to take some account of the cyclical position of business with a view to selecting a period characterized by fairly "normal" (that is, neither extremely prosperous nor extremely depressed) business conditions. Since the entire period 1928–1950 to be included in the present index is characterized by rapid industrial growth (with the exception of the war years), 1934 would seem to be as typical and in this sense as "normal" a year as any. Moreover, 1934 is much to be preferred to 1926–27 (the base-weight year for the official index of industrial production) as a weighting year, because it falls more nearly midway in the period for which output is being measured and is thus less open to criticism. Standards of efficiency of productive processes, range of products, and general price level are likely to be more representative of the other years included in the index.

Computing Pay-Roll Weights for Individual Industries and Products

Comparative pay rolls are the basis for the weights for individual industries and products. Unfortunately, Soviet statistical sources do not present data for the annual sums of wages and salaries and pay-roll taxes classified by separate branches of industry. In order to obtain the annual pay roll for separate industries and industrial processes, it was necessary to multiply annual average employment figures by appropriate wage rates. The first step was to obtain the most detailed classification of employment and of wage and salary data by industry that was available.

At this point a completely unexpected difficulty was encountered. An examination of the available employment data revealed that, for the period 1927–28 to 1936, Soviet statistical sources give two different and conflicting sets of figures for the labor force in large-scale industry. Both sets of statistics on the labor force in large-scale industry were prepared by the Central Statistical Administration (which during the 1930's was called the Central Administration of National-Economic Accounting). One set of data was prepared by the *labor division* of the Central Statistical Administration, the other set by the *industrial division*. The main responsibility for collecting and publishing labor statistics — these include data on employment, wage rates, days and hours worked, labor turnover, and the like — belonged to the labor division. The industrial division, on the other hand, was charged with collecting and publishing data on the volume and value of industrial production, costs of production, power supply to industry, and others. (The same division of function was observed between the labor division and other branch sections [construction, agriculture, etc.] of the Central Statistical Administration.)

In view of the importance to the planning and administration of industry of correlating these two broad types of statistics having to do with industrial performance, it is most surprising that the industrial and labor divisions as late as 1938 and possibly even well into the 1940's had not agreed on a common set of criteria for defining large-scale industry. Had the industrial division, more or less as a formality, not included in its questionnaire on production a question regarding the average annual number of workers in the industrial establishment concerned, no aggregate figures for employment directly comparable to output statistics would exist.

Differences in criteria for "large-scale industry." Let us examine the reasons for differences in coverage in the employment statistics prepared by the industrial and labor divisions of the Central Statistical Administration. The industrial division included industrial coöperatives and the lumbering, timber flotage, and fishing industries in its definition of large-scale industry. All these were excluded according to the labor division definition, since they were regarded as separate branches of the economy for purposes of planning the distribution of labor resources.

The labor division accepted as its criterion for "large-scale" the old criterion for "census" industry (adopted by a decree of the Council of People's Commissars, January 4, 1919); namely, enterprises having no fewer than 16 workers (interpreted to include workers, apprentices, and minor service personnel) with mechanical motive power or 30 without. The industrial division, while accepting the same criterion as a starting point, adopted an additional set of special criteria for power stations, brick factories, glass factories, printing establishments, tanneries, flour and grain mills, breweries, and soft drink plants, and, in addition, included all enterprises of the mining and metallurgical industry and all enterprises of industries formerly subject to the excise tax administration, such as distilling.[4]

Finally, the labor division included in large-scale industry only those industrial establishments which were administered as independent industrial enterprises, while the industrial division included, as well, enterprises engaged in activities of an industrial type but administratively subordinated to parent organizations classified in construction, agriculture, trade, transport, and communications. Thus, for example, while collective farm workshops for the repair of agricultural machinery or repair shops for automobiles and trucks located in garages and motor pools were classified by the division of labor statistics with agriculture and auto-transport, respectively, the industrial division classified these establishments with industry.

The fact that the number of workers classified in large-scale industry by the industrial division in 1934 was 48 per cent larger than the number of workers in large-scale industry according to labor division statistics is a measure of the importance of differences in these two sets of criteria. Differences in the statistics for the average number of workers vary considerably among industries, however, so that any general statement regarding these differences may be quite misleading with respect to particular industries. Individual industry differences in the two sets of statistics are indicated by the employment coverage adjustment coefficients given in Table B, below.

Computing pay rolls from labor division statistics. The labor division statistics for employment and wage rates have to be taken as the point of departure in calculating pay rolls for separate industries and processes, since these statistics are far more complete in this regard than those of the industrial division. Employment statistics published by the labor division are classified by five main categories of industrial personnel (that is, workers, apprentices, engineers and technical personnel, administrative personnel, and minor service personnel). These labor division data on employment are contained in two statistical tables in *Trud v SSSR* (Labor in the USSR) for 1934, a handbook of labor statistics published by the Central Statistical Administration. One table gives the annual average number of employees in each of these categories classified by fourteen main industrial groups plus a miscellaneous category.[5] These major industrial groups are further subdivided into thirty separate industries. The second table presents a further classification of the employment data by industry for July 1, 1934.[6] To obtain a maximum number of subclassifications for separate industries and processes, it was necessary to make use of both sets of employment data in calculating pay rolls. This, of course, raises the question of differential seasonal swings in employment peculiar to specific industries and of making some statistical correction to avoid distortion on this account in relative weights for the various industries. No separate adjustment was made to allow for seasonal factors, however, since it was felt that the adjustment for differences in employment coverage (discussed below), as between industrial-division and labor-division statistics of employment, included as adequate an adjustment for seasonal factors as available data permit.

Wage data by industries for each of the five categories of industrial personnel for 1934 are likewise given in *Trud v SSSR* for 1934.[7] In some instances, however, wage data are not presented in the detail by industry and subprocess for which employment data are given. Thus, for example, while employment in the chemical industry on July 1, 1934 is given for the divisions of basic chemicals, aniline dyes, artificial fibers, other chemicals, pharmaceutical chemicals, wood chemistry, and paints and varnishes, the average wage for each of the five categories of industrial personnel is given only for the chemical industry as a whole. In such cases employment in each of the industrial subdivisions was multiplied by the appropriate average wage rate for the industry as a whole, and the separate pay rolls for each of the five types of industrial personnel were then summed to obtain pay rolls for each of the several subdivisions within the industry.

This procedure, based as it is on the average wage for the industry, results in an accurate recomputation of the aggregate pay roll for the entire industry. The division of the aggregate pay roll among the subdivisions of the industry obtained by this computation need not correspond, however, to the actual distribution of the aggregate pay roll among these subdivisions. To the extent that there are marked variations in the wage rates for each specific category of industrial personnel among the subdivisions of the industry as a whole, multiplying employment by the average wage rate distorts the distribution of the aggregate pay roll among the subdivisions.

Thus while the index of output for the industry as a whole enters the general index of industrial output with the appropriate value-added weight, it is possible that some distortion is present in the index for the industry as a whole as a result of distortions in the relative weights applied to the quantity relatives for individual product series in constructing the industry index. Wage rates for any one category of industrial personnel (for example, workers, apprentices) probably show considerably less variation among the subprocesses of a single industry (such as chemicals) than among separate industries (such as chemicals, textiles, ferrous metals, and others). It seems likely, therefore, that no serious distortions are introduced into the general production index by the procedure just described.

A third method of calculating pay rolls has been followed in the case of the textile industry and the food industry. In these two industries both employment and wage data were given on an individual basis for certain major processes within the industry, while for less important processes only the employment data were given on an individual basis. There was thus a choice between calculating all subprocess pay rolls on the basis of average wages for the entire industry or calculating the major subprocess pay rolls on the basis of wages specific to those processes and minor subprocess pay rolls on the basis of average wages for the industry as a whole. The choice was made in favor of the latter alternative out of a desire to observe the highest degree of accuracy possible for the major series for purposes of later analysis. With pay rolls for the major processes within the industry correctly computed, the aggregate pay roll should not suffer much distortion. It cannot be denied, however, that the choice between these two alternatives rests to a considerable extent simply on the predilection of the writer.

One other general comment about the calculation of pay rolls from the labor division statistics is in order. The wage data used are average monthly wages rather than average annual wages. These monthly wages were *not* converted to annual wages before calculating pay rolls, since the only effect of this operation would have been to multiply all succeeding computations by a factor of twelve.

Employment coverage adjustment. The difficulty with the pay rolls calculated from the labor division data is that for many industries these labor division data are less inclusive in their coverage than the output series for which the pay-roll data are to be used as weights. The employment data for large-scale industry prepared by the industrial division of the Central Statistical Administration are published in *Socialist Construction in the USSR.*[8] This industrial division likewise prepared the output statistics which are used in constructing the present index, so that presumably the employment data published by this division correspond more closely in coverage to the output series than do the employment data prepared by the labor division. The employment data published by the industrial division are incomplete, however, since only the average annual number of *workers* in industry is shown (that is, no figures are given for administrative and technical personnel, apprentices, and minor service personnel). Furthermore, the industrial division publishes no statistics on wages. Therefore, in computing the pay-roll weights for the new production index both the industrial and labor division data are used in combination.

First, pay rolls are computed from employment and wage data given by the labor division as indicated above. Then the number of workers in a given industry or industrial process as given in the labor division statistics is compared to the number of workers in the same industry or process as given in the industrial division statistics, and the ratio of one to the other is calculated. The pay-roll figure calculated from employment and wage data prepared by the labor division is then multiplied by this ratio to adjust the pay-roll figure to one comparable in coverage to the output series.

This procedure faces both theoretical and practical hazards. Since the entire adjustment depends on a comparison of the number of workers rather than total employment, the assumption has to be made that the proportion of workers to each of the four classes of industrial personnel is approximately the same in a given industry under either the labor division or the industrial division definition of that industry. Stated otherwise, the assumption is that the ratio of workers employed to each of the other classes of employees remains fairly constant on the average, regardless of the size of the industrial establishment concerned. This assumption is not strictly valid. Probably the ratio of workers to other personnel increases somewhat in the smaller industrial establishments in which all work is done by hand tools. This means that there is a general overstatement of the pay rolls adjusted for employment coverage. Another qualification having the same implication is that probably personnel in the smaller industrial establishments receive a somewhat lower wage than those in the same employment category in the large establishments.

Two considerations indicate that distortions introduced into the weighting system by these factors are likely to be small. First, to the extent that overstatement of pay rolls is to approximately the same degree in all industries, its effect on relative weights is unimportant. There seems to be no reason to expect very wide differences among the industries in this respect. Second, the share of workers in total pay rolls in most industries was considerably more than 60 per cent so that the distortions stemming from the ratio of workers to other personnel have no influence at all on a considerable portion of each pay roll.[9]

The practical hazard referred to above is that of matching accurately the industry classifications used in reporting employment data by the labor division and in reporting employment and output data by the industrial division. In most industries, the matching was fairly straightforward, and the problem was further reduced by making comparisons for as detailed a classification by product as possible, for example, basic chemicals, pharmaceutical chemicals, and others, instead of for the chemical industry as a whole. In a few industries, however, and particularly in machinery, a more devious method was employed. Since the construction of the machinery index is discussed in detail in Appendix C and complete details for all industries are contained in Appendix B, no further space will be devoted to the problem of the adjustment for employment coverage in this section.

It may be well, however, to make one further comment about the problem of adjusting for seasonal influences in the July 1, 1934 employment data. As was previously mentioned, no adjustment separate from the employment coverage adjustment has been made for seasonal factors. Since the industrial division statistics for employment are the *annual average* number of workers per industry, adjusting pay rolls in relation to this criterion, in effect, takes seasonal differences into account along with differences in coverage.

Estimating pay-roll taxes. The comparative pay-roll weights for each industry include pay-roll taxes. Published Soviet industrial statistics do not provide data on the ruble amounts of pay-roll taxes paid, classified by industry. Nevertheless, it is possible to estimate these sums for the weighting year 1934 for all large-scale industry classified by over 40 industries and industrial groups from their percentage relation to the annual pay roll in these industries.[10] Reference is to data on the structure of production costs in industry which permit a comparison of *pay rolls* as a percentage of total factory costs of production with the *pay-roll tax* as a percentage of total factory costs of production. Thus, if pay rolls are 10 per cent of factory costs of production and pay-roll taxes are 2.5 per cent of costs of production, pay-roll taxes are 25 per cent of pay rolls, and the pay-roll figure is multiplied by an adjustment coefficient of 1.25 to estimate pay rolls inclusive of the pay-roll tax.

Published Soviet statistics showing the structure of factory costs of production are based on cost data for the enterprises administered by the industrial commissariats in 1934. According to data published in the *Plan for the National Economy* for the year 1936, the gross output of large-scale industry in 1934 valued at prices of 1926–27 was 50,600 million rubles, while that of the enterprises of the all-union and local industrial commissariats was 40,588 million rubles.[11] Thus the cost tables are based on approximately 80 per cent of the output of large-scale industry in 1934. This coverage is the basis for the assumption that the cost structure for the enterprises of the industrial commissariats was typical of that for all enterprises in any particular branch of industry.

The Soviet statistics on which the pay-roll tax estimates are based do not provide in every case as detailed a classification by industry and process as is available for wages and salaries. Therefore, when the cost data did not permit the calculation of a pay-roll tax coefficient for the specific industrial subdivision or process concerned, the pay-roll tax coefficient for the more inclusive industrial category given in the cost tables was applied to all the sub pay rolls in that category. Thus, for example, the pay-roll tax coefficient for *machinery as a whole* is the only available pay-roll tax coefficient for all machinery items. In other cases, primarily food and textiles, the pay-roll tax was estimated for some items by specific pay-roll tax coefficients; for others, by the general pay-roll tax coefficient for the industry as a whole. Details of these computations are given in Appendix B.

Estimate of pay-roll taxes for individual processes and products by means of a general coefficient for the industry as a whole involves the assumption that the ratio of salaries and wages to pay-roll taxes is fairly similar among the separate processes. Since the factors affecting social insurance costs and thus the pay-roll tax (such as working conditions and composition of the labor force) are much more similar within a single industrial group than among such groups, this assumption probably does not do undue violence to the facts.

Imputing Value-Added Weights to Quantity Series

The three major operations in computing net value-added weights for the production series have already been discussed. These operations were: (1) computation of pay rolls from labor division wage and employment data, (2) adjustment for employment coverage, and (3) adjustment to include pay-roll taxes. In some cases, the end result of these three operations was a weight directly assignable to the quantity relative for a specific product. In other cases, it was desirable to split up the weight so obtained among the relatives for two or more products produced by the given industry or process. Methods employed in splitting group weights among the products constituting the group are the subject of this section.

The preferred method was to obtain from technical literature unit cost data for the different products included in the group, and to divide the group weight among the various products in proportion to the share that estimated total labor costs of each product were to estimated total labor costs for the group. Thus, for example, the total weight for the ferrous metals industry was divided among the three constituent series for pig iron, steel and rolled steel on the basis of unit wage costs (including pay-roll taxes) per ton for each of these three types of products. Unit cost data are for production by the Southern Metallurgical Trust in the year 1930. Production of pig iron, steel and rolled steel in tons in 1934 was multiplied by the wage cost per ton of each product. Then total wage costs of each product were expressed as a percentage of aggregate wage costs for the three products. The total adjusted pay roll for ferrous metals was then divided among the three series in accordance with these percentages (see Appendix B for details and sources). In numerous instances, however, the technical information on unit costs necessary to this method was not available.

The second method used in assigning group weights to subseries was a variant of the unit cost approach just described. In the absence of data for unit labor costs, data for the number of man hours required to produce a unit of product were substituted when available. The number of units of product of each type produced in 1934 were multiplied by their respective man-hour requirements in that year and the group value-added weight was subdivided among the constituent product relatives in accordance with the estimated share of each in total requirements of productive man hours. This method, which was used in several branches of the machinery industry, is described in more detail in Appendix C on the construction of the machinery index.

Group weights also were assigned to subseries on the basis of the number of workers engaged in the production of each of the various products of the subseries. Thus, the total adjusted pay roll for an industry or industrial group was subdivided among constituent product series in proportion to the share of each product in the annual average number of workers employed in the industry. This was the basis, for example, for assigning the total weight for nonferrous metals to the constituent series for the production of copper, aluminum, zinc, and lead.

In some instances, no satisfactory basis could be found for the subdivision of a group weight among the several quantity relatives for products produced in that industrial group. This situation has been handled in three different ways, depending on the circumstances involved.

In a few instances, the entire weight for the group has been assigned arbitrarily to a single subseries judged to be either representative or of predominant importance. Perhaps the outstanding example of this is the assigning of the entire pay-roll weight for the production of "equipment for heavy industry" to the production series for tons of rolling mill equipment produced. In effect, this means that the quantity relative for the production of tons of rolling mill equipment is taken to represent the movement of production of equipment for the mining, metallurgical, and chemical industries. This is not too satisfactory an assumption, and it is fortunate for the reliability of the revised production index that there are relatively few such drastic assumptions involved in its construction.

A second method employed when no satisfactory basis could be found for subdividing a group weight was to attempt to find a common denominator for the physical products concerned. The most important example of this method is the aggregation of steam and water turbines, steam engines, stationary and marine diesels, and motor vehicle and tractor engines in terms of kilowatt capacity. The assumption here is that the cost of each of these types of prime movers varies approximately in proportion to the kilowatt capacity, and that the cost per kilowatt of capacity is the same regardless of type and size of the equipment concerned. This, too, is an extreme assumption and can scarcely be true in practice. The hope is, however, and it is scarcely more than that, that the assumption is not too much in error for the quantity relative computed on this basis to be at least an approximate indicator of the general trend in the production of these types of equipment.

The third method used when group weights could not be further subdivided was to construct a group index from the quantity series for the various products composing the group and unit values for these or similar products derived from the United States *Census of Manufactures*. (See below, pp. 49–50.)

One other problem which had to be faced in assigning weights to the quantity relatives for individual product series should be mentioned. In a few instances, principally in the food and machinery industries, it proved possible to compute net value-added weights for products or product groups for which no physical product series could be located in Soviet statistical sources. This was the case, for example, for milling, tea, coffee, wines and liquors in the food industry, and for pumps and compressors, control and measuring instruments, and "equipment for the food industry" in the machinery industry. This situation was handled in one of two ways, largely by rule of thumb. If it did not, for one reason or another, seem unreasonable that the production of the missing items had moved in harmony with the general index of the industry concerned, the net value-added weight for the missing items was imputed to the available quantity relatives for the products of the industry, in proportion to the existing weight carried by each of these series. If such an assumption appeared to be unjustified, the weight for the item was simply eliminated and the total weight for the industry concerned correspondingly reduced.

The group and individual product weights which resulted from the operations just described are presented in Table B. The table shows both the absolute weights in thousands of rubles and the relative weights which add to 100 per cent. While the general methods involved in the derivation of these weights have been described in the foregoing pages, the reader who is interested in the exact derivation of any specific weight will wish to consult Appendix B.

Physical Product Series

The physical product series to which these weights are applied have been collected from a variety of published volumes of official Soviet industrial statistics. Some of the production data were obtained with relative ease from statistical abstracts, other data were found only after painstaking and time-consuming search through the pages of economic and technical journals, yielding sometimes only a figure at a time. Appendix A gives a source for every production figure which is used in this study. While most of the comments regarding these production data are specific to the particular series concerned, a few general remarks are in order.

Many of the production data for years prior to 1931 are on a fiscal-year basis rather than a calendar-year basis. The Soviet fiscal year corresponded to the crop year and ran from October 1 to September 30. Prior to 1931, only data for peat, electric power, ore mining, coke, soap, matches, lumber, plywood, leather footwear, butter, and cigarettes are consistently available on a calendar-year basis. The major shift to a calendar-year basis occurred in 1931 although a number of product series, especially in the food and textile industries, were transferred from a fiscal-year to a calendar-year basis in 1930.

It would be desirable to have the revised index unequivocally on a calendar-year basis for the years prior to 1931 to facilitate comparison with the official index and with Soviet labor-force data, both of which are published on a calendar-year basis. However, two considerations argued against any statistical adjustment to transfer Soviet production series from a fiscal-year to a calendar-year basis. First, any such attempt would of necessity involve fairly arbitrary assumptions regarding the distribution of the production of many varieties of products over the four quarters of the year. Without accurate information regarding the seasonal pattern of production for the various commodities, it is not at all clear that an attempted adjustment would yield more accurate figures for years prior to 1931 than the mixed calendar-fiscal-year data actually employed. The second consideration had to do with the awkwardness which would arise in attempting to shift the final fiscal year to a calendar-year basis. Most Soviet production series pass from a fiscal-year to a calendar-year basis without providing data on the output of the fourth quarter of the calendar year in which the fiscal year ends. Any procedure adopted to estimate the output of the missing fourth quarter, especially in view of the lack of information on the seasonal distribution of output, would again be fairly arbitrary.

Since it is not clear that an adjustment to transfer output data for numerous series prior to 1931 from a fiscal-year to a calendar-year basis would in fact reduce the ambiguity of the annual period in these years, no such attempt has been made in the construction of the revised index. Instead, data for some commodities on a fiscal-year basis have been used interchangeably with those for other commodities on a calendar-year basis (for example, data for the fiscal year running from October 1, 1927 to September 30, 1928 have been used interchangeably with data for the calendar year 1928). If this were true of all the product series, the revised index would lag three months behind the calendar-year data for years prior to 1931. In a period of rapid industrial expansion such as characterized Soviet industry in the late 1920's, three months might make an appreciable difference in the volume of production for a selected twelve-month period. Since the revised index takes a twelve-month fiscal year as its base and the latter shifts forward to a calendar-year basis after 1930, the question arises whether the revised index may not exaggerate the growth of Soviet industrial output from 1928 as compared to an index which is uniformly on a calendar-year basis. The possibility is a real one, although it does not appear to be of more than minor quantitative importance.

An estimate of the maximum effect of substituting fiscal-year for calendar-year data in the base year of the revised index can be obtained on the assumption that output in each of the initial two fiscal years was distributed equally in the four quarters of the year. One fourth of the output in the fiscal year 1927–28 may then be subtracted and one fourth of the output in the fiscal year 1928–29 added to obtain an estimate of output in the calendar year 1928. Since the revised index shows 1928–29 at 120 per cent of 1927–28, this procedure will yield a new base for the revised index in the calendar year 1928 which is 5 per cent larger than the value for the fiscal year 1927–28. To anticipate results presented in Chapter 4 this shift to the calendar year 1928 as a base would reduce the value of the revised index in 1937 from 371 per cent to 354 per cent of 1928, and would affect other post–1930 index values similarly. This change, however, overstates the adjustment. Since a number of the product series which enter the revised index are already on a calendar-year basis, the actual extent to which the revised index departs from a calendar-year basis in its base year is less than the amount of the difference in industrial output in the fourth quarter of 1927 and the fourth quarter of 1928.

In subsequent discussion of the revised index and comparison with other measures of Soviet industrial growth and with population and labor-force data, no adjustment has been attempted for discrepancies in fiscal versus calendar years prior to 1931. Whenever appropriate, however, the reader is reminded of this fact by footnotes to the text or tables.

A second general comment regarding physical quantity series has to do with the treatment of gaps in some series in the decade 1927–28 to 1937. Wherever possible, these gaps were filled by simple interpolation, usually by taking the arithmetic average of the preceding and succeeding years. In other instances, the main series for a given industry was extrapolated on the basis of a dominant or representative subseries. Thus, for example, the production series for glass of all types has been extrapolated on the basis of the production series for window glass alone. In some cases, it was possible to link two series for the output of related products to obtain a more complete coverage by years than that offered by either of the individual series. An example of this occurs in the food industry with the linking of the series for "processing of fruits and vegetables" with that for "canning."

For some industries, it has been found advisable to substitute homogeneous input series for heterogeneous output series. Thus the consumption of crude oil by the petroleum refining industry is taken to represent the trend in output of that industry instead of the more accurate and less tractable (from a weighting viewpoint) several series for gasoline, kerosene, benzene, and others. The consumption of rubber is taken to represent the output trend for the rubber goods industry, and the consumption of ferrous metals in the production of agricultural machinery is made the basis for an extrapolation of that series for the years 1936 and 1937.

Gaps remained in some production series for the period 1927–28 to 1937 even after the exercise of considerable ingenuity, since there were cases in which the available data by no stretch of the imagination provided a reasonable basis for estimate. For the decade 1927–28 to 1937 the general procedure followed in these instances was to calculate the production index for the industry in which the incomplete product series was contained on the assumption that the output of the incomplete series had moved in harmony with the general index for the industry net of these series. This decision was implemented statistically by omitting from the base-year value totals for the industry, those items for which no data were available in the given year. Thus, the comparison of given-year and base-year output was made only for selected series, while the quantity relative so calculated was taken to represent the entire industry inclusive of the missing series, and was given the full weight for the entire industry in the general index of production.

There were, of course, any number of products which had to be omitted entirely from the production index. Some omissions resulted from lack of physical production data, others from inability to calculate satisfactory value weights.

The product coverage of the revised index drops sharply after 1937, reflecting the decline in the volume of economic statistics published by the Soviet government. There is no way of knowing with any certainty how well movements in the published output series reflect changes in production of other products. The representativeness of the revised index for the years after 1937 clearly is open to question. For this reason, missing production series have been omitted completely from the index after 1937. No attempt has been made to assign the value weights for missing series to available product series for the same industry. The problem of measuring changes in Soviet industrial output after 1937 is discussed in greater detail in Chapter 5.

Production Index for the Machinery Industry

The large variety of products produced by the machinery industry greatly complicated all phases of the construction of the machinery index. In addition to the usual problems and procedures encountered and employed in other industries, the machinery index required the introduction of some methods not used in any other industry. In particular, assignment of value weights to the individual product series for machinery was a difficult problem.

An exception to the general weighting methodology has been made for six branches of the machinery industry: agricultural implements and equipment, textile machinery, construction and road building machinery, hoisting and handling machinery, metal-cutting machine tools, and a miscellaneous group consisting of sewing machines, typewriters, motorcycles, and bicycles. There was no single dominant or representative series in any of these subgroups, and in no instance was there a measure of output in conventional units to serve as a common denominator for the physically diverse collection of products. Therefore, in order to avoid having to omit these important products from the revised production index, subindices were constructed for each of the above types of machinery using unit values computed from the United States *Census of Manufactures* as weights. Once these subindices were obtained, they were reweighted by Russian pay-roll weights (available for each of the subseries as a whole) and thus assimilated to the general methodology of the production index.

Not only does the machinery index involve certain unique procedures which require discussion, but it provides instructive examples of most of the procedures employed in calculating production indices for other industries. For these reasons a more detailed discussion of the construction of the machinery index is included in Appendix C to this volume.

The General Production Index

The general production index is the arithmetic mean of weighted quantity relatives for the individual products and industries, that is, the sum of the weighted product and industry relatives for each year was divided by the sum of the weights to obtain the finished index with base year 1934 equal to 100.

Summary and Critical Appraisal of Statistical Procedures

If, for purposes of criticism, the statistical procedures involved in the construction of the new index are divided into two general categories, (1) the selection of output series and (2) the derivation of net value-added weights for output relatives, it is at once clear that most of the unique statistical procedures followed in constructing the new index come under the second heading. Most of the shortcomings of the output series have their parallels in any production index which relies on imputed rather than earned weights. Input series have been substituted for output series, various conventional units of measurement have been used instead of physical units. The physical output series which are used do not reflect fully the increase in the degree of fabrication over time, although this defect may be compensated in part or entirely in the Soviet case by a deterioration in quality of some products. These devices and laments are familiar to the student of production indices, since they are largely unavoidable if indices of the physical volume of production are to be computed at all.

The derivation of weights for the revised index is a considerably more complicated procedure, however, than is usually required. The principal reason for this is, of course, the absence in published Soviet industrial statistics of compiled statistics for value-added in industrial groups, industries, and processes. Nothing comparable in richness of statistical detail to the United States *Census of Manufactures* with its statistics for value-added by manufacture, value of product, cost of materials, and wages classified by industry and product is published for Soviet industry. Moreover, the standardization of industrial classifications and census criteria which has been achieved in the United States was noticeably absent in Soviet statistics of industry prior to the 1940's. These facts have necessitated not only the preliminary computation of industrial pay rolls from wage and employment data (in themselves not always as detailed as one would wish), but the adjustment of these pay rolls for differences in the concept of large-scale industry as defined by the industrial and labor divisions of the Central Statistical Administration and their further adjustment to include pay-roll taxes in addition to basic wage and salary payments.

It has been the writer's purpose to expose the shortcomings in these operations to the critical view of the readers. The more important of these shortcomings are: (1) the multiplication of employment in a particular process by the average wage for the entire industry in computing pay rolls, (2) the use of employment data for July 1, 1934 as well as average figures for the entire year, (3) the problem of matching accurately the industrial classifications used in labor division statistics with those used in industrial division statistics, and (4) the computaton of pay-roll tax adjustment coefficients from data on the structure of costs of production calculated for enterprises of the industrial commissariats only, rather than for all large-scale industry, and the application of a general pay-roll tax coefficient for an entire industry to estimate pay-roll taxes for a specific subdivision of that industry. When group net value-added weights had been calculated by the foregoing methods, the problem of imputing group weights to individual product series was tackled by fairly conventional methods, the one innovation perhaps being the use of unit cost, and unit labor requirement data as guides to the assignment of weights to individual series.

Clearly the net value-added weights which are obtained as the result of this series of statistical operations are more subject to error than if they had been taken directly from the compiled and published statistics of a reliable government agency. Just as clearly this latter alternative simply did not exist for the Soviet Union. While the statistics used are from official sources, they are subject to gaps which it has been the purpose of the statistical procedure described in this chapter to bridge. The adjustments which have been made, in many cases, are substantial as study of Appendix B will reveal. Nevertheless, the writer believes that the revised production index gives a reasonably accurate picture of changes in the physical volume of production of Soviet industry, especially for the decade 1928–1937, and is a demonstrably better index for this purpose than the official Soviet production index.

4

Production of Soviet Large-Scale Industry, 1927–28 to 1937

The 1934 value-added index of Soviet industrial production may be conveniently set forth through a comparison with the official Soviet index. Discrepancies between the two indices may arise, however, from a multiplicity of causes, so that no precise attribution of degrees of divergence to particular causes may be expected.

The official Soviet index for large-scale state and coöperative industry (excluding lumbering and fisheries) and the 1934 value-added index for large-scale industry (excluding lumbering but including fisheries) for the years 1928–1937 are shown in Table 4.

Included in the revised index of Soviet industrial production for the years 1928–1937 are 137 separate product series. Many of these are for specific product types; others represent the combined output of a number of physical products aggregated in terms of some common physical characteristic or conventional unit of measurement. Seventy-six of these 137 product series are machinery items; the remaining 61 are nonmachinery items representing the whole range of industrial production and a considerable portion of mining.

Although the revised index avoids a number of the specific defects of the official index, its usefulness as an accurate measure of movements in the physical volume of Soviet industrial production may be vitiated by incomplete coverage for industry as a whole or by nonrepresentative and erratic measures of the output of individual industries. These problems are examined below.

General Coverage

The gross value of output of Soviet large-scale industry in the year 1934 measured in the constant prices of the year 1926–27 was 50,568 million rubles.[1] The gross value of output at 1926–27 prices of the industries included in the revised production index (either by direct representation among the quantity relatives or in the net value-added weights imputed to these series) was 36,064 million rubles. Thus, by this admittedly inadequate measure, the revised production index covers in the base year 1934 approximately 71 per cent of industrial output included in the official index. The principle on which the revised index has been constructed, however, is net value-added rather than gross value. Ideally, therefore, it is more appropriate to inquire what proportion of *net value-added* by industry in 1934 is represented by the output series included in the revised index.

TABLE 4

Production Indices for Soviet Large-Scale Industry, 1928–1937

Year	Revised Index [a] (per cent of 1934)	Official Index [b] (per cent of 1934)
1928	46.6 [c]	32.8
1929	54.8 [c]	41.3
1930	62.8 [c]	53.7
1931	72.7	67.0
1932	76.0	76.6
1933	82.8	82.9
1934	100.0	100.0
1935	123.6	123.6
1936	146.0	162.0
1937	160.3	180.6

[a] This version of the revised index excludes lumbering but includes fisheries both of which were also excluded from the official index.
[b] The official index has been shifted from a 1913 to a 1934 base.
[c] Values represent fiscal rather than calendar years.
Source (for the official index) — *SSSR i kapitalisticheskie strany* (USSR and the Capitalist Countries; ed. Ia. A. Ioffe; Moscow-Leningrad; Gosplanizdat, 1939), p. 127.

Net value-added in industry as a whole may be estimated for 1934 by expanding the industrial pay roll to include pay-roll taxes and by making an upward adjustment to allow for the difference in coverage between industrial division and labor division statistics of employment in industry.[2] A figure of 12,586.8 million rubles is given as the annual pay roll for employees in large-scale industry by *Trud v SSSR*, 1936.[3] This figure has been adjusted upward by 48 per cent to 18.6 billion rubles to allow for the difference in coverage between labor statistics and industrial statistics for employment (and thus pay rolls) in large-scale industry. An upward adjustment of 48 per cent was established by comparing the average annual number of workers in large-scale industry in 1934 according to labor statistics (4,993,100) [4] with the average annual number of workers in large-scale industry in 1934 according to industrial statistics (7,404,000). Pay rolls in 1934 were 26.5 per cent of factory costs of production in large-scale industry, while pay-roll taxes were 5.2 per cent of these costs.[5] Thus pay rolls plus pay-roll taxes in 1934 were a magnitude equal to 119.6 per cent of pay rolls [(26.5 + 5.2) /26.5 = 1.196]. Total net value-added in large-scale industry in 1934 can then be estimated at 22.2 billion rubles (18.6 billion rubles times 1.196 = 22.2 billion rubles). This amount must be divided by twelve before it can be compared to the sum of the net value-added weights for the new index.[6] One-twelfth of 22.2 billion is 1.85 billion. The sum of the net value-added weights for the revised index is 989 million rubles. Thus the coverage of the revised index in terms of net value-added in large-scale industry in 1934 is 53.5 per cent (989/1,850 = .535).

If the distribution of the average annual number of workers by industry is accepted as an approximation to the distribution of net value-added in specific industries, a second calculation of the coverage of the revised index in terms of net value-added is possible. The annual average number of workers in large-scale industry as a whole in 1934 was 7,404,000.[7] Of these, 3,237,900 were employed in branches of industry which are omitted from the revised index. Thus by this measure, the revised index covers 56.3 per cent of net value-added in industry in 1934

$$\left(\frac{7,404,000 - 3,237,900}{7,404,000} = .563\right).$$

Variation in Coverage Among Industries

To assess the reliability of the revised index as an indicator of movements in the physical volume of production for all large-scale industry, it is necessary to know something of the growth patterns and relative importance in terms of net value-added of the branches of industry which have been excluded from the revised index relative to the branches of industry which have been included. This poses a problem, since the exclusion of the omitted series arises from a lack of satisfactory output data in some cases and the difficulty of calculating net value-added weights

TABLE 5

Average Annual Number of Workers as of 1934 in Branches of Large-Scale Industry Included and Excluded in the Revised Production Index

	Average Annual Number of Workers	
	Included	Excluded
1. Power stations	76.7	
2. Coal mining	422.8	
3. Crude petroleum production	26.5	
4. Peat extraction	114.7	
5. Oil shales		1.4
6. Ore mining	131.2	
7. Nonmetallic minerals		134.6
8. Lumber industry		974.5
9. Coke industry	27.8	
10. Petroleum refining	13.9	
11. Illuminating gas		1.4
12. Chemicals	160.3	
13. Stone, clay, and glass products		2.4
a. Mineral building materials	137.3	81.6
b. Glass industry	70.7	
c. China and pottery		26.5
14. Ferrous metals	310.5	
15. Nonferrous metals	42.7	
16. Metalworking industries		
a. Repair plants		623.2
b. Machinery	611.5	380.3
c. Metal wares		257.3
d. Structural steel parts and welding		16.2
17. Abrasives, graphite		6.1
18. Rubber	47.1	
19. Asbestos		1.6
20. Woodworking		
a. Sawmill and plywood	193.9	
b. Other		156.7
21. Paper	45.3	
22. Printing and publishing		84.2
23. Textiles	768.9	107.3
24. Needle industries		283.0
25. Leather industry	30.9	
26. Artificial leather		2.2
27. Leather goods (excluding footwear)		16.3
28. Fur industry		28.8
29. Boots and shoes	157.6	
30. Grease, tallow, soap, and perfume	18.4	
31. Food industry	673.2	
32. Miscellaneous		111.0
33. Statistical discrepancy		25.5
TOTAL	4,081.9	3,322.1

SOURCE — *Socialist Construction in the USSR*, 1936, pp. 42–47.

in others: precisely the data which are needed to make the intended comparison. Nevertheless, it is possible to make some estimates of the growth patterns and the importance in terms of net value-added of the omitted branches of industry which, while below the standards set for inclusion in the revised index, serve adequately in the present context. The approach used is to accept the average annual number of workers employed in a branch of industry as an approximate indication of its importance in terms of net value-added and to use official statistics for the gross value of output for the branch as an indication, though inflated, of the growth pattern in the branch.

Table 5 shows the average annual number of workers employed in industry in 1934, classified by major branches of industry and divided into the categories "included" and "excluded" with reference to the revised production index. It will be remembered that the Soviet definition of industry includes lumbering and mining as well as manufacturing. An inspection of this table reveals that the more important omissions are lumbering, repair plants, a part of machinery, metal wares, needle trades, nonmetallic minerals, a part of textiles, wood working other than sawmills and plywood, publishing, and miscellaneous. The first five of these are the most important and will be discussed in some detail.

The lumbering industry was excluded from the revised production index because calculation of an appropriate net value-added weight was considered too risky. Soviet statistical sources provide data which may be taken as an indication of the change in the physical volume of production of the lumber industry for the years 1929–1937. These data for the quantity of lumber removed from forests measured in millions of cubic meters are presented in Table 6.

The production of the lumber industry increased only 211 per cent from 1929 to 1937 compared to an increase of 291 per cent in the revised production index for these years. Including lumbering in the revised index, therefore, would have resulted, other things being equal, in a smaller increase in total industrial output over the period than is indicated by the revised index net of the lumber industry. According to rough estimates, had lumbering been included in the revised index, it would have carried approximately 13 per cent of the total weight on a net value-added basis.[8] Thus it would have had an important retarding effect on the rate of growth displayed by the revised index net of lumbering. It must be noted, however, that the official index presented above also omits lumbering so that the lumbering industry is no key to the discrepancy between the revised and the official index.

For needle trades, the only available production indicator is the gross value of output at 1926–27 prices given in official Soviet statistics. These data are shown for the years 1928–1934 and 1937 in Table 7. These figures indicate an increase of 355 per cent from 1928 to 1934, while the revised

TABLE 6

Output of the Lumber Industry, 1929–1937
(lumber removed from forests)

Year	Quantity (mil. cu. meters)	Index (per cent of 1929)
1929	95.5	100
1930	147.2	154
1931	159.8	167
1932	164.7	172
1933	173.3	181
1934	181.3	190
1935	203.2	213
1936	202.5	212
1937	201.5	211

SOURCES — 1929–1935 from *Socialist Construction in the USSR*, 1936, p. 189; 1936 from *Narodnokhoziaistvennyi plan Souiza SSR na 1937 god*, 1937, pp. 94–95; 1937 from *Sotsialisticheskoe stroitel'stvo Soiuza SSR 1933–1938* (Moscow, 1939), p. 70.

production index shows an increase of only 113 per cent in the same period. Apparently, including needle trades in the revised index, if this were possible, would pull the general index up at least a few degrees. What is of particular interest about these official statistics for the needle trades is the peculiar pattern of the increase. The bulk of the increase was attained by 1930, and from 1931, the trend was actually downward. The figure for 1937, while somewhat less inclusive than the others in coverage, indicates clearly that nothing approaching the growth of the early years was achieved in the later years. This peculiar growth pattern means clearly but one thing. The growth in the gross value of output of the needle trades shown for the early years is the result, not of genuine expansion of the needle trades, but of statistical manipulation.

It is now well known that one source of inflationary bias in the official index of production of large-scale industry is "the transfer of formerly small-scale industrial enterprises into the category of large-scale industry, a process of some importance in the years of the First Five Year Plan."[9] This transfer occurred both as a result of changes in statistical criteria for large-scale industry and as a result of the organization and amalgamation of small privately run shops into larger establishments. The latter process was particularly easy to carry out in the needle trades where the capital equipment required is negligible. In short, the needle trades are a prime example of the particular type of inflationary bias cited above, and the official figures for gross value of output in this industry are not a reliable guide even to the general trend of growth in this industry. There can be little doubt, however, that the actual growth of the industry was markedly less than that shown in the official figures. It is not at all unlikely that including an accurate measure of the net value-

TABLE 7

Gross Output of the Needle Trades, 1928–1937

Year	Millions of 1926–27 rubles	Index (per cent of 1928)
1928	449	100
1929	822	183
1930	1,629	363
1931	2,195	489
1932	2,142	477
1933	2,069	461
1934	2,043	455
1937	1,927[a]	429[a]

[a] The figure for 1937 is for the People's Commissariat of Light Industry only.
SOURCES — 1928–1934 from *Socialist Construction in the USSR* (Moscow, 1936), p. 49; 1937 from *Tretii piatiletnii plan razvitiia narodnogo khoziaistva Soiuza SSR 1938–1942*) (Moscow, 1939), p. 209.

added to manufactures by the needle trades, had this been possible, would have left the general production index very little changed from what it is without the needle trades.

Repair shops, the omitted part of the machinery industry (consisting for the most part of "shipbuilding," "other transportation equipment," and "various other equipment"), and metal wares are all branches of the Soviet metalworking industry. Taken together, they account for approximately 38 per cent of net value-added in Soviet industry not covered by the revised production index. Moreover, taken together, they comprise 67.6 per cent of total net value-added to manufactures by the metalworking industry in 1934, judging from figures for the annual average number of workers employed. Clearly, this is a potential source of serious distortion in the machinery-metalworking index and in the production index for industry as a whole. To assess its importance, we must know something of the probable movement of the physical volume of production in these branches. The only production indicators for these branches of the metalworking industry are the official series for the gross value of their output at constant 1926–27 prices. Table 8 presents these data for the only three years for which such a classification of the official gross value figures was obtainable.

TABLE 8

Gross Output of the Metalworking Industry, 1932–1934
(Official figures at 1926–27 prices)

Year	Machinery Included [a]		Machinery Excluded [a]		Metal Wares		Repair Shops		Total Metalworking	
	(million rubles)	(% of 1932)	(million rubles)	(% of 1932)	(million rubles)	(% of 1932)	(million rubles)	(% of 1932)	(million rubles)	(% of 1932)
1932	4,388	100	1,873	100	1,681	100	1,355	100	9,408	100
1933	5,254	120	2,171	116	1,695	101	1,605	118	10,822	115
1934	6,648	152	2,801	150	2,062	123	1,993	147	13,611	145

[a] Reference is to coverage of the revised index for machinery.
SOURCE — *Sotsialisticheskoe stroitel'stvo SSSR* (Moscow, 1936), pp. 8–11.

With the exception of metal wares, the subseries move in quite close harmony, although the series for machinery items included in the new index (largely by direct representation but in part by imputing of weights) shows a slightly greater increase than the others from 1932 to 1933. A comparison of the revised index for the machinery industry with the index based on the official figures for the value of gross output of the same branches of the machinery industry (shown above) for the years 1932–1934 is presented in Table 9.

If we assume that a revised index for all metalworking (had it been possible to construct one) would have borne the same relation to the official index for all metalworking as the revised index for machinery bears to the official index for the same branches of machinery, then the index for all metalworking for these three years would have been as follows: 1932 — 100; 1933 — 121; 1934 — 135.

Two factors have to be considered in assessing the reasonableness of this assumption: (1) the amount of inflation in the respective branch indices, and (2) the shift in the relative importance of the several branches with the change to net value-added rather than gross value. It is probable that the official gross value of output figures for repair shops are particularly subject to an upward bias as a result of the common practice of valuing repair work at current prices rather than actual 1926–27 prices.[10] Moreover, on the basis of net value-added, repair shops carry approximately one-third of the total weight for the metalworking industry. Metal wares, even in the official statistics, show a relatively small increase. The

TABLE 9

Production Indices for Machinery, 1932–1934
(per cent of 1932)

	1932	1933	1934
Revised Index for Machinery	100	126	141
Official Index (same coverage)	100	120	152

metal wares branch carries approximately 14 per cent of the total net value-added weight for machinery in the base year. That part of the machinery industry proper which has been omitted from the revised index consists of shipbuilding, other transportation equipment (this does *not* include railroad rolling stock or motor vehicles), and "various other equipment." The Soviet Union purchased a considerable portion of its merchant tonnage abroad during these years, so that it is not likely that shipbuilding expanded as rapidly as other branches of machinery. The other two categories are too nondescript for even an intelligent guess as to their growth pattern. Perhaps the safest assumption is that they moved with the index of machinery output as computed for the revised index.

On balance, then, it seems fairly certain that a production index for the entire metalworking industry, had it been possible to compute one, would have shown no greater growth for these years than the revised index for the machinery industry, and quite possibly a somewhat smaller increase. Expanding the coverage for the metalworking industry would, however, have an important effect on the general production index, since the expanded coverage would result in approximately tripling the net value-added weight for one of the most rapidly expanding industries in the Soviet industrial economy.

Later in this chapter an attempt is made to adjust the revised index to allow for the defects in coverage which have just been discussed. First, however, it is desirable to compare the indices for *specific industries* used in constructing the revised general index of industrial production with the official figures for the gross value of output of these industries, to uncover and analyze any important differences, and in this way to check the accuracy of the production indicators for individual industries which have been used in the revised index.

A Comparison of Revised and Official Indices for Specific Industries

Both the official Soviet and the revised production indices for specific industries are presented in Table 28.* The official Soviet indices have been computed from data for the gross value of output for the various branches of industry given in millions of rubles at 1926–27 prices. The revised indices, in some cases (for example, coal), are simply quantity relatives computed from the physical production series in Table A, and in other cases (for example, machinery), are the arithmetic mean of quantity relatives for a number of subseries weighted in proportion to net value-added in the particular subprocess in the base year 1934. In general, as one might expect, there is fairly good correspondence between the Soviet value indices and the revised indices for single-product or one major-product industries. Examples of this are coal mining, iron-ore mining, cement, sawmills and plywood, and boots and shoes. The change from gross value to net value-added as a measure of relative importance has almost no effect internal to these industries. Also, they are industries in which new product bias is absent or at a minimum. The two industries of this type, for which the correspondence between the revised and the official indices is poorest, are manganese-ore mining and matches. Since the ore content of manganese ore was very stable over the decade in question, and matches would seem to be a fairly standardized product, the writer has no explanation for these discrepancies.

For those multiple-product industries for which single inputs or single major products were allowed to stand for the more complex output, the correspondence between the revised indices and the official indices in most instances is close enough to be reassuring; that is, it is well within

* See Tabular Section, p. 189, below.

the range and generally in the direction of the correction for new-product bias which was intended. Examples here are the glass industry, the paper industry, petroleum refining, and the grease, tallow, soap, and perfume industry.

The most important and most interesting pairs of production indices, however, are those for the multiple product industries or industrial groups such as chemicals, ferrous metals, machinery, food, and textiles. Taken together, these five industries comprise 62.33 per cent of the assigned net value-added weights in the base year 1934. Their accuracy collectively and individually, therefore, is critical to the reliability of the revised index. Let us consider them in turn.*

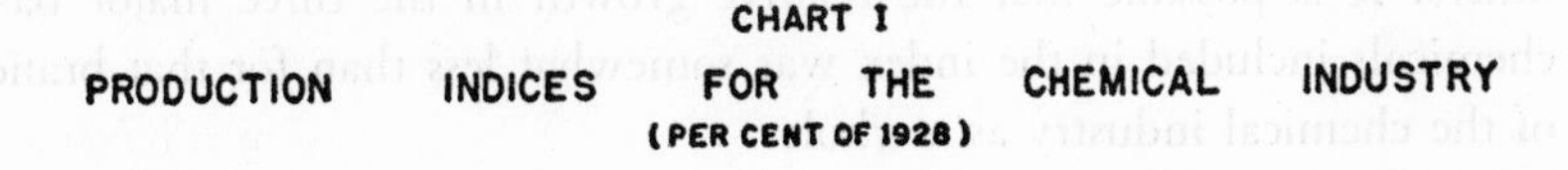

CHART I
PRODUCTION INDICES FOR THE CHEMICAL INDUSTRY
(PER CENT OF 1928)

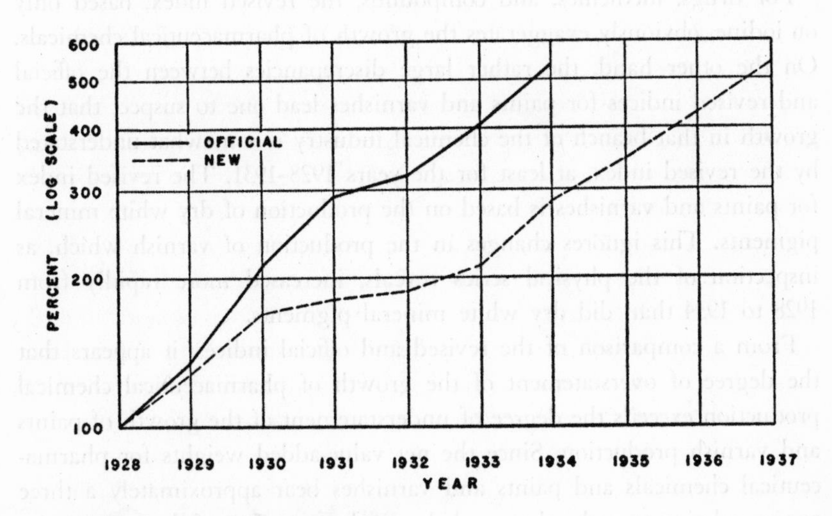

SOURCE: DATA FROM TABLE 28

Chemical industry. The official index for the chemical industry as a whole exhibits a more rapid rate of growth than the revised index for the chemical industry throughout the years 1928–1933, while from 1933 to 1934 the rate of growth in the two indices is identical. No official data for the gross value of output of the chemical industry are available for

* Ratio scale charts are presented for each industry discussed in detail. For convenience in visual appreciation, the base year has been transferred from 1934 to 1928.

the years 1935–1937. Three subseries for the chemical industry are likewise available for comparison: basic chemicals; drugs, medicines, and compounds; and paints and varnishes. No comparison is possible for synthetic dyes or for artificial fibers, since official data are lacking for these branches.

That the revised index for basic chemicals lags behind the official index may perhaps be explained on two grounds. In part, it may show less growth because of the elimination of the new product bias. Another factor, however, is the fact that the revised index is based only on superphosphate, soda ash, and sulphuric acid, while omitting numerous other chemicals such as sodium sulphate, hydrochloric acid, bicarbonate, and others. It is possible that the relative growth in the three major basic chemicals included in the index was somewhat less than for that branch of the chemical industry as a whole.

For drugs, medicines, and compounds, the revised index, based only on iodine, obviously exaggerates the growth of pharmaceutical chemicals. On the other hand, the rather large discrepancies between the official and revised indices for paints and varnishes lead one to suspect that the growth in that branch of the chemical industry is somewhat understated by the revised index, at least for the years 1928–1931. The revised index for paints and varnishes is based on the production of dry white mineral pigments. This ignores changes in the production of varnish which, as inspection of the physical series reveals, increased more rapidly from 1928 to 1934 than did dry white mineral pigments.

From a comparison of the revised and official indices, it appears that the degree of overstatement of the growth of pharmaceutical chemical production exceeds the degree of understatement of the growth of paints and varnish production. Since the net value-added weights for pharmaceutical chemicals and paints and varnishes bear approximately a three to two relation to each other, on balance, the net effect of these two series on the chemical industry production index is probably a slight upward bias. This, in turn, may be more than offset by the possible understatement of growth in basic chemicals. This latter is not too certain, however, and with aniline dyes and artificial fibers missing from the analysis, it is impossible to state the direction of the over-all bias in the revised chemical industry index with any confidence.

CHART II

PRODUCTION INDICES FOR THE FERROUS METALS INDUSTRY

(PER CENT OF 1928)

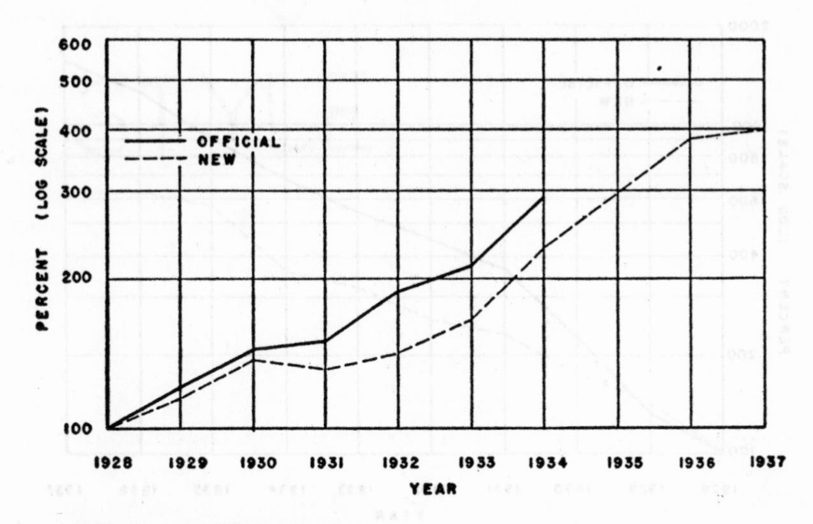

SOURCE: DATA FROM TABLE 28

Ferrous metals. The revised index for the production of ferrous metals is the weighted arithmetic mean of quantity relatives for the production of pig iron, steel, and rolled steel. A comparison of this index with the official index reveals that the major discrepancy occurs in the year 1931, for which the revised index shows an actual decline while the official index shows a small increase. Since all the physical series for ferrous metals output show an actual decline in this year, it would appear that the official index is incorrect when it indicates an increase in production for 1931. That it does so, may have its explanation in the inclusion in the official index of relatively small quantities of special steels or rolled products at extraordinarily high prices. A second possible explanation may lie in the relation of gross measures of output to net value-added measures from which double-counting, possibly of considerable importance in the ferrous metal industry, has been removed.[11] While the rates of growth in the two indices are about the same in the period 1928–1930, the revised index stands at a higher level relative to the base year 1934 than does the official index. This, it will be observed, follows the pattern set by the chemical industry.

CHART III

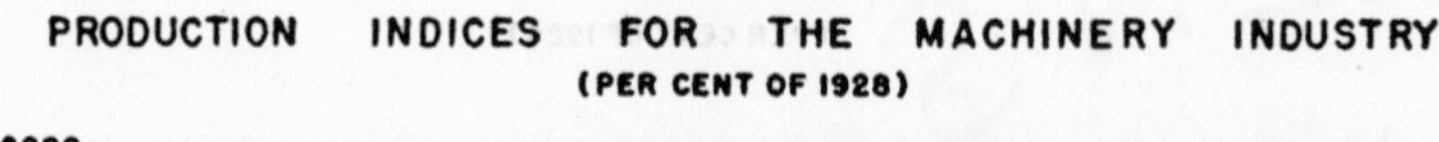

PRODUCTION INDICES FOR THE MACHINERY INDUSTRY
(PER CENT OF 1928)

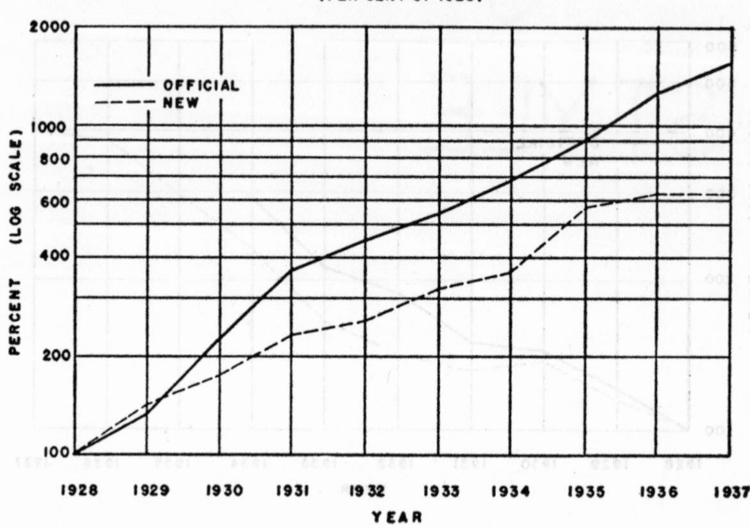

SOURCE: DATA FROM TABLE 28

Machinery. The machinery industry is the case par excellence for new product bias (that is, for the bias caused by including new products in the production index at the exaggerated current prices of the first high-cost period of production). It is not surprising, therefore, that the official index for the machinery industry displays a much more rapid growth pattern than the revised index for most years, with 1935 a marked exception.

The increase of 56.7 per cent in the revised index from 1934 to 1935 is accounted for primarily by marked increases in that year of two important subindices within the machinery index: an increase of 84 per cent in the index for railroad equipment and an increase of 158 per cent in the index for equipment for the mining, metallurgical, and chemical industries. The index for railroad equipment is compounded of six subseries, and the writer claims for it a fairly high degree of reliability. In the case of the index for equipment for the mining, metallurgical, and chemical industries, a somewhat different situation exists. Owing to lack of data for determining relative weights, the entire weight for this group of machinery products has been assigned to a single quantity relative, namely, that for the production of rolling-mill equipment in metric tons. Thus, the sharp increase in the production of rolling-mill equipment from 1934 to 1935 enters the general index for machinery products with the combined net value-added weight for the mining, metallurgical, and chemical equipment producing branches of the machinery industry. There can be little question that the development of the revised index from 1934 to 1935 would be more gradual if it were possible to give the production of equipment for the mining and chemical industries more adequate representation in the revised index. The use of quantity relatives for rolling-mill equipment for the production indicator for equipment for the mining, metallurgical, and chemical industries probably tends to introduce an upward bias in the revised machinery index, since this quantity relative undoubtedly exaggerates the growth of the combined output of these branches of the machinery industry.

Two subseries for the machinery industry also are available for comparison. The difference between the official and the revised index for the production of tractors may be due almost entirely to the omission of tractors produced in the Kirov plant from the official series.[12] The difference between the official and the revised index for motor vehicles appears to arise from a difference in the relative weights assigned to different models of vehicles. Since a tenfold increase from 1931 to 1932 in the physical production of 2.5-ton trucks results in a 441 per cent increase in the revised index for motor vehicles and only an 87 per cent increase in the official index, it is clear that 2.5-ton trucks are assigned a greater relative weight in the revised index than in the official index. The 2.5-ton trucks in the revised index carry a net value-added weight which has been computed for trucks from 2.5 to 4 tons. In fact, in the base year 1934 for which the weights were computed only 4-ton trucks were produced in this class. Thus, the relative weights for the class are actually those for 4-ton trucks. When applied to the production of 2.5-ton trucks, they may exaggerate the relative importance of these trucks in the total of value-added with the result that the growth in the production of motor vehicles may be exaggerated in those years when the output of 2.5-ton trucks was numerically large. Owing to the pattern of production of 2.5-ton trucks, this factor is of special importance in the revised index only in the year 1932.

ndex for machinery shows a slightly greater annual in-
official index in 1929 and in 1933. Otherwise, except for
t undoubtedly exaggerates the increase in output, the
s at a less rapid rate than the official index. This is
would expect of an index from which a considerable
of the new product bias has been removed.

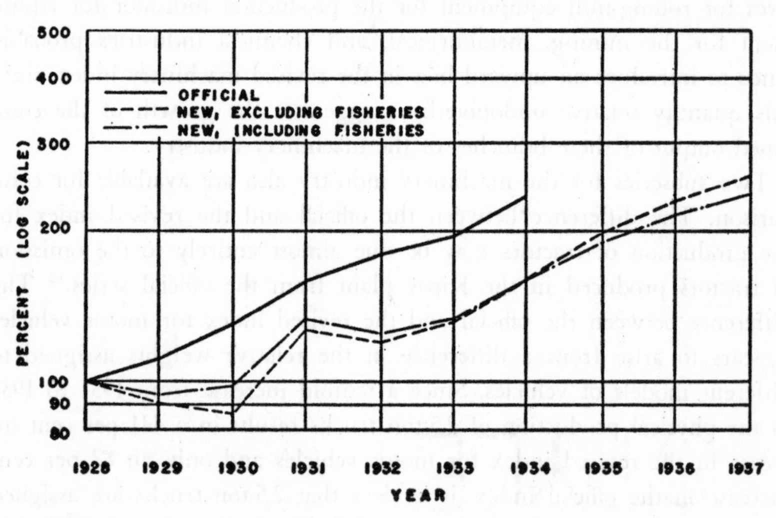

SOURCE: DATA FROM TABLE 28

Food industry. Comparison of the revised and official indices for the food industry is complicated by certain mutual exclusions in coverage. The official index excludes fisheries, while the revised index has been computed in two versions, one including and the other excluding fisheries. Further, while milling and distilling are included in the weights for the food industry in the revised index, specific quantity relatives for these two branches of the food industry are lacking.

Another factor of importance in comparing the revised and official indices for the food industry is the shift in the relative importance of fisheries, milling, and distilling when the index is transferred from a gross value to a net value-added basis. The per cent of gross value of output at 1926–27 prices for the food industry as a whole in 1934 accounted for by these branches was, respectively: fisheries — 4.7; milling — 17.4; distilling — 11.7. The per cent of the share of each of these branches in the net value-added in the food industry in 1934 (as computed in Table B, below) was, respectively: fisheries — 13.5; milling — 3.3; distilling — 6.3. Fisheries, milling, and distilling were all established, relatively mature industries at the beginning of the decade 1928–1937. Their influence, therefore, is to retard the rate of growth in an index of production for the food industry for these years. Milling and distilling are of much reduced importance in the revised index (both because weights are on a

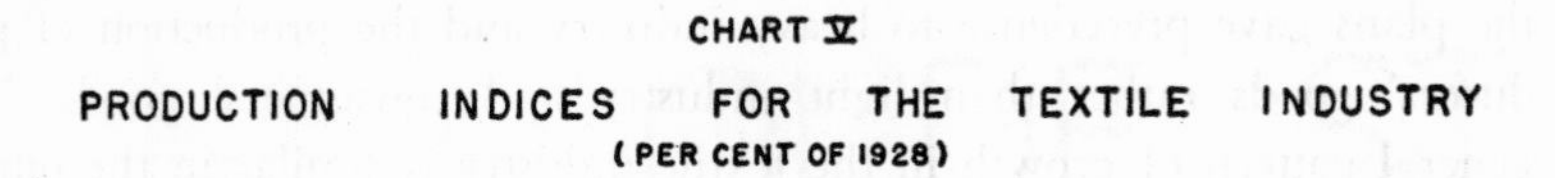

CHART V
PRODUCTION INDICES FOR THE TEXTILE INDUSTRY
(PER CENT OF 1928)

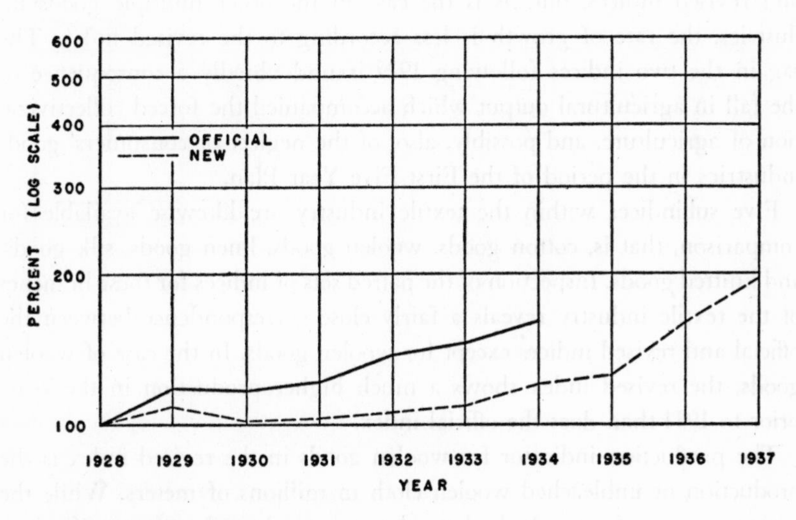

SOURCE: DATA FROM TABLE 28

value-added rather than gross-value basis and because there are no quantity relatives for milling and distilling) but fisheries are magnified in importance (because of value-added weights).

Both versions of the revised index for the food industry reveal a slower increase in output than the official index. The revised index which excludes fisheries, as one would expect, indicates a more rapid increase in output than the index which includes fisheries.[13] Nevertheless, the divergence between the revised and official indices for the food industry is less pronounced than for other multiple product industries, such as chemicals or machinery. This is in accord with expectations, since new product bias in the food industry may be presumed to have been of much less importance than in chemicals or machinery.

Textile industry. The decade growth in the textile industry according to either the official index or the revised index is moderate. This was to be expected. The textile industry was one of the most mature industries in the Soviet economy at the beginning of the First Five Year Plan, and the plans gave precedence to heavy industry and the production of producers' goods rather than light industry and consumers' goods. The general pattern of growth in the textile industry is similar in the official and revised indices, but, as is the case in the other multiple goods industries, the rate of growth is less according to the revised index. The sag in the two indices following 1929 is undoubtedly a consequence of the fall in agricultural output which accompanied the forced collectivization of agriculture, and possibly, also, of the neglect of consumers' goods industries in the period of the First Five Year Plan.

Five subindices within the textile industry are likewise available for comparison, that is, cotton goods, woolen goods, linen goods, silk goods, and knitted goods. Inspection of the paired sets of indices for these branches of the textile industry reveals a fairly close correspondence between the official and revised indices except for woolen goods. In the case of woolen goods, the revised index shows a much higher production in the years prior to 1934 than does the official index.

The production indicator for woolen goods in the revised index is the production of unbleached woolen cloth in millions of meters. While the various sources from which these data were taken do not specify, it is presumed that reference is to linear rather than square meters. Linear meters do not take into account changes in width and weight, so that changes in these dimensions of the cloth reduce the accuracy with which a linear measure reflects changes in the value of output. On the other hand, changes in the grade and quality of cloth may well have been the source of new product bias in the official index. In the absence of further evidence, the writer feels that the question as to the relative accuracy of the official and revised indices for the woolen-goods industry must remain open. The woolen-goods branch of the textile industry carries one-tenth of the total net value-added weight for the textile industry as a whole in the revised index. From this, it is clear that the general pattern of the revised index for textiles would not be greatly modified even by the complete substitution of the official index for the revised index of woolen goods.

The comparison of the revised and official indices for the five important multiple product industries — chemicals, ferrous metals, machinery, food, and textiles, does not reveal any startling or erratic discrepancies. Although there are marked differences in the revised and official indices for these industries, the differences are those which are to be expected in view of the known inflationary bias in the official index. It may be concluded that the problem of outright omission of certain branches of industry from the revised index is likely to be a greater source of error than misrepresentation of those industries which are included by the product series selected to portray their growth.

Adjusting the Revised Index for Coverage

It has been shown that in terms of general coverage, the industries included in the revised index account for approximately 54 per cent of total net value-added in Soviet large-scale industry in the base year 1934. Among the omissions of major importance are lumbering, repair plants, a part of machinery, and needle trades. The omission of lumbering results in a more rapid rate of growth in the revised index than would have been the case had lumbering been included. The effect of the omission of needle trades is more difficult to judge in the absence of any reliable production indicator for this branch of industry. The omission of metal wares, some branches of the machinery industry, and repair shops is judged to have resulted in a machinery index which is somewhat inflated relative to an index for the full metalworking industry, but in a general index for large-scale industry which is somewhat too low because of the underweighting of an important industry which expanded more rapidly than industry as a whole. No analysis has been attempted of the effect of other numerous but less important omissions such as nonmetallic minerals, woodworking other than sawmills and plywood, a part of textiles, and miscellaneous other small industries.

The major source of possible distortion in the coverage of the revised index appears to be the underweighting of the metalworking industry. The purpose of the present adjustment is to correct this defect. It is assumed that the revised index net of machinery is fairly representative of the production movements of all industry except metalworking. The revised machinery index is accepted as representing the movements in the physical volume of production for the entire metalworking industry. These two indices, shown in Table 10, are then combined on the basis of revised net value-added weights, and their arithmetic mean is taken as the index for large-scale industry adjusted for coverage.

TABLE 10

Revised Production Indices for Metalworking and Other Large-Scale Industry, 1928–1937
(per cent of 1934)

Year	Metalworking	Other Large-Scale Industry
1927–28	27.5	51.2
1928–29	39.1	58.6
1929–30	48.3	66.3
1931	64.6	74.7
1932	70.9	77.2
1933	89.5	81.2
1934	100.0	100.0
1935	156.7	115.7
1936	172.4	139.7
1937	172.0	157.6

The revised weights for these two indices were calculated from Table 5 above, on the assumption that the average annual number of workers employed in branches of industry is an approximate guide to the distribution of net value-added by branches. In the base year 1934 the average annual number of workers employed in large-scale industry was 7,404,000. Of these, 4,081,900 were employed in branches of industry included in the original coverage of the revised index. Omissions from the metalworking industry alone accounted for 1,277,000 workers, so that 2,045,100 workers were employed in other branches of industry omitted from the index. Since the original coverage for the machinery industry was for branches which employed 611,500 workers, the ratio of complete coverage to actual coverage for metalworking is 308.8 per cent [(1,277 + 611.5)/611.5 = 3.088]. For the remainder of industry, the ratio of complete coverage to actual coverage is 158.9 per cent [(3,470.4 + 2,045.1)/3,470.4 = 1.589].

These two ratios are then applied as correction coefficients to the original net value-added ruble weights for the machinery index (191 million rubles) and for the index for other industry (798 million rubles). This operation results in a net value-added ruble weight for metalworking of 590 million rubles (191 × 3.088 = 589.8) and for other large-scale

TABLE 11
Production Indices for Large-Scale Industry, 1928–1937
(per cent of 1934)

Year	Revised Index		Official Index[a]
	Unadjusted	Adjusted for Coverage	
1928	46.6[b]	43.7[b]	32.8
1929	54.8[b]	52.4[b]	41.3
1930	62.8[b]	60.6[b]	53.7
1931	72.7	71.5	67.0
1932	76.0	75.2	76.6
1933	82.8	83.8	82.9
1934	100.0	100.0	100.0
1935	123.6	128.7	123.6
1936	146.0	150.1	162.0
1937	160.5	162.2	180.6

[a] For source for official index, see notes to Table 4, p. 54.
[b] Values represent fiscal rather than calendar years.

industry of 1,268 million rubles (798 × 1.589 = 1,268). Taking the sum of these ruble weights as 100 per cent, the per cent of total weights assigned to metalworking is 31.75 per cent [590/(1,268 + 590)] and for other industry 68.25 per cent [1,268/(1,268 + 590)]. The separate indices for production in the metalworking industry and in other industry are then weighted by these percentage weights, and their arithmetic mean taken to obtain the final general index adjusted for coverage. This adjusted version of the revised index is presented in Table 11 along with the unadjusted version of the revised index and the official index.

The increased importance of the rapidly expanding metalworking industry in the adjusted version of the revised index results in a higher rate of growth for the over-all index of Soviet industrial output. With 1928 as the base year, the adjusted version of the revised index registers 371 in 1937 compared to 344 for the unadjusted version of the revised index and 551 for the official index. The discrepancy between the revised and official indices in the years 1928–1932 and 1936–1937 has become somewhat less with the adjustment for coverage, but the general configuration is the same. The adjusted version of the revised index may exhibit a slightly too rapid growth pattern for the decade owing to the omission of the lumbering industry and because the revised machinery index taken to represent the production of the entire metalworking industry probably exaggerates the growth of that industry.

The correction for coverage ignores the problem of variation in coverage over time. Sufficient data for an adequate analysis of this problem are not available. The only year other than 1934 for which it has proved possible to calculate the coverage of the revised index is 1932. In that year (judging from the per cent of the average annual number of workers employed in branches of industry included in the index), the unadjusted version of the revised index accounted for 56 per cent of value-added in Soviet large-scale industry as compared to 56.3 per cent in 1934. The time elapsed between these two measures of coverage is not sufficient to permit any judgment of actual trend in coverage over the decade. It is probable, however, that the coverage of the revised index increases somewhat during this period. Owing to the Soviet preference for production statistics which point to a rapid growth in industrial output, it is likely that both production and pay-roll data are more readily available for those industries which expand most rapidly. If true, this would introduce an upward bias in the revised index relative to an ideal standard, since the importance of rapidly expanding industries in the index would be greater than in the economy.

A Comparison of the Revised and Official Indices for Large-Scale Industry

The two versions of the revised index of Soviet industrial output along with the official index are shown in Chart VI, on the next page. In the discussion which follows, all reference to the revised index is in terms of the version which has been adjusted for coverage.

The official index for *large-scale state and coöperative industry* (excluding lumbering and fisheries) has been chosen for purposes of comparison with the revised index in order to minimize differences in coverage.[14] The output of private industry and of all small-scale industry is supposed to be excluded from this official index. The physical quantity series underlying the revised index likewise are for large-scale state and coöperative industry.

CHART VI

PRODUCTION INDICES FOR LARGE-SCALE INDUSTRY

(PER CENT OF 1928)

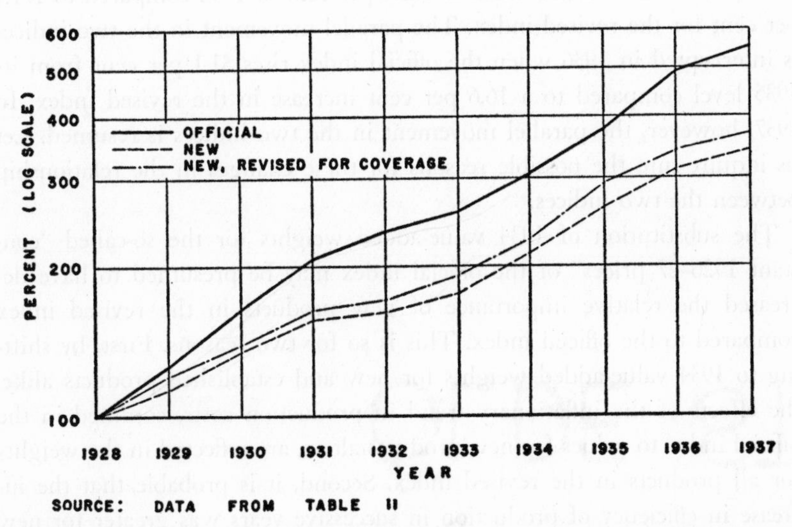

SOURCE: DATA FROM TABLE II

The revised index is a value-added index, while the official 1926–27 index is a gross value index. Since the ratio of value-added to gross value varies from product to product and industry to industry, there is no *a priori* reason why two such indices should move together even if based on the same year and computed for identical product coverage. Nevertheless, it appears that the divergence between the two indices may be attributed primarily to other causes, at least in the period 1928–1937.

Discrepancies, due neither to differences arising from the use of value-added rather than gross value weights nor to differences in coverage, must be due to substitution of weights based on 1934 value relationships in Soviet industry for the system of temporally mixed weights employed in the official Soviet index. This may have been the most important source of discrepancies between the 1934 value-added index and the 1926–27 official index during the period 1928–1937.

The official index for the production of Soviet large-scale industry registers an increase from 100 in 1928 to 551 in 1937, while the revised index rises from 100 to 371. There are some interesting differences in the relationship between the two indices for different years within the decade. The greatest discrepancy between the two indices develops during the first five years. By 1932, the official index has climbed to 233.5 per cent of its 1928 level compared to 172.1 per cent for the revised index. The two indices undergo a parallel development from 1932 to 1935. The 1935 level of the official index is 161.4 per cent of 1932 compared to 171.1 per cent for the revised index. The parallel movement in the two indices is interrupted in 1936 when the official index rises 31.1 per cent from its 1935 level compared to a 16.6 per cent increase in the revised index. In 1937, however, the parallel movement in the two indices is resumed. Let us inquire into the possible reasons for these changes in the relationship between the two indices.

The substitution of 1934 value-added weights for the so-called "constant 1926–27 prices" of the official index may be presumed to have decreased the relative importance of new products in the revised index compared to the official index. This is so for two reasons. First, by shifting to 1934 value-added weights for new and established products alike, the effects of the inflationary trend in production costs, confined in the official index to values for new products alone, are reflected in the weights for all products in the revised index. Second, it is probable that the increase in efficiency of production in successive years was greater for new products than for established products. Therefore, unit costs of production should be lower for new products relative to established products in 1934 than in any preceding year. Both of these factors tend to reduce the relative importance of new products in the revised index.

Compared to the 1934 value-added index, the official index may be said to be subject to an inflationary bias arising from the manner in which new products were valued. The degree of inflation in the official index thus increases *pari passu* with any increase in the proportion of the value of new products to the total value of all products.

The years of the First Five Year Plan (1928–1932) were characterized by a very rapid expansion in the production of new products by Soviet industry. Each successive year witnessed not only the further expansion in output of new products introduced in previous years, but also the introduction of additional types of new products never produced before by Soviet industry. Therefore, for the years of the First Five Year Plan it is reasonable to explain the divergence between the official and the revised indices on the basis of the removal of the new product bias from the 1934 value-added index.

The more detailed analysis undertaken earlier in this chapter revealed that the differences between the official and revised indices for these years (1928–1932) are due largely to differences in the subindices for machinery, chemicals, food, and textiles. There is a fairly close correspondence between the subindices for industries with such relatively simple products as coal, iron ore, cement, glass, sawn lumber, paper, boots and shoes, and petroleum. But for the four multiple product industries, namely, machinery, chemicals, food, and textiles, the rate of growth in output indicated by the official index is above that shown by the revised index.

It must not be overlooked that the possibility of inadequate product coverage by the 1934 value-added index is greater for a multiple product industry than for a single product industry. But the similarity in the over-all development of the official and revised indices in the years 1932–1935 suggests that inadequate product coverage is not the major cause for the differences between the official and revised indices in the period 1928–1932.

Both the machinery and chemical industries were young, rapidly expanding industries during the First Five Year Plan. Many of their products were completely new to Russian industry. It is not surprising to discover that the divergence between the official and revised indices is greatest in their case. Some new products were likewise being introduced into the food industry (for example, canned foods and margarine), but were undoubtedly much less important than in machinery or chemicals. In the textile industry, product change probably was much less pronounced and more in the nature of changes in styles of clothing and weights and widths of cloth than in the development of entirely new products. Among these four industries, the rank ordering according to greatest divergence between official and revised indices, most rapid rate of growth, and greatest probable incidence of new products is identical.

For the period 1932–1935, the official index continues at an inflated level relative to 1928 as compared to the revised index. But the year-to-year developments in the two indices are quite similar, and the three-year increase in the official index of 61.4 per cent is slightly less than the 71.1 per cent increase in the revised index. Is it possible that for some reason the effect of new product bias on the official index has been reduced in these years?

Clearly, so long as new products are included in the official index at inflated values, the increase in production *from base year to given year* will be exaggerated. Inflationary distortion of the increase in output *from one given year to the next,* however, depends not on the degree of inflation relative to the base year, but on changes in the degree of inflationary bias between the two given years. A constant degree of inflationary bias implies a similar constancy in the share of new products in total value of production.

The annual expansion in the relative importance of new products in an economy undergoing intensive industrialization is likely to be greatest in the early years of the process while the basic structural change in the composition of industry is being accomplished. This is so both because the new products of last year are no longer new this year, and because the number of types of products produced by modern industry, while very large, is by no means infinite. Therefore, there is a limit to the process of introducing new products year after year. A further restriction is occasioned by technical complementarity among products. Certain products cannot be produced without certain other products, and these must be available in more or less definite proportions.

In the case of Soviet industry, it is possible that the basic structural changes attendant upon industrialization were largely accomplished in the years of the First Five Year Plan, or, at least, that a plateau in development had been reached by about 1932. It is even more likely that the number of *new types* of products introduced annually declined during the 1930's. In the early years of its intensive effort at industrialization, the Soviet Union, borrowing from the more advanced technology of the West, had a vast reservoir of techniques and products to draw on which were in fact new to the Soviet economy. As the Soviet economy moved closer to the technological frontier, however, the number of new *types* of products introduced annually probably tended to decline.

It is quite possible, therefore, that the similarity in the official and revised indices for the period 1932–1935 is caused by a decline in the annual increment in the share of new products in the total value of output of Soviet industry. If this is so, the degree of inflationary bias in the official index may have remained fairly constant over these years, with the result that the official index does not distort production movements in this period.

This hypothesis is strengthened by the possibility of explaining the sharp rise in the official index relative to the revised index in 1936 by reference to two special developments in that year.

The first of these was the general review of constant 1926–27 prices undertaken in 1936 by the Central Statistical Administration and the issuance of uniform, country-wide price lists for the first time.[15] The method by which this revision was carried out and the relationship of the revised to the original 1926–27 prices have not been made clear. It is known that uniform nation-wide prices replaced divergent regional prices, and that a greater allowance was made for style and quality. Was the effect of these revisions to increase or decrease the value of a given aggregate of physical products relative to its value at the old 1926–27 prices? Without more information, it is possible only to speculate.

Note, however, the dilemma confronting authorities who were intensely interested in presenting to the world a picture of rapid and uninterrupted growth in industrial output if lower 1926–27 prices were approved. Either the actual increase in industrial production in 1936 relative to 1935 and earlier years would have been understated, or it would have been necessary to revise the pre-1936 production totals and thus admit their bias. On the other hand, if higher 1926–27 prices were approved, both of these unpleasant contingencies could be avoided and a handsome increase in output in 1936 would result. The effect of this latter course would have been precisely a sudden and unwarranted increase in the official index for the year 1936 (when the revised prices were first incorporated) relative to 1935 and earlier years, followed by a return to a more moderate rate of increase in 1937 relative to 1936. If the latter course was actually followed, it provides one explanation for the sudden spurt in the official index relative to the revised index in 1936.

The second event which may help to explain the sudden increase in the official index for 1936 was the reduction in subsidies to heavy industry and the accompanying general upward revision in current prices for producers' goods which occurred in that year.[16] As a result of the rise in prices for the products of heavy industry, those new products which entered the production index in 1936 and subsequent years, as well as that part of industrial production which was customarily valued at current prices (such as repair shop work), were valued on the basis of a substantially higher level of prices than goods for which the "constant 1926–27 prices" had been established prior to 1936. Therefore, the increment in new-product bias in 1936 may have been somewhat larger than in the years 1932–1935.

Both of the special developments in the year 1936 would have exerted their major influence on comparisons between 1936 and earlier years. By 1937, their effects had been incorporated in the official index so that the comparison between 1936 and 1937 should have been little affected by them. This may explain the similarity between the increases in the official and revised indices in this year.

5

Production of Soviet Large-Scale Industry, 1937–1951

Limitations on available data make the construction of an independent index of Soviet industrial output an especially dubious procedure for the years since 1937. Beginning in 1938, the Soviet government, presumably impelled by the considerations of military security, sharply curtailed the publication of annual production statistics for Soviet industry. Since World War II this policy has been continued in somewhat modified form. Annual production data are now published for a number of products in the form of percentage increases from an unspecified absolute figure for an earlier year. By carefully sifting Soviet sources for these earlier years Western scholars have discovered base-year production data in absolute terms making it possible to reconstruct output series in absolute quantities for a limited number of commodities.[1]

Not only are the underlying data less reliable for the years 1940 and 1946–1951 than for 1928–1937 but the coverage of the revised index is sharply reduced from 137 commodity series in the base year 1934 to 22 product series in the years 1940 and 1946–1950 and only 18 product series in 1951. Moreover, some exceedingly risky adjustments to the post-1937 values of the revised index have been undertaken in an attempt to overcome deficiencies in product coverage. Consequently, the reader is warned emphatically that the revised index must be considered provisional for the post-1937 period until such time as more ready access to detailed Soviet production data provides an opportunity to verify and supplement data presently available.

The 22 product series which enter into the revised index in the years 1940 and 1946–1950 are coal, crude oil, electric power output, pig iron, steel, rolled steel, cement, paper, glass, cotton cloth, woolen cloth, silk cloth, soap, sugar, vegetable oils, fish, canned goods, confections, beer, cigarettes, tractors, and motor vehicles. In the year 1951, tractors, motor vehicles, glass, and soap disappear from this list. The most important omissions are chemicals, nonferrous metals, the bulk of machinery production, and military products.

Data from the Soviet annual production plan for 1941 have been utilized to compute an index value for the year 1941.[2] The *1941 Plan* was intended by Soviet authorities only for restricted domestic circulation. Therefore, it contains much more detailed production statistics than have appeared in published Soviet sources since the middle 1930's. The obvious drawback to the statistics in the *1941 Plan* is that they represent planned rather than actual performance. As a result of the economic chaos precipitated by the invasion of the German armies in June of 1941, it is probable that the 1941 plan targets exceed actual performance by 60 per cent or more. Nevertheless, the plan targets are useful as an approximation to the *expected* capacity of Soviet industry in the year 1941. Thus, the significance of the index value for 1941 computed from these plan data is that of a benchmark based on more comprehensive production statistics against which the index values for 1940 and 1946–1951 computed from the 22 selected product series may be tested. The 1941 index value for the revised index is based on 89 product series, compared to 137 for the base year 1934. Of these, 43 series represent machinery items and 46 are nonmachinery items as compared to 76 machinery items and 61 nonmachinery items in 1934.

There is no satisfactory way of knowing how representative the 22 selected product series are of total Soviet industrial output in the years after 1937. For the years 1929–30 to 1937, the 22 selected product series account for a fairly stable portion of the value-added in Soviet industry as measured by the revised index, that is, between 45 and 49 per cent. The rise in industrial output from 1929–30 to 1937 measured by the 22 selected series is 149 per cent compared to 155 per cent for the revised index before adjustment for coverage and 167 per cent after adjustment for coverage. The revised index (selected series) thus lags slightly behind the more comprehensive versions of the revised index in this period.

The planned production data for 1941 provide the only basis for comparison between the revised index (selected series) and any more comprehensive version of the revised index later than 1937. Taking 1934 as 100, the index value for the 22 selected series in 1941 is 175, while for the more comprehensive version of the revised index (89 product series) the index value for 1941 is 180. Although this is an insignificant discrepancy, it is not particularly reassuring with respect to the representativeness of the 22 selected series. Products omitted from both revised indices could make both indices inaccurate indicators of changes in Soviet industrial production.

An official index for the output of all state and coöperative industry valued at the so-called "constant 1926–27 prices" has been reconstructed by Western scholars from announced percentage increases in Soviet industrial output. This index, of course, is highly suspect for reasons which have already been discussed.[3] Nevertheless, something can be learned by a comparison of the official and revised indices.

The official index for all state and coöperative industry and the revised index (selected series) are shown in Table 12. It is apparent at once that a very large discrepancy between the two indices develops in the period 1937–1940. In column four of Table 12, the discrepancy between the two indices is measured by the ratio of the official index to the revised index. As measured by this ratio, the discrepancy between the two indices is 41 per cent by the year 1940. The general order of magnitude of the discrepancy between the two indices is fairly constant from 1941 through 1949 save for the year 1945. A further noticeable increase occurs in 1950–51.

The divergence between the official and revised indices from 1937 to 1940 is striking as compared to their parallel development in the period of the Second Five Year Plan (1932–1937). The discrepancy between the two indices from 1932 to 1937 is only 9 per cent measured by the ratio of the official index to the revised index. Moreover, the entire discrepancy during the period 1932–1937 may be due almost entirely to the special price revisions of 1936.[4] But for these price developments, the increase registered by the official index might have been slightly *less* than that shown by the revised index.

There are several possible explanations for the divergence between the official and revised indices. First, as has beeen mentioned, there is no logical reason why a gross value index should duplicate the movements of a value-added index. Nevertheless, the similarity in the two indices for the years 1932–1937 reduces the likelihood that the difference between value-added and gross value weights is a principal factor in explaining the discrepancy after 1937.

Second, the discrepancy between the official and revised indices in 1940 and later years may result from an increase in the degree of inflationary bias in the official index. Although the degree of inflationary bias appears to have been fairly constant over the period 1932–1937, it may

TABLE 12

Indices of Soviet Industrial Output, 1937–1951
(per cent of 1937)

Year	Official	Revised (Selected Series) [a]	Official ÷ Revised
1937	100	100	100
1938	111.0	—	—
1939	129.5	—	—
1940	144.7	102.6	141
1941	169.5 (Plan)	115	147
1942	108.0	—	—
1943	126.8	—	—
1944	150.5	—	—
1945	133.1	63	211
1946	111.4	73	153
1947	134.6	89	151
1948	170.7	111	154
1949	204.0	134	152
1950	250.3	154	163
1951	292.3	177	165

[a] This index is the weighted mean of quantity relatives for the twenty-two product series mentioned in the text. In the food indusry for the years 1946 and 1947 it is assumed that missing series for the output of canned goods, confections, beer, and cigarettes moved with the weighted average for sugar, vegetable oils, and fish caught. In 1951 missing series for tractors, motor vehicles, glass, and soap are assumed to have moved with the weighted mean increase of the remaining eighteen product series relative to 1950.

SOURCES for official index (all state and coöperative industry) — 1937–1940 from Alexander Gerschenkron, "The Soviet Indices of Industrial Production," *The Review of Economic Statistics*, November 1947, p. 218; 1941 (Plan) from *Gosudarstvennyi plan razvitiia narodnogo khoziaistva SSSR na 1941 god*, p. 9; 1942–1943 from Alexander Gerschenkron, Review of N. Vosnesenski, *Voyennaya ekonomika SSSR v period otechestvennoy voyny* in *The American Economic Review*, Sept. 1948, pp. 649–657; 1944–1951 from percentage increases relative to 1940 given by G. M. Malenkov in his *Report of the Central Committee of C.P.S.U.(B) to XIX Congress of the Party*.

have increased in subsequent years. Such an increase could have occurred as a result of an increase in the relative importance of "new" products which first entered Soviet production in the first two five year plans (1928–1937) or as a result of the development and introduction of completely new product types in the years after 1937. The strongest inflationary bias would have resulted from the introduction of completely new product types, since these would have been "priced in" to the official index at even higher price levels relative to 1926–27 than those of previous years.

Third, the complete omission of a number of products from the revised index is undoubtedly an important source of divergence between the revised and official indices. The similarity in the revised and official indices in the period 1932–1937 and the similarity in the 1941 values for the two versions of the revised index (that is, the 89-product index and the 22-product index), suggest that the omitted products were new rather than established products. Clearly, the omission of these products by the revised index results in an estimate of the increase in Soviet industrial production which is too low. The inclusion of these products in the official index, on the other hand, may be presumed to have caused a further inflation of that index.

The omission of new products from the revised index causes that index to understate the growth in Soviet industrial output when the share of the omitted products in total output is increasing, and to overstate the increase in the volume of production when the share of the omitted products in total output is decreasing. When the share of the omitted products in total production is constant, changes in the revised index approximate percentage changes in total production. It may be noted that the greatest divergences in the movements of the official and revised indices occur in years presumably marked by industrial mobilization and industrial reconversion (for example, 1937–1940 and 1945).

It is necessary to make some allowance for the omission of new products from the revised index for the years 1940–1951. The method which has been used is not very satisfactory, but it appears to be the best available. A number of sweeping assumptions are involved and some exceedingly cavalier estimates are made.

With reference to the product coverage of the *more comprehensive version* of the revised index for planned output in 1941, it is assumed that the omission of all final products specific to military use constitutes the major gap in product coverage and is the only omission for which an adjustment in the revised index is required. It is further assumed that such divergence between the official and more comprehensive revised indices, as cannot be accounted for by the omission of military products, results from a continued increase in the inflationary bias in the official index rather than from differences in gross value and value-added weights.

Any increase in the inflationary bias in the official index is the consequence of a further increase in the relative share of products introduced after 1926–27 and valued at inflated price levels. New product types appearing for the first time after 1937 (and before 1946) are assumed to be primarily in the nature of war-time substitutes in all branches of industry except metalworking and machinery.[5]

The problem is to estimate military production by Soviet industry in 1937 and 1941 and to adjust the revised production index for the omission of these products. The bulk of Soviet military production is accounted for by the Ministries of Aviation, Shipbuilding, Armaments, and Munitions, and is included with machinery and metalworking production.[6] Table 13 presents official data at "1926–27 prices" for the value of machinery and metalworking output and the value of output of the four Defense

TABLE 13

Soviet Metalworking and Military Production, 1937–1941
(billions of 1926–27 rubles)

Year	Metalworking	Military	Ratio of Military to Metalworking (per cent)
1937	27.5	5.5[a]	20.0[a]
1938	33.6	11.6	34.5
1939	40.6	16.9	41.5
1940	48.4	—	
1941	61.0	31.9	52.0

[a] Estimated.

SOURCES — Metalworking: 1937 from Gosplan, *Tretii piatiletnyi plan razvitiia narodnogo khoziaistva Soiuza SSR (1938–1942)* (The Third Five Year Plan of Economic Development of the Union SSR; Moscow, 1939), p. 197; 1938 from TsUNKhU, *Sotsialisticheskoe stroitel'stvo Soiuza SSR (1933–1938 gg)* (Socialist Construction of the Union SSR, 1933–1938; Moscow, 1939), p. 36; 1939 from a statement by N. Voznesensky, *The Growing Prosperity of the Soviet Union* (New York: Workers Library Publishers), p. 43, that the output of the machinery and metalworking industry in 1940 was 119 per cent of 1939; 1940 from a statement in Voznesensky, op. cit., p. 7, that the output of the machinery and metalworking industry in 1940 was 176 per cent of 1937; 1941 Plan from a statement in Voznesensky, *op. cit.*, p. 13, that the output of the machinery industry planned for 1941 was to be 126 per cent of 1940.

Military production: 1938, 1939, 1941 official data for the four Commissariats of Defense quoted in N. Jasny, *The Soviet Price System* (Stanford University Press, 1951), p. 115. Data for 1939 and 1941 are "planned," *The indicated 5.5 billion rubles of military production in 1937 is an arbitrary estimate* based on a rough backward extension of the percentage trend.

Ministries. In the absence of official statistics, the value of military production in 1937 has been estimated by a rough backward extension of the percentage trend.

Table 14 compares the increase in nonmilitary machinery production from 1937 to 1941 according to official data (as modified by the military production estimate for 1937) and according to the more comprehensive version of the revised index. The implication of the decline in nonmilitary machinery production indicated by the revised index is that the increase in military production was greater than the increase in productive capacity in the metalworking industry and was achieved in part by the conversion of existing capacity. Thus, the 31 per cent increase in the official index for nonmilitary machinery production is presumed to reflect an increase in inflationary bias rather than an increase in physical volume of output. The extent of this bias may be expressed by the ratio of the official machinery index to the revised machinery index in 1941; that is, 131/96 = 1.37 or an inflationary bias of 37 per cent.

If the same degree of inflationary bias relative to 1937 is assumed to characterize official totals for military production, an adjusted official figure for production of the entire metalworking industry in 1941 (Plan) of 44.5 billion 1926–27 rubles is obtained (total production of metalworking at 1926–27 prices [61.0 billion rubles] divided by 1.37).

Official totals for all industrial output except metalworking increase from 68 billion 1926–27 rubles in 1937 to 101 billion 1926–27 rubles in 1941 (Plan) or by 50 per cent compared to the 18 per cent increase indicated by the revised index for all industrial output except metalworking. If the 1941 (Plan) total for all industrial production except metalworking is reduced to the level of 18 per cent in excess of 1937 rather than 50 per

TABLE 14
Soviet Machinery and Metalworking Production Excluding Military Production, 1937 and 1941
(per cent of 1937)

Year	Official Index	Revised Index
1937	100	100
1941	131	96

SOURCES — Official: Calculated from Table 13; Revised: Calculated from data in Appendices A and B. Products missing from data for either year have been omitted from the calculation.

cent, the revised 1941 value becomes 81 billion 1926–27 rubles. The adjusted total value for all industrial output in 1941 (Plan) is the sum of metalworking (44.5 billion 1926–27 rubles) and nonmetalworking production (81 billion 1926–27 rubles) or 125.5 billion 1926–27 rubles.

The adjusted total for all industrial production including military production in 1941 (125.5 billion 1926–27 rubles) is 30 per cent above the level of total industrial production in 1937 (95.5 billion 1926–27 rubles). The comprehensive version of the revised index which omits military production indicates an increase in Soviet industrial output from 1937 to 1941 of 11 per cent. Thus, the omission of military production from the comprehensive revised index may result in an understatement of the increase in Soviet industrial output from 1937 to 1941 of 17 per cent (130/111 = 1.17). The revised index based on 22 selected-product series increases by 15 per cent from 1937 to 1941 (Plan). This version of the revised index thus may understate the increase in Soviet industrial production from 1937 to 1941 (Plan) by 13 per cent (130/115 = 1.13).

The order of magnitude of the discrepancy between the official index and the revised index (selected series) in the years 1940–1949 is fairly constant with the exception of the year 1945. (See Table 12, p. 84 above.) This suggests that the degree of understatement relative to 1937 may be relatively constant in the revised-index values for 1940, 1941, and 1946–1949. A further increase in the understatement of the revised index may occur in the years 1950 and 1951 when the discrepancy between the official and revised indices again increases.

This estimate for the degree of understatement in the revised index after 1937 is painfully rough and ready. The assumptions underlying the adjustment are open to question. Military products probably account for the majority of new products but scarcely for all. Thus, the entire discrepancy between the official and revised indices for all production except military should not be assigned to inflationary bias in the official index. Some must result from the omission of new civilian products from the revised index. On the other hand, the inflationary bias in the value of military production in 1941 relative to 1937 probably exceeded rather than equalled the inflationary bias in civilian production because of the higher proportion of new products in military production. These are compensating errors, the net effect of which is uncertain.

The application of an upward adjustment derived from *1941 Plan* data to all years from 1940 to 1951 is very crude. Implicit in this procedure is the assumption that products included in the revised index accounted for a fairly constant proportion of the value of total industrial production in this decade. This assumption is suggested by the roughly parallel development of the revised and official indices from 1940 to 1949, excepting the turbulent years 1942–1945. In 1950 and 1951, the gap between the official and revised indices widens appreciably. The timing suggests an increase in the share of military items in total output in connection with the Korean War, but this cannot be proved.

TABLE 15

Indices of Industrial Production, 1928–1951
(per cent of 1927–28)

Year	Revised Index	Official Index	Year	Revised Index	Official Index
1928	100[a]	100	1939	—	714
1929	120[a]	126	1940	430	797
1930	139[a]	163	1941	482	934
1931	164	204	1944	—	829
1932	172	234	1945	263	733
1933	192	253	1946	304	614
1934	229	305	1947	375	742
1935	295	377	1948	464	941
1936	344	494	1949	560	1120
1937	371	551	1950	646	1380
1938	—	612	1951	742	1610

[a] Values for 1928–1930 represent fiscal rather than calendar years.
SOURCES — Revised index: 1927–28 to 1937 from Table 11, p. 84; 1937–1951 from Table 12, p. 84 (adjusted upward by 13 per cent). Official index: 1928–1937 large-scale industry excluding lumbering and fisheries from Table 11, p. 74; 1937–1951 from Table 12, p. 84.

The adjustment to the post-1937 values of the revised index of Soviet industrial output affects comparisons between production in the periods 1928–1937 and 1940–1951 and *not within these periods.* Table 15 compares the official and revised indices of Soviet industrial production for the entire period 1928–1951. The index values for the years through 1937 are for large-scale industry. For years later than 1937, the official index of the production of all state and coöperative industry is linked to the official index of large-scale industry, and the revised index based on 22 selected series (adjusted upward by 13 per cent) has been linked to the revised index for large-scale industry. Official totals relate to the territory of the Soviet Union of the given year. No adjustment to the revised index has been made for territorial changes.

6

Other Measures of Soviet Industrial Growth

This study is not the first attempt at an independent appraisal of Soviet industrial development. The problem of improving on the biased official measures of Soviet industrial output has interested a number of Western scholars. Their efforts to recompute value indicators of Soviet industrial growth may be classified conveniently into two main types: those which use Soviet value relationships, and those which use value relationships from other countries. Important among the former group is the work of Naum Jasny and that of the Deutsches Institut für Konjunkturforschung; among the latter, the work of Alexander Gerschenkron, Colin Clark, and Demitri Shimkin.[1] In addition, James H. Blackman has prepared an index of Soviet transportation ton-kilometers which is of interest because of the established covariation of transportation and industrial production indices in countries other than the Soviet Union.[2]

The very existence of these other general measures of Soviet industrial growth invites their comparison to the index of industrial production computed in this volume. At first thought it might appear that the check of mutual consistency should provide a test of the accuracy with which the various measures reflect the pattern of Soviet industrial development. In a very broad sense, this is probably true, since the extent of agreement among these various independent measures of Soviet industrial growth is greater than between any one of them and the official Soviet index of industrial output.

Yet, there are also marked discrepancies among the various indices of industrial production, minerals consumption, and freight transportation. This chapter has been written to discuss and consider the implications of these similarities and differences for the individual and collective validity of these indices. For the most part, the conclusion must be that each index is a rule unto itself and is to be judged in accordance with its specific purpose and the success with which the investigator has been able to carry through his particular statistical design.

All of the comprehensive measures of Soviet industrial growth which are discussed are shown in Table 16. The only published portion of Professor Gerschenkron's work is a dollar index of Soviet machinery output for the period 1927–28 to 1937. This dollar index is compared to the machinery component of the revised production index in Table 17.

It is apparent from Table 16 that the revised production index, the

TABLE 16

Indices of Soviet Industrial Growth, 1928–1950
(per cent of 1928)

Year	Industrial Production					Minerals Consumption	Freight Transportation
	Official (large-scale industry)	Revised (large-scale industry)	Jasny (all industry)	Clark	Institut		
1928	100	100[a]	100	100		100	100
1932	234	172	165	128		171	184
1937	551	371	287	311		357	363
1940	797	430	330–350	340		400	422
1946	614	304	238	—		386	337
1950	1380	646	411	—		586	615
			per cent of 1929				
1929	100	100[b]			100		
1932	186	143			135		
1937	437	309			292		

[a] 1927–28.
[b] 1928–29.

SOURCES — Official Production index for large-scale industry valued at "constant 1926–27 prices" from Table 15, p 89; Revised Production index for large-scale industry with 1934 wage and salary weights as an approximation to value-added from Table 15, p. 89; Jasny's production index of total industrial production obtained, according to the author, by deflating the value of industrial output at current prices by an index of industrial prices, 1928–1946 from Naum Jasny, *The Soviet Economy During the Plan Era* (Stanford University Press, 1951), p. 22; 1950 from Naum Jasny, "A Close-up of the Soviet Fourth Five-Year Plan," *Quarterly Journal of Economics*, May 1952, pp. 139–171; Clark's production index showing industrial output obtained by weighting selected production series by Clark's "international units" (U.S. dollars at their average purchasing power over 1925–34), from Colin Clark, *The Conditions of Economic Progress* (2d ed.; London: Macmillan and Co., 1951); Production index computed by the Deutsches Institut für Konjunkturforschung combines physical output series by means of a weighting system which utilizes both employment data by branch of industry in 1932 and fixed capital invested in the individual branches of industry as of January 1, 1933 (from *Weekly Report* of the German Institute for Business Research [Institut für Konjunkturforschung], Berlin, April 30, 1940, p. 44); Minerals Consumption computed from the gross value of Soviet minerals consumption valued at 1937 United States dollar prices from Demitri B. Shimkin, *Minerals — A Key to Soviet Power* (Harvard University Press, 1953), p. 320; Freight Transportation volume in billions of ton-kilometers including railroad, river, domestic maritime, motor, air, and petroleum pipeline, from James H. Blackman, "Transportation" in Abram Bergson (ed.) *Soviet Economic Growth* (Row, Peterson and Company, 1953), p. 128.

Institut für Konjunkturforschung production index, and the indices of freight transportation and minerals consumption are in substantial agreement as to the general orders of magnitude of changes in the volume of Soviet industrial activity over the years 1928 to 1950. The production indices computed by Naum Jasny and by Colin Clark, however, indicate lower rates of growth.

Minerals Consumption and Industrial Production

Demitri B. Shimkin's mineral-consumption index is based on the gross value of Soviet mineral consumption valued at 1937 United States dollar prices. The index consists of 21 production series and is estimated by Shimkin to cover 90 per cent or more of the value of Soviet mineral consumption (other than gold, silver, stone, sand, and gravel).[3]

In an unpublished manuscript, *Mineral Consumption and Economic Development in the United States and the Soviet Union*, Shimkin and Gregory Grossman have examined the relationship of minerals consumption to industrial output in the United States and the Soviet Union.[4] In the United States they discovered that for the period 1899 to 1932, the index of minerals consumption increased somewhat more rapidly than an index of value-added in manufacturing, but that after 1932 manufacturing output tended to increase in relative terms somewhat faster than mineral consumption. The two indices tended to move quite consistently together, both cyclically and secularly, over the fifty-year period 1899 to 1949, though with differing amplitudes of fluctuation.

These findings for the American economy suggest that a similar, not necessarily identical, functional relationship may exist between minerals consumption and industrial production in the Soviet economy. This possibility has been examined and confirmed by Shimkin and Grossman.[5] Their finding is based on a comparison between the minerals-consumption index in 1937 U.S. dollar prices and a variety of estimates of growth in Soviet industrial output for the decade 1927–28 to 1937. The production estimates employed range from a 2.6-fold increase to a 3.6-fold increase, and the authors have adopted as a working figure a threefold increase in Soviet industrial output (large-scale and small-scale). On this basis, the index of minerals consumption by the Soviet economy rises more rapidly than the index of industrial production for the period 1927–28 to 1937.

No attempt will be made to examine directly the validity of the particular relationship between Soviet minerals consumption and industrial output established by Shimkin and Grossman.[6] The problem of the rationale for such a relationship, however, is of considerable interest as is a comparison between the minerals consumption index and the revised index of Soviet industrial production computed in this volume.

Shimkin has mentioned two limitations on the usefulness of the index of minerals consumption as a measure of actual minerals consumption in Soviet industry.[7] First, the index explicitly measures consumption of minerals by the entire economy and not just the industrial sector. Second, the consumption of primary metals only is included with recovery from scrap excluded. The effect of the first factor is not readily ascertainable. Presumably, however, scrap recovery of metal was increasingly more important in the 1930's and 1940's than in 1928, so that its omission results in a progressive, though not necessarily important, understatement of minerals consumption by the Soviet economy. These limitations on the minerals-consumption index for the purpose of comparison with an index of industrial production are noted, but will be temporarily ignored in the discussion which follows.

In the simplest case, that of the relationship of the amount of a single mineral consumed in the production of a single product, output of product will increase more rapidly than input of mineral if productive efficiency increases as a result of increased skill in using the mineral (less waste) or as a result of a mineral-saving technical innovation. A second possibility turns on the definition of the unit of measurement of the mineral. Unless the definition specifies constant quality (for example, metal content of ore or caloric content of coal), apparent changes in the relation of mineral input to product output may result from changes in mineral quality. Thus, product output might increase relative to non-quality-defined mineral input as a result of improved-quality mineral or more efficient primary processing of the mineral. Declines in productive efficiency or in mineral quality would require greater increases in mineral input than in product output.

In the case of two (or more) products utilizing a single mineral in constant but unequal quantities per unit of output, changes in the ratio of physical units of product A produced relative to product B will cause changes in mineral consumption relative to total output. A shift in product composition toward the more "mineral intensive" type of product will result in a more rapid increase in mineral consumption than in industrial production and vice versa. In order to determine which product is the more "mineral intensive," the two physically dissimilar products must be expressed in terms of a common denominator, usually value. Under one system of value weights, product A may be more mineral intensive than product B. Under another system of value weights, the reverse may be true. Therefore, the system of relative value weights (for example, prices) will influence the subsequent relative development of the output index relative to the mineral input series.

A third range of possibilities is opened up when two (or more) minerals are required to produce a single industrial product. In this case, a minerals consumption index cannot be expressed in physical terms but involves the use of measures of relative importance, again presumably value. The system of relative value weights adopted will indicate which mineral is more expensive per unit of weight. This will determine whether the index of minerals consumption increases more or less rapidly than the physical output series with changes in the proportions in which the minerals are required per unit of output. Substitution of one mineral for another as a productive factor in the one product case may result from changes in the relative current prices of the minerals or from technical innovation. When there are two or more products, the composition of minerals consumption may change also in response to changes in product composition.

There are thus a multiplicity of factors at work to determine the relationship of an index of industrial output to an index of minerals consumption. Since there is no common tendency in the influence of these factors, it is impossible to say *a priori* whether an industrial-output or minerals-consumption index should increase more rapidly in a period of industrial expansion.

The relationship is no more predictable with particular reference to Soviet experience. From 1928 on, there were marked shifts in the composition of industrial output. In broad terms, the shifts favored producers' goods relative to consumers' goods. In general, producers' goods are more mineral intensive than consumers' goods, so that this suggests a more rapid increase in minerals consumption than in industrial output. But the degree of mineral intensity for different producers' goods is by no means identical, and there were also major changes in the structure of producers' goods output. The tremendous increase in the relative importance of the machinery industry, characterized by a relatively high ratio of value-added to gross value (as an indicator of the ratio of value of product to value of minerals consumed), must have operated as an important offset to the increase in mineral intensity in industry as a whole.

Much depends also on the factors of increased technical efficiency, possible depletion of mineral resources, changes in composition of minerals consumption, and the relative value weights employed in constructing the index of minerals consumption and industrial production. Moreover, there is the circumstance already noted that the index of minerals consumption omits recovery of scrap and embraces mineral use for the entire economy rather than for industry alone. Faced with all these uncertainties, it would be unwise to attempt to predict the exact relationship of the indices of minerals consumption and industrial production for the Soviet economy.

The high degree of consistency, however, in the fluctuations of the United States indices of minerals consumption and industrial production over the fifty-year period 1899 to 1949 studied by Shimkin and Grossman does suggest one observation. In view of these findings for the United States the relationship between the revised index of Soviet industrial production and the index of minerals consumption (see Table 16) appears to be much more plausible than that between the official index of industrial production and the index of minerals consumption.

Transportation and Industrial Production

The relationship between an index of industrial production and an index of freight transportation measured in ton-kilometers is even more complex than that between minerals consumption and industrial production. The factors which may produce changes in the physical inputs per unit of value output mentioned in the foregoing discussion are still at work (for example, factor substitution and changes in the composition of output). In addition, there are transportation requirements for intermediate and final products. There may also be variations both in the ratio of total materials and products transported to those consumed or produced and in the distance over which this tonnage is carried. Finally, as in the case of the minerals-consumption index, the index of transportation ton-kilometers is influenced by developments in other sectors of the economy (for example, agriculture and trade) as well as by industrial developments.

There is no reason for the unit transportation requirements for a variety of products to be in the same ratios as their unit values, yet this is a necessary condition for identical changes in transportation and production indices, with a given change in product composition. Moreover, changes in transportation requirements are functions not only of changes in volume and composition of industrial output, but also of changes in specialization in production, population densities and like factors which affect the distance over which goods are moved.

Empirical studies of the relationship between indices of industrial production and transportation in the United States have revealed a high degree of consistency in the covariation of the two indices, as might be expected.[8] No precise and unvarying relationship, however, has been found to exist.

The Transport Division of the United Nations Economic Commission for Europe has examined the relationship between freight traffic indices and production indices for a number of European countries. They observe, "At first sight it might well be expected that there should be a direct relation between indices of traffic and indices of production and of imports. On more detailed examination, however, it becomes apparent that there is no direct and inevitable ratio between indices of general economic activity, which are based on values, and those of traffic, which are based on the weight of goods, because the various sectors of production and trade are not necessarily affected in the same manner, or to the same extent, by changes in the level of economic activity."[9]

Thus, as in the case of the minerals-consumption index, the multiplicity of different influences acting without common tendency on the relationship of the transportation and production indices makes prediction of the pattern of this relationship impossible. If the empirical investigations into this relationship in the United States and European countries may be taken as a rough guide, however, it appears that the revised production index stands in more plausible relation to the transportation index than does the official production index.

Other Indices of Soviet Industrial Production

The three other independent appraisals of Soviet industrial production (prepared by Naum Jasny, Colin Clark, and the Institut für Konjunkturforschung) shown in Table 16 also have the virtue of standing in more credible relation to the indices of mineral consumption and freight transportation than does the official production index. Only the production index computed by the Institut für Konjunkturforschung, however, is in fairly close agreement with the revised production index computed in this volume. Jasny's and Clark's computations result in indices which are considerably lower than the revised production index. It is useful to examine the causes of the similarities and differences.

(a) Production index of the Institut für Konjunkturforschung. The index of industrial production computed by the Deutsches Institut für Konjunkturforschung resembles the revised production index in its use of a weighting system based on Soviet rather than foreign production relationships.[10] The Institut index is supposed to combine 47 physical quantity series by means of a weighting system utilizing both employment data by branch of industry in 1932 and fixed capital invested in the individual branches of industry as of January 1, 1933. Unfortunately, the published results of this study are confined to indices for a few broad classes of goods and an over-all index. Only fourteen of the constituent physical output series are named, and the means of reconciling the double weighting criteria is not discussed. Consequently, the index is not subject to critical evaluation. Moreover, the study ends with the year 1939.

The paucity of published details concerning the Institut production index does not permit an explanation of the differences between this index and the revised index. Presumably, differences in the two indices may be traced both to dissimilarities in the systems of relative weights and to differences in product coverage.

Although the Institut has not explained the method of combining employment and fixed capital weights, the resulting weights must accord a greater measure of relative importance to those industries in which the capital-labor ratio is relatively high than is given to these industries under the system of wage and salary weights utilized in the present study. Nevertheless, the underlying rationale of both weighting systems is fairly similar, so that the similarity in the resulting production indices is not surprising. One may speculate that the major differences in product coverage occur in the multiple product industries such as machinery, chemicals, food, and textiles where the available Soviet data on fixed capital may not have allowed the imputation of weights on a detailed product-for-product basis.

(b) Colin Clark's production index. Colin Clark has calculated an index of Soviet industrial output for the years 1913 and 1921–1940.[11] This index is composed of twelve physical quantity series: cotton cloth, woolen cloth, trucks, passenger cars, locomotives, freight cars, aluminum, copper, lead, paper, cement, and gold. These series are valued and aggregated in terms of "International Units" (that is, average dollar prices of the years 1925–1934).

Clark computed this index of Soviet industrial production as a minor step in the much more comprehensive scheme of international comparisons of real national income per capita for a large number of countries. Specifically, Clark's purpose in computing the index of industrial production was to serve as a guide to the interpolation of national income data. He states:

> The remainder of the national income is interpolated by means of an index of industrial production. Certain basic materials and fuels have been omitted. Their inclusion would have given the index so strong an upward bias that it would not have served its purpose. It must be remembered that this index is only required for the interpolation of figures of real national income which have already been deduced from quite different sources.[12]

From this statement, it seems clear that Clark is not interested in defending his computation as a painstaking independent appraisal of changes in the volume of Soviet industrial output. He is careful to point out both that the index has been prepared as an aid in a particular statistical maneuver, and that certain products have been excluded deliberately to secure a more modest increase in industrial production than would otherwise have been the case. Clark is rather vague on the precise reasoning involved in this decision, but this need not concern us in this study.

The version of Clark's index shown in Table 16 omits gold. Had gold been included, the index would have registered 296 per cent of 1928 in the year 1937 rather than 311 per cent. To test for the influence of different relative weights employed in combining the individual physical output series by Clark and in the present study, an attempt has been made to compute a revised index using the same physical series contained in Clark's index but weighted by wage and salary weights. To this purpose, weighted quantity relatives for fireburned copper, lead, aluminum, paper, cement, cotton cloth, motor vehicles, and railroad equipment have been combined in a single index. This appears to represent substantially the same set of products as those contained in the version of Clark's index which omits gold. For 1937, this revised index registers 266 per cent of 1928 compared to 311 per cent for Clark's index.

Not all of this difference is assignable to different relative weights for the output series. Clark apparently makes no allowance for changes in the composition of output of trucks, locomotives, and freight cars by size and type. His lead-production series shows no production in 1928, although lead was produced in that year. Finally, even some of the single-product series, such as cotton cloth and aluminum, differ in Clark's index from those employed in this study. No attempt has been made to explain these discrepancies in the physical series, since Clark does not cite sources.

It does seem obvious, however, that the usefulness of Clark's index as a general measure of Soviet industrial development is qualified by its highly restricted and somewhat arbitrary product coverage. Clark is quite forthright on this point. The only justification for discussing the shortcomings of the index in this detail is that at times less cautious use of Clark's index has been made by other writers than by its author.

(c) Naum Jasny's index of Soviet industrial production.[13] This index of Soviet industrial production, like that of Clark, was computed by its author as a part of a larger design, the calculation of Soviet real national income. Jasny's approach, in principle, is to estimate the value of Soviet industrial output for different years at current prices and to deflate these values by price indices based on the crop year 1926–27.[14] In application, the method has been modified by a liberal admixture of estimate and "expert appraisal" to overcome or by-pass obstacles raised by inadequate statistical information.

Part of the difference between Jasny's index and the revised index of Soviet industrial production may be explained quite simply. First, Jasny's production index is intended to represent production developments in *all* Soviet industry — state-owned, industrial coöperatives, and private, large-scale as well as small-scale enterprises — whereas the revised index covers only large-scale state and coöperative industry. Total production of *all* Soviet industry increased less rapidly than large-scale industry even according to official Soviet statistics.[15] Second, Jasny's data for 1928 are on a calendar-year basis, while those for the revised index are on a fiscal-year basis. Since the fiscal year closed three months earlier than the calendar year, production in the twelve months represented in the fiscal year may be presumed to have been somewhat less than that for the calendar year (owing to a strong growth trend).[16] Therefore, other things equal, Jasny's index should show somewhat less expansion in industrial output by 1937 than should the revised index.

It does not appear likely, however, that all of the discrepancy between Jasny's index and the revised index is due to differences in base year and coverage. Despite the ingenuity of Jasny's approach to a perplexing problem, certain aspects of his actual or implied statistical procedures raise questions as to the validity of his results. Critical evaluation of his findings is complicated by the omission from the published version of his work of a number of the statistical steps which are crucial to its accuracy.

Jasny's first task was to obtain reasonable estimates of the value of Soviet industrial production at current prices. This he did by inflating wage costs to total costs of production by means of the percentage relation of wage costs to total costs. This is a promising approach, but it has to be very carefully handled. There are a number of pitfalls in Soviet statistics of both kinds (that is, pay rolls and cost percentages) arising out of the question of precise definition of categories, per cent of total labor force or industry covered, and so on. None of the data or calculations involved in this process has been published by Jasny.

A much larger and more important problem is that of securing appropriate price indices to deflate the production totals at current prices. It is no exaggeration to say that the task of providing reliable price indices for Soviet industrial products equals and perhaps exceeds the task of computing an index of Soviet industrial production to which this entire volume has been devoted.

The Soviet government has published no price indices since 1931. Therefore, the investigator must painstakingly assemble a large volume of detailed, representative prices not only for a single year, but also for a number of years. He must be concerned with product comparability and with the problem posed by the introduction of new products. Finally, he must combine these prices in general price indices by means of appropriate weights. In short, he must face all the problems involved in the detailed construction of price indices beginning from the raw data.

Jasny has attempted this major project as but one step in an even more comprehensive investigation. It is by no means certain that his efforts have met with success.

Jasny has published the price data which underly his indices.[17] It appears doubtful whether the prices included in the indices cover a sufficiently broad and varied selection of products to give the indices a truly representative character. Moreover, some of the prices on which the price indices are based are simply "estimated."[18]

Even graver doubts are aroused by Jasny's approach to the weighting problem in combining the prices into price indices. Jasny states that "weights [are] estimated throughout except for building materials."[19] The weights are nowhere made explicit, nor is the procedure followed in making the estimates explained, save to say that weights are "output of state industry."[20]

It may be reasonable to assume that the output weights are taken from the year 1926–27, since this is the base year for the price indices.[21] If this is the case, then prices of new products, to the extent that they are included at all, would be given a relatively small weight compared to prices of established products. Moreover, there is a strong possibility that, for the most part, the prices of products first introduced by Soviet industry in years subsequent to the late 1920's have been omitted entirely from the price indices. Yet, it is precisely the prices of new goods which, over the years covered by the index, should reflect most markedly the cost decreases occasioned by improved techniques and increased scale of production. As a result, the actual rise in the level of Soviet industrial prices may well be exaggerated by Jasny's price indices. Any exaggeration of price increases by the price indices would produce underestimation of the increases in the volume of industrial production at constant prices obtained by deflating current costs by the price indices.

Another problem in selecting appropriate prices arises in connection with the definition of costs of production. In Soviet statistical practice, costs of production are calculated net of profits and turnover (or sales) taxes on final products.[22] In the logic of the situation, it appears likely also that costs of production are computed before the incidence of subsidies on final products. Therefore, prices of final products entering into the price indices also should be net of profits, subsidies, and turnover taxes. Such prices are not readily available, so that Jasny found it necessary to estimate them from retail prices which are gross of profits, subsidies, and turnover taxes. He states that the turnover taxes have been removed from the retail prices, but he does not indicate how this desirable result has been achieved.[23] The problem of allowing for profits and subsidies is completely ignored.

Jasny does not discuss the composition of Soviet prices in the year 1926–27 with respect to the effects of taxes, profits, and subsidies on price structure in that year. Yet, the value of Soviet industrial output in 1928 computed in these prices is accepted by Jasny as the value base for his production index.

Constant 1926–27 prices are referred to by Soviet writers as "wholesale prices f.o.b. factory" (*otpusknye tseny frankozavod*).[24] Customarily, the wholesale prices paid to enterprises are net of turnover taxes but gross of subsidies and profits.[25] Therefore, the current prices comparable to 1926–27 prices also should be gross of subsidies and profits. This poses a dilemma. Current prices used in computing the price indices should include the effects of subsidies and profits so as to maintain comparability with Soviet prices of the year 1926–27. But the price indices used as deflators for total costs of production of Soviet industrial output at current prices should be formed from current prices net of subsidies and profits.

To the extent that subsidies and profits varied only in direct proportion to prices, price indices computed net and gross of profits and subsidies might be very similar. Presumably, they would not be identical, owing to the differential weighting of prices with different gross to net ratios. In fact, however, the history of Soviet price developments has been characterized by great shifts in the relative importance of profits and subsidies as price-forming factors. Thus, for example, subsidies were very important in 1932 but had been sharply reduced by 1937, while profits were relatively small in 1932 and more important in 1937. Therefore, other things equal, for 1932, when subsidies were relatively more important, Jasny's price index may understate price increases and the production index may overstate production increases, while for 1937 the reverse may be true.

Actually, it is not at all clear that Jasny obtained the 1932 value for his production index by straightforward deflation of current costs of production by the price index. Since none of the work is shown, any statement about his actual procedure is hazardous. But he hints that the production value for 1932 may have been calculated somewhat less precisely than that for 1937. He writes:

> The rate of inflation of the "unchangeable 1926–27 prices" was much greater in the 2d than in the 1st Plan Period. But contrary to the inflation ratio established for both Plan Periods together [i.e., for 1937], which is based on rather thorough analysis, partly unpublished, the apportioning of this inflation ratio between the 1st and the 2d Plans was effected rather arbitrarily.[26]

By "inflation ratio" Jasny presumably means the difference between the official index of industrial production and his own calculations. The implication is that the 1932 value of Jasny's production index was established "rather arbitrarily."

Regardless of whether or not Jasny's price indices are appropriate deflators for current costs of production, it appears that the omission of profits and subsidies from production costs, and their inclusion in the official Soviet production totals at 1926–27 prices for 1928 (the value base for Jasny's production index), introduces an arbitrary element into the resulting measure of production changes.

On balance, the problems posed by the weighting system employed, proper representation of prices of new products, and the handling of profits, subsidies, and turnover taxes suggest that the production index prepared by Jasny may be characterized by a downward bias for the period 1928 to 1937. This may explain the much lower index value obtained by Jasny for 1937 than by the minerals consumption, freight transportation, and revised industrial production indices.

A further major discrepancy between Jasny's production index and the minerals consumption, freight transportation, and revised industrial production indices develops in the decade 1940–1950. The latter indices all increase from 45 to 50 per cent, while Jasny's index increases from 18 to 22 per cent, depending on whether the 1940 data are adjusted to postwar territory.

The earlier discussion of factors affecting the relationship of industrial production, minerals consumption, and freight transportation led to the conclusion that no precise function governs these relationships. Nevertheless, it does not seem unreasonable to expect a somewhat greater similarity among them than is evidenced by Jasny's production index.

Indeed, a perplexity arises in connection with Jasny's production index for the years after 1940. In *Soviet Prices of Producers' Goods*, Jasny has published a price index for "all industrial goods, tax free." [27] Presumably, this index served as the deflator for the value of industrial output at current costs in estimating industrial output at constant prices. This price index, however, does not extend beyond the year 1940. In an adjoining passage Jasny states: "In the absence of any data on turnover taxes in the postwar years, it seems advisable to abstain from further estimation of the prices of total industrial production." [28]

The reader is forced to consider the possibility that the production index for the years after 1940 has been computed without the aid of the price index as deflator. But Jasny does not provide any explanation of the actual procedure employed. Until this explanation has been made, there appears to be cause to reserve judgment on the accuracy with which Jasny's estimates reflect changes in Soviet industrial output in the postwar years.

Indices of Soviet machinery output. Professor Alexander Gerschenkron has undertaken a comprehensive recomputation of the rate of growth of Soviet industrial output during the period 1927–28 to 1937. To date, only the portion of the study dealing with the production of the Soviet machinery industry has been published.[29]

Professor Gerschenkron has searched Soviet sources for comprehensive and consistent data on Soviet machinery output in physical quantities. These physical data are then weighted by United States 1939 dollar prices for similar products to permit the computation of over-all value aggregates. The value aggregates in constant prices serve as the basis for an index of the physical volume of Soviet machinery output. The approach is especially noteworthy for its painstaking revaluation of individual product types undertaken in preference to the mass conversion of value aggregates by means of a few selected price ratios. The method has the advantage of securing temporal homogeneity in the prices used, and of making possible direct Soviet-American comparisons of the absolute level of machinery output.

Professor Gerschenkron's dollar index of Soviet machinery output differs from the machinery component of the revised production index prepared in this study in two major respects. First, the systems of value weights applied in the two indices are different. Professor Gerschenkron's study employs U.S. dollar prices of 1939, while the revised machinery index is weighted in an approximation to net value-added in Soviet industry in 1934. Second, there are differences in product coverage by the two indices, resulting from the particular limitations of each weighting system. Each machinery index includes some products omitted by the other.

Since the relative importance of different products is different under the two weighting systems, changes in the composition of Soviet machinery output would produce unlike responses in the two machinery indices even if the product coverage were identical. Professor Gerschenkron has ventured a generalization on the effects of replacing a weighting system based on Soviet prices with U.S. 1939 dollar prices. He believes that

> . . . applying 1939 machinery prices of the advanced American economy as weights to Soviet machinery output over a period of years should result *in a rate of growth lower than the one that would be shown by any index of Soviet machinery output based on Russian prices.*[30]

This view is not entirely correct. It depends upon a particular relation in the structure of relative prices in the two economies, and this necessary condition may not always be satisfied. What is necessary is that the prices of products newly introduced by Soviet industry, whose output is rapidly expanding, should be relatively higher in the Soviet price system than in the U.S. 1939 dollar price system.

The Soviet machinery industry was backward both in product types and methods in the late 1920's compared to the U.S. machinery industry. Since costs of production typically are higher when a product first enters production than after it has become well established, Soviet prices for those new products, whose output was rapidly expanding, presumably were higher relative to established products than the prices of similar products in the United States. Therefore, Professor Gerschenkron's statement is correct for what might be termed the "preindustrialization" Soviet price structure.

During the years subsequent to their first appearance, however, the prices of these new products of the Soviet machinery industry may be expected to have declined relative to the prices of established goods. There would appear to be no inherent limitation to this process to cause it to stop short of achieving in time a structure of relative prices in the Soviet machinery industry comparable to those in the U.S. machinery industry. In fact, given proper conditions of differential changes in productive efficiency in different product lines, the prices of the same products might eventually be lower compared to the general level of prices in the machinery industry in the Soviet Union than in the United States.

To apply Professor Gerschenkron's criterion, it is necessary to know how far this change in price structure has proceeded. Probably Professor Gerschenkron's statement is still true when applied to Soviet prices of the year 1934. Even so, it is of little help in the present instance, since the weights for the revised index are an approximation to value-added while those for the dollar index are gross values. Substantial variations in the ratio of value-added to gross value for different products are to be expected. Thus, there appear to be no grounds for prediction of the influence of the two different sets of value weights on the relationship of the two machinery indices.

The effects of the differences in product coverage are equally elusive. The use of dollar price weights made possible the application of more detailed product-by-product weighting than was possible using Soviet pay-roll weights. It was for this reason that U.S. dollar prices were employed for some subseries of the machinery index in the present study. For the period 1927–28 to 1937, the revised machinery index covers 76 machinery products, while the dollar index includes 128 machinery products. Part of this difference, however, is apparent rather than real.

The dollar index follows the principle of "earned weights," while the revised index uses "imputed weights."[31] Under the system of earned weights, each physical quantity series is given a weight in proportion to the value or value-added of that particular product alone. When imputed weights are employed, the procedure is to establish the general value or value-added weight for the entire industry in question and to subdivide this general weight on the basis of relevant criteria among the available quantity relatives for the products produced by that industry.

On occasion, when imputed weights are used, it is possible to utilize production series which are expressed in conventional rather than physical units. Thus, for example, the production of steam and water turbines, steam engines, stationary and marine diesels, and motor vehicle and tractor engines is represented in the revised index by a single series for the aggregate kilowatt capacity of all these prime movers. Quantity relatives computed from the kilowatt capacity series have been assigned the aggregate value-added weight for all these engines. Thus, some of the individual series constituting the revised machinery index, in fact, represent more than a single product.

Nevertheless, even allowing for the representation in the revised index of several products by a single series in conventional units, there is no question but that a wider and more detailed coverage of Soviet machinery products has been achieved in the dollar index. It is impossible, however, to assess the effects of differences in coverage on the divergence between the two indices without an excessive computational effort.

Professor Gerschenkron's dollar index of Soviet machinery and the revised index machinery component are compared in Table 17. No attempt will be made to explain the discrepancies between the two indices

TABLE 17

Dollar and Revised Indices of Soviet Machinery Output, 1927–28 to 1937 (per cent of 1927–28)

Year	Dollar Index	Revised Index
1927–28	100	100
1928–29	142	142
1929–30	211	175
1931	263	235
1932	264	257
1933	298	325
1934	361	363
1935	457	570
1936	490	625
1937	525	625

SOURCES — Dollar index from Alexander Gerschenkron, *A Dollar Index of Soviet Machinery Output, 1927–28 to 1937* (The RAND Corporation, 1951), p. 29. Revised index from Appendix D.

beyond emphasizing that they are due both to differences in the weighting systems employed and to differences in product coverage. Comparison of the revised and dollar indices with the official Soviet machinery index and an index of Soviet machinery output computed by the Deutsches Institut für Konjunkturforschung serves to accentuate the similarities rather than the differences between the revised and dollar indices. This comparison is made in Table 18. The years are the only ones for which the index prepared by the Deutsches Institut für Konjunkturforschung has been published. Even allowing for differences in product

TABLE 18

Indices of Soviet Machinery Output, 1928–29 to 1937

Year	Revised Index (per cent of 1928–29)	Dollar Index (per cent of 1928–29)	Institut Index (per cent of 1929)	Official Index (per cent of 1928–29)
1928–29	100	100	100	100
1932	181	186	217	348
1933	229	210	343	413
1937	440	370	681	1108

Sources — Revised index from Appendix D; Dollar index from Gerschenkron, *A Dollar Index*, p. 29; Institut für Konjunkturforschung index from *Weekly Report* of the German Institute for Business Research, Berlin, April 30, 1940, p. 44; Official index: the Soviet index for the large-scale machinery industry adjusted by Gerschenkron to a fiscal year 1928–29 rather than a calendar year 1929 base, from Gerschenkron, *op. cit.*, pp. 29, 340–341.

coverage and in the weighting systems employed, the much greater similarity between the revised and dollar indices than between the other two indices cannot be merely fortuitous. It must result in part from the use of more appropriate and more self-consistent systems of value weights.

Conclusion

If this discussion of other measures of Soviet industrial growth leads to any general conclusion, it is that in judging the significance of differences among the various measures, due regard must be had both for the specific purposes for which the individual measures have been computed and for the theoretical principles and statistical procedures which underlie them. Each measure must be judged by its own standards. For the most part, comparisons between the revised production index and the other measures of Soviet industrial growth can neither confirm nor deny the validity of the revised index as an acceptable measure of Soviet industrial production.

7

Aspects of Soviet Industrial Development

The record of Soviet industrial development is impressive. From the inauguration of the First Five Year Plan to the end of the Fourth Five Year Plan, Soviet industrial production expanded about six and one-half times. This great increase was achieved despite the terrible devastation of Soviet industry in World War II.

To assess this record of Soviet achievement both an analysis of internal economic relationships and the use of international comparisons as standards of performance are appropriate. Either approach is much beyond the scope of this volume. Nevertheless, a brief excursion into both areas of analysis will be undertaken for two reasons. First, to call the Soviet industrial achievement "impressive" implies a standard of measurement. Despite many conceptual and statistical hazards, such a standard involves international comparisons. Second, both an index of labor productivity in Soviet industry and an index of industrial consumers' goods per capita of population are readily computed with the aid of the revised index of industrial output. The index of labor productivity indicates the extent to which the growth of industrial production has depended on increased labor efficiency rather than an increase in the size of the industrial labor force and provides some insight into the elements of Soviet past and possible future industrial performance. The index of industrial consumers' goods per capita is a more significant measure of the direct benefits of Soviet industrial growth to the Soviet citizen than is a general index of Soviet industrial production.

Labor Productivity in Soviet Large-Scale Industry

The official Soviet measure of industrial labor productivity has both defects and limitations which render it an unsatisfactory tool of economic analysis. The official index is calculated by dividing the annual gross output of large-scale industry valued at "constant 1926–27 prices" by the average annual number of workers (*rabochie*) in large-scale industry.[1] Thus, the inflationary bias in official production statistics at 1926–27 prices is carried over to the official index of labor productivity. A further feature of the official index, at least for the years 1928–1935 and quite possibly for all years, is that it includes only the enterprises of the industrial commissariats rather than all large-scale enterprises. The enterprises of the all-union and local industrial commissariats produced about 80 per cent of the output (valued at 1926–27 prices) of large-scale industry in 1934.[2]

The reason for thus limiting the coverage of the official index of labor productivity has been stated succinctly in *Sotsialisticheskoe stroitel'stvo* (Socialist Construction) for 1936.

> Data for output per worker are given for the enterprises of the industrial commissariats (Heavy Industry, Wood Industry, Light Industry, Food Industry, Procurement, and the Moving Picture Industry). Comparison of data for the number of workers and output for all large-scale industry does not represent correctly changes in the productivity of labor. A large number of comparatively small-scale enterprises which barely satisfy census criteria have been added in recent years to those enterprises which meet the criteria for large-scale industry, especially in connection with the socialization of small-scale industry.
>
> An increase in the size of small-scale industry is doubtless accompanied by an increase in the productivity of labor in these enterprises, but the level of their productivity is, of course, significantly below the average level in large-scale industry. Therefore, the inclusion of a large number of small-scale enterprises in the totals with large-scale industry according to formal census criteria retards the rate of growth of output per worker in comparison with actual changes in labor productivity. For this reason data on labor productivity are presented for the enterprises of the industrial commissariats, the composition of which is more stable and homogeneous.[3]

This is not an unreasonable argument, although it applies equally well to the measurement of industrial output. Exclusion from production statistics of the numerous small-scale enterprises newly classified as "large-scale" during the process of "socialization" after 1928, however, would have *reduced* the rate of increase in industrial output. The official Soviet attitude toward economic statistics may be reflected by the selection in each case of that statistical procedure which yielded results most laudatory of Soviet industrial achievement.

A final limitation is that the official productivity index is calculated on a man-year basis. It reflects but does not distinguish between increases in productivity per man hour and changes in numbers of man hours worked per year. Yet the significance of these two types of increases in man-year productivity is quite different. Perhaps the most important distinction is that increases in man-year productivity resulting from increases in working hours have an absolute upper limit, while increases in man-hour productivity resulting from technical and organizational improvements presumably have no such limit and are the main vehicle of secularly rising living standards.

The revised index of the productivity of workers in Soviet large-scale industry has been calculated by dividing the revised index of industrial production (Table 15, p. 89) by the number of workers in Soviet large-scale industry. Some comment is required on the manner in which statistics were obtained for the number of workers in large-scale industry.

A distinction has been drawn previously between the employment statistics prepared by the industrial and labor divisions of the Central Statistical Administration.[4] The labor division was primarily responsible for statistics on employment, wages, hours, labor turnover, and the like. The industrial division bore the main responsibility for preparing statistics on industrial production. Census criteria and industrial classifications adopted by the two divisions did not coincide. Consequently, the only employment statistics directly comparable in coverage to the production statistics prepared by the industrial division are those collected by the industrial division itself. The industrial division, however, required enterprises to report only the number of workers (rabochie) employed and did not seek information on the number of engineers and technicians, salaried personnel, service personnel, and apprentices.

The official index of labor productivity in Soviet industry is computed in terms of the value (at 1926–27 prices) of gross output per worker. This fact suggests that the index of labor productivity may be based on industrial division employment statistics. There is, however, no direct and conclusive evidence on this point. In any case, it is appropriate to use industrial division employment statistics in conjunction with the revised production index, since the latter is based on physical output data prepared by the industrial division of the Central Statistical Administration.

No consistent annual statistics on the industrial labor force have been published since 1936. Comprehensive and clearly identifiable industrial division statistics for the number of workers in Soviet large-scale industry are available only for the years 1928–1935. One "preliminary" figure was published for 1936. After 1936 the distinctions between employment in *large-scale* industry and in *all* industry and between *industrial* division and *labor* division employment statistics are not made in Soviet publications. Indeed, the writer is not aware of any published figures which even separate workers (rabochie) from other employees in industry for years later than 1937 with the exception of planned totals in the *1941 Plan*.

TABLE 19

Workers in Soviet Large-Scale Industry, 1928–1950

Year	Number of Workers (1000)	Year	Number of Workers (1000)	Year	Number of Workers (1000)
1928	3,699	1935	8,027	1940	9,384[b]
1929	4,154	1936	8,322[a]	1946	8,515[b]
1930	4,996		8,669[b]	1947	9,198[b]
1931	6,037	1937	8,870[b]	1948	10,200[b]
1932	6,951	1938	9,198[b]	1949	10,800[b]
1933	6,901	1939	9,198[b]	1950	11,900[b]
1934	7,404				

[a] Indicated by Turetskii as "expected."
[b] Estimated by constructing an index of the number of workers in Soviet industry from a comparison of official indices of labor productivity (Table 20, p. 113) and industrial output (Table 15, p. 89) and multiplying the number of workers in 1935 by the values of this employment index for the respective years.
SOURCES — 1928–1935 from *Sotsialisticheskoe stroitel'stvo* (Socialist Construction; Moscow, 1936), p. 3; 1935–1936 from Sh. Turetskii, 'Ekonomicheskaia effektivnost' osvoeniia novoi tekhniki'' (Economic Effectiveness of Mastering the New Technique), *Planovoe khoziaistvo*, no. 8, 1936, p. 81.

After 1940, with the single exception of the *1941 Plan*, no published Soviet source has indicated so much as what portion of the total nonagricultural labor force is employed in industry as distinguished from other nonagricultural sectors of the economy.

In view of these circumstances, annual changes in the number of workers employed in Soviet large-scale industry from 1936 to 1950 have been estimated by dividing the official index of industrial production for these years by the official index of the productivity of labor. This procedure is done in ignorance of the precise coverage by industrial establishments of either official index. Presumably, the official production index covers all industrial production regardless of size of establishment and whether socialized or private (private industry was negligible). It is not known whether the official productivity index for these years was computed as formerly only for the enterprises of the industrial commissariats or whether the base was broadened to include all industry. Thus, it is possible that the estimated number of workers in Soviet large-scale industry for years later than 1935 is subject to some error. It does not appear likely that the error would exceed 10 per cent, and it may well be smaller. Actual and (after 1935) estimated numbers of workers in Soviet large-scale industry are presented in Table 19.

The revised index of labor productivity in Soviet industry is compared in Table 20 to the official index and to an unofficial index computed from

TABLE 20

Indices of the Productivity of Labor in Soviet Large-Scale Industry, 1928–1950
(per cent of 1928)

Year	Revised Index	Official Index	Varga's Index
1928	100	100	100
1929	107	112.9	111.6
1930	103	123.9	121.0
1931	100	133.3	120.1
1932	92	136.8	115.9
1933	103	148.7	128.3
1934	114	164.6	145.3
1935	136	186.0	—
1936	147	225.8	—
1937	155	245.9	—
1938	—	272.9	—
1939	—	318.5	—
1940	169	324.6	—
1946	132	270.4	—
1947	151	305.6	—
1948	169	351.4	—
1949	192	397.1	—
1950	201	444.7	—

SOURCES — Revised Index: derived from the revised index of industrial production, Table 15, p. 89, and data on number of workers in Soviet industry from Table 19, p. 112; values for the revised index for 1928–1930 have been obtained by combining fiscal-year output with calendar-year labor force data. Official Index: assembled from official sources and presented by Walter Galenson, "Industrial Labor Productivity," Table 6.2 in Abram Bergson (ed.), *Soviet Economic Growth* (Row, Peterson and Co., 1953), p. 195. Varga's Index: Based on official statistics of output and labor force in Soviet large-scale industry exclusive of the lumber industry, timber flotage, fisheries, and railway repair shops, E. Varga, *Kapitalizm i sotsializm za 20 let* (Capitalism and Socialism During 20 Years), Partizdat Ts.K.V.K.P. (b), 1938, p. 59. For coverage of the output data used by Varga, see *Socialist Construction in the USSR* (Moscow, 1936), p. 4.

official statistics by a Soviet economist, E. Varga. All three indices measure changes in *productivity per man year*. Measured by the revised index, the productivity of Soviet industrial labor in 1950 was about double the 1928 level, while the official index indicates a level four and one-half times that of 1928. Changes in the two indices are roughly similar in the Second and Fourth Five Year Plans and in the wartime drop in productivity from 1940 to 1946. Major discrepancies between the two indices mark the years of the First and Third Five Year Plans.

In 1932 productivity of Soviet industrial labor measured by the revised index actually was below the 1928 level, whereas the official index shows a 37 per cent increase. From 1929 to 1932, the revised index registers annual declines in productivity, whereas the official index shows steady, though in some years small, increases. According to the revised index, no significant increase in Soviet industrial labor productivity occurred until 1934. From 1934 to 1937, however, productivity registered rapid gains.

In the three prewar years of the Third Five Year Plan (1938–1940), the official index indicates a 32 per cent increase in labor productivity, while the revised index shows a bare 9 per cent increase. Both the official and revised indices of productivity drop from 1940 to 1946 and then rise fairly rapidly during the postwar industrial recovery. In both indices the prewar level of productivity per man year is regained in 1948. By 1950 the revised index stands 19 per cent above the prewar level and 30 per cent above 1937. For the official index, the 1950 level is 37 per cent above prewar and 81 per cent above 1937.

Varga's index of labor productivity has been computed from official statistics of output and employment, and differs from the official index only in the scope of its coverage of industrial establishments. The official index includes only the establishments of the industrial commissariats, while Varga's index includes *all* "large-scale" enterprises in "Census Industry," that is, Varga's index includes the small-scale establishments recently reorganized and reclassified by census criteria as large-scale enterprises. Although Varga's index is more comprehensive in coverage by size of enterprise, it is less comprehensive than the official index by industrial coverage. Varga's index for "Census Industry" excludes fisheries, lumbering, and railway repair shops which are included in the official index for "large-scale" industry. Nevertheless, output indices for "large-scale" and for "Census Industry" are very similar, so that the productivity indices for these two categories of large-scale industry probably would be very similar if computed for establishments of the same size.[5]

Varga's index is of interest as corroborative evidence of the decline in productivity of Soviet industrial labor in the early 1930's revealed in the revised index. The decline in Varga's index begins a year later and is less severe than that indicated by the revised index. Both Varga's index and the revised index reflect the effect on average productivity in these years of the reorganization of small-scale, low productivity industrial establishments into larger units satisfying the census criteria for "large-scale" industry. But Varga's index, unlike the revised index, is subject to an upward bias arising from the use of inflated official production values at 1926–27 prices.

All of the preceding productivity changes have been computed in terms of output per man year. No allowance has been made, therefore, for changes in the average number of man hours worked per year due to changes in the normal work week, overtime, holidays, and vacations. Soviet labor statistics have never reported systematically on changes in average man hours worked per year. Nevertheless, for the period 1928–1937 changes in average man hours worked per year in large-scale industry may be estimated from a comparison of two official Soviet indices of labor productivity: one in terms of output per man year, the other in terms of output per man hour.[6] Presumably, the only difference between these two indices arises from changes in average man hours worked per year, so that an index of changes in average man hours worked per year may be obtained by dividing the index of productivity per man year by the index of productivity per man hour. In Table 21 the index of average man hours worked per year for the years 1928, 1932, and 1937 has been obtained in the manner just described. The index is at best an approximation, since the Soviet statisticians in adjusting the man-year index for changes in days per year and hours per day were forced to extrapolate data for the number of working hours per day for the years 1932 to 1937.[7]

Estimates of changes in the average number of hours worked per year subsequent to 1937 are even more problematical than for earlier years. No comprehensive statistics recording these changes are available. The best that can be done is to allow for the change in the statutory work week. By a decree of June 26, 1940 the normal work week was changed from a seven-hour day every five days out of six to an eight-hour day every six days out of seven.[8] On an annual basis, this is equivalent to a change from 40.8 hours to 48 hours per calendar week or an increase of 18 per cent in weekly or annual hours worked. Since the change became legally effective only after the first six months of 1940, the increase in average annual hours worked in 1940 has been taken as 9 per cent rather than 18 per cent relative to 1937. In 1950 the extended work week was effective throughout the year, so that an increase in average annual hours

TABLE 21
Index of Average Man Hours Worked Per Year in Soviet Large-Scale Industry, 1928–1950
(per cent of 1928)

Year	Index
1928	100
1932	91
1937	93
1940	101
1950	110

SOURCES — See text.

worked of 18 per cent relative to 1937 is assumed. The index values in Table 21 for 1940 and 1950 have been extrapolated from 1937 on this basis.

The revised index of labor productivity per man hour in Table 22 has been calculated by correcting the revised index of productivity per man year for these estimated changes in average annual man hours worked per year. Clearly, the index must be regarded simply as an approximation. Detailed corrections for changes in actual man hours are not possible without more information regarding actual overtime, legal holidays, vacations, and the like. Nevertheless, as an approximation the man-hour index of labor productivity is informative.

The outstanding increase in the man-hour productivity of the Soviet industrial worker came during the period of the Second Five Year Plan (1932–1937). During this brief period, man-hour productivity in Soviet industry increased at an average annual percentage rate of 10.5. During the years of the First Five Year Plan and the three prewar years of the Third Five Year Plan, man-hour productivity in Soviet industry remained virtually unchanged. From 1928 to 1940 man-hour productivity increased by 67 per cent or at an average annual percentage rate of 4.4. This may be compared to the 4.2 average annual percentage rate of increase in man-hour productivity in American manufacturing (excluding mining) for the period 1919 to 1939 indicated in Solomon Fabricant's study, *Employment in Manufacturing 1899–1939*.[9] Over the longer period 1899 to 1939 Fabricant finds an average annual percentage rate of increase in man-hour productivity in American manufacturing of 2.9.

From 1940 to 1950 man-hour productivity in Soviet industry increased by 11 per cent or at an annual average percentage rate just slightly in excess of 1 per cent. Considering the handicap of wartime destruction

TABLE 22

Revised Index of the Productivity of Soviet Workers Per Man Hour in Large-Scale Industry, 1928–1950

(per cent of 1928)

Year	Index
1928	100
1932	101
1937	167
1940	167
1950	183

SOURCES — Computed by correcting the revised index of productivity per man year (Table 20, p. 113) for changes in average annual hours worked (Table 21, p. 116).

and disorganization, this is a creditable gain. Moreover, there is no reason to expect future gains in man-hour productivity in Soviet industry to be limited to the level of the war decade 1940–1950. Gains in man-hour productivity from 1948 to 1950 probably closely paralleled gains in productivity per man year and thus may have been annually about 9 per cent. However, if allowance is made for the increase in average annual man hours from 1940 to 1948 of approximately 9 per cent, it must be noted that man-hour productivity in 1948 still was some 8 per cent below the level of 1940. Thus, a part of the increase from 1948 to 1950 simply represented recovery to prewar performance levels. The increase in productivity per man year and (in the absence of any known changes in average annual man hours) also per man hour from 1949 to 1950 was 4.7 per cent or of the same general order of magnitude as during the period 1928–1940.

The pattern of productivity changes during the Five Year Plans as indicated by the revised index can be given a meaningful economic interpretation and has some interesting implications both for future Soviet industrial development and for countries embarking on industrialization programs. The decline in productivity per man year from 1928 to 1932 can be attributed to a decline in average man hours worked per year in this period. The failure, however, of *man-hour* productivity to rise during the First Five Year Plan requires further explanation in view of the emphasis in these years on capital investments and modernization of industrial techniques.

Although heavy capital investments in Soviet industry were made during the First Five Year Plan, it appears likely that a considerable portion of this effort was directed into building construction which would not immediately be reflected in increased labor productivity. Moreover, for the more complex types of industrial equipment there was undoubtedly a considerable incubation period between the start of construction and the actual availability of the equipment and facilities for use in production. Also, it must be recognized that the extremely rapid expansion of the industrial labor force in these years was accomplished only by bringing into industry large numbers of peasant farmers completely unskilled in industrial techniques and unfamiliar with an industrial regimen. Thus, a considerable dilution of the average skill level in industry could scarcely have been avoided.

The great leap in productivity per man hour during the years of the Second Five Year Plan (1933–1937) is an outstanding achievement for Soviet industry. The abruptness of the increase in these five years, preceded and followed by insignificant or, at most, fairly conventional rates of growth in other years, constitutes a highly unusual phenomenon. One hypothesis may be offered in explanation.

The rapid gains in productivity in the years 1933–1937 undoubtedly reflect the increasing availability of new plants and equipment as investments undertaken in earlier years reached fruition, and the increasing familiarity of the new industrial workers with their tasks. The more gradual increase (both absolute and percentage-wise) in the number of industrial workers in the Second than in the First Five Year Plan also undoubtedly contributed to productivity differences. These factors, however, do not emphasize sufficiently the nature of the underlying change in Soviet industry accomplished in the First Five Year Plan which made possible the unusual achievement of the Second Five Year Plan.

The program of the First Five Year Plan was directed not only to an expansion of Soviet industry, but also to a drastic change both in its technological base and in its interbranch structure. The Second Five Year Plan continued to build on this base, but it was during the First Five Year Plan that the basic changes in technology and industrial structure were accomplished. The First Five Year Plan was the period during which Soviet industry was converted from the nineteenth to the twentieth century. It was a period also during which the new industrial labor force required by industry was recruited and trained. These processes did not come to a halt during the Second Five Year Plan, but the grand metamorphosis of Soviet industry had occurred and the fruits of the achievement were harvested during the Second Five Year Plan. In a sense, the spectacular growth in industrial output, labor force, and productivity which characterized Soviet industry in the years 1928–1937 represents the bonus collected by the underdeveloped Soviet economy as a result of its backwardness.

The sharp decline in rates of growth of output, labor force, and productivity in Soviet industry after 1937 reflects in part the unavoidable slowing down of rates of technological and structural change incident to industrialization as the backward Soviet economy achieved more modern form and, in part, the reallocation of labor and investment accompanying economic and military mobilization. With the induction of increasing numbers of males of prime working age from industry into the armed forces and their replacement in industry by women, adolescents, and older workers, there must have been a noticeable reduction of the average level of skill and experience in the industrial labor force. Temporary loss of productive facilities during the process of conversion of industry from civilian to military products, the transfer of workers to new jobs in armament factories, and the curtailment of the civilian investment program in favor of expansion in armaments could not have failed to retard the growth in industrial labor productivity. In the official index the retarding effects of these factors on the growth of output and labor productivity are offset by the inflation of official production totals because of the high valuation of the increasing volume of military production as well as the continuous increase in new product bias in production totals for civilian goods. These particular distortions are absent from the revised index. On the other hand, the crude nature of the allowance for military production in the revised index does not permit its acceptance as any final standard of accurate measurement.

It appears unlikely that the bonus to backwardness collected by Soviet industry in the first two Five Year Plans can ever be claimed again in comparable degree. This hypothesis has interesting connotations for the future growth of Soviet industry. So long as Soviet industrial technique in the broad sense — embracing both technology and human organization — lags behind that of the United States, it is not unreasonable to expect a more rapid rate of industrial progress in the Soviet Union than in the United States. A trail once blazed is more readily followed. But, short of a vast technological revolution, Soviet industry will not have the opportunity to duplicate its feats of the first two Five Year Plans in the future. Soviet industry appears to have spent most of its inheritance in surplus agricultural labor and Western technology, and must now live more on its own current ingenuity with such assistance as the still sizable gap between Soviet and American technical and organizational refinements may provide through further borrowings.

Soviet centralized control over the rate and direction of investment will continue to influence the future rate of growth of Soviet industrial output. In a recent stimulating study, "Capital Formation and Allocation," Norman M. Kaplan has found that the rate of formation of industrial capital in the Soviet Union during the Five Year Plans exceeds that in any period of the economic development of the United States.[10] Dr. Kaplan finds indications that this result has been obtained in the USSR not by devoting a higher proportion of gross national product to investment than has been customary in the United States, but by directing a larger proportion of total investment into the industrial sector of the economy.[11] Moreover, owing to the more youthful age composition of Soviet industrial capital to date, and the consequent smaller requirements for replacement, the ratio of net to gross investment has been higher in Soviet than in American industry.

With increasing maturity of the age composition of Soviet industrial capital, the ratio of net to gross investment must decline unless there is a further major increase in the rate of investment in industry. In view of competing investment requirements of other sectors of the economy and consumption requirements of the Soviet population, no such major increase in the rate of investment in Soviet industry appears probable.

Thus, the passage of time may be expected to reduce this particular advantage enjoyed by Soviet industry in the race for capital accumulation and industrial expansion.

Soviet controls over the direction of investment presumably will continue, however, to favor industry relative to other sectors of the economy and within industry to favor producers' goods relative to consumers' goods. Thus, it is likely that the rate of net capital formation and thus of capital accumulation in Soviet industry will continue to exceed that in American industry. From this, however, it does not follow that the further expansion of Soviet industrial capital will be accompanied by increases in industrial production in similar proportion to those increases which accompanied capital expansion in the First and, more especially, the Second Five Year Plans.

Capital expansion may be of the capital widening or capital deepening varieties. Capital widening implies a duplication of existing capital facilities and a proportional increase in other factors of production, especially labor. Capital deepening implies an increase in the amount of capital employed with given quantities of other productive factors and thus the necessity for accompanying technical change. During the first two Five Year Plans capital expansion in Soviet industry embraced both capital widening and capital deepening to an unusual degree. Capital deepening was accomplished through the introduction of new industrial techniques primarily borrowed from abroad and was reflected in the sharp increase in man-hour productivity of industrial labor. Capital widening was facilitated by the induction of large numbers of surplus farm laborers into the industrial labor force. In the future, however, both types of capital expansion in Soviet industry face limitations.

The future rate of technological change in Soviet industry, even allowing for further borrowings, is certain to be much less than in the first two Five Year Plans, simply because relatively less remains to be borrowed. This is another way of saying that, in the future, gains in labor productivity in individual industries will be more gradual. Capital widening, on the other hand, is likely to be limited by a reduced intake of labor into the industrial labor force, since there is considerable evidence of the disappearance of a labor surplus and its replacement by a labor shortage.[12] Capital deepening on an industry-wide basis can, of course, be achieved by capital widening in capital intensive industries. This form of capital deepening is of more limited consequence than across-the-board capital deepening. Moreover, it faces the obstacle of requiring additional supplies of industrial labor (since it requires capital widening) and it is limited by the desirability of further change in the composition of industrial output. Thus, although Soviet economic controls may make possible a more rapid rate of expansion in industrial capital than is likely to occur in the United States, the effectiveness of this additional investment will be limited by the adequacy of the supply of additional industrial labor and the rate of technological progress.

The peculiar pattern of changes in productivity per man hour in Soviet industry suggests one other observation with respect to the potentialities of industrial development in backward economies. A determined government favored with adequate supplies of labor and natural resources can make great initial progress in a relatively short span of years with the introduction of the major elements of modern industrial technique. Following the dramatic changes of the initial phase, however, there ensues a period of more gradual change during which progress consists of the introduction of technological and organizational refinements. Machinery and major industrial processes may be imported, but the subtleties of industrial organization, both technical and human, especially the latter, have to be learned through experience and this takes time. A nation may stride with seven league boots the first rough mile of industrialization, but this must give way to steady slogging at a more moderate pace on the long road to the summit of industrial progress.

Production of Industrial Consumers' Goods

The direct benefits of industrialization to the average citizen are measured more appropriately by the production of consumers' goods than by total industrial production. It is no secret that the rapid rate of Soviet industrial expansion is due in part to a policy of favoring the development of producers' goods industries and thus investment at the expense of consumers' goods industries and consumption. Official Soviet statistics distinguish between the production by Soviet industry of producers' and consumers' goods. In 1950 the index for producers' goods stood at 21.7 times its 1928 level, while that for consumers' goods registered 6.7 times its 1928 level. But the defects of Soviet production statistics extend to the index of industrial consumers' goods production, so that there is reason to question the validity of the increase claimed.

A revised index of the production of consumers' goods by Soviet large-scale industry has been calculated from production series for textiles, leather footwear, food, matches, and the grease, tallow soap, and perfume industry, using 1934 pay-roll weights. This revised index of consumers' goods is compared to the official Soviet index in Table 23. The revised index increases 158 per cent from 1928 to 1950 compared to an increase of 568 per cent in the official index. Only in the years of the Second Five Year Plan are there comparable increases in the two indices. In all periods increases are greater or decreases less measured by the official index.

TABLE 23

Indices of the Production of Consumers' Goods by Soviet Large-Scale Industry, 1928–1950

(per cent of 1928)

Year	Revised Index	Official Index	Year	Revised Index	Official Index
1928	100	100	1940	225	543
1932	125	190	1946	109	360
1937	237	405	1950	258	668

SOURCES — Revised index: 1927–28 to 1937 calculated by weighting the indices for matches, textiles, leather footwear, food, and the grease, tallow, soap, and perfume industry in Appendix D, by their respective value-added weights in 1934 from Appendix B, 1937–1950 calculated from the weighted quantity relatives for food, textiles, and grease, tallow, soap, and perfume industry. Official index: large-scale industry 1928–1934 from *Sotsialisticheskoe stroitel'stvo* (Socialist Construction; Moscow, 1936), p. 3; 1935–1937 calculated from percentages in *SSSR i kapitalisticheskie strany* (USSR and the Capitalist Countries; ed. by Ioffe), p. 4; all industry 1937 from Gosplan, *Tretii piatiletnii plan razvitiia narodnogo khoziaistva Soiuza SSR* (Third Five Year Plan of Economic Development of the Union SSR; Moscow, 1939), p. 197; 1940 from N. Voznesensky, *The Growing Prosperity of the Soviet Union* (New York: Workers Library Publishers), p. 14; 1946–1950 from percentage increases relative to 1940 given by G. M. Malenkov in his *Report of the Central Committee of C.P.S.U. (B) to XIX Congress of the Party.*

For both the official and revised indices the coverage changes after 1937, so that post-1937 indices are linked to pre-1937 indices.

Relative changes in per capita production of industrial consumers' goods are of greater interest than changes in total volume of consumers' goods production. Table 24 contains estimates of Soviet population for selected years since 1928 taken from postwar studies of Soviet population made by Frank Lorimer and Warren Eason. The postwar estimates are subject to revision when and if more comprehensive population data become available. Possible errors in the present estimates are unlikely to exceed 5 per cent.

Table 25 shows the official and revised indices of the production of industrial consumers' goods per capita. In 1950 the official index indicates a per capita production of industrial consumers' goods approximately five times as great as in 1928, while the revised index is about twice its 1928 level. Even more interesting is the relationship of levels of production in some of the intervening years. The official index declines only during and immediately after the war. By 1950 it is above the level of 1940 and well above the level of 1937. Even in 1946 it is well above 1928 and 1932, although about 25 per cent below 1937. The revised index, on the other hand, registers a decline from 1937 to 1940 and falls below even the 1928 level in 1946. By 1950 it has regained at best the level of 1940 but is still 10 per cent or more below the level of 1937.

Neither the revised nor official index is in any sense a measure of changes in standards of living of the Soviet population. Major omissions in this respect are agricultural products consumed without industrial processing,

TABLE 24

Population of the Soviet Union, 1928–1950

Year	Number (millions)	Index (per cent of 1928)
1928	150	100
1932	158	105
1937	163	109
1940 (prewar territory)	174	116
1946	193	129
1950	200–205	133–137

SOURCE — Numbers for 1928–1940 from Frank Lorimer, *The Population of the Soviet Union: History and Prospects* (Geneva: League of Nations, 1946), pp. 135, 183. The figure for 1940 is a population projection for the January 1939 area and does not include Soviet annexations in Eastern Europe after September 1, 1939; 1946, 1950 from Warren W. Eason, *Trends and Prospects of the Soviet Population and Labor Force* (The RAND Corporation, March 1952), pp. 23, 32.

housing, and numerous services including education, social insurance, health services, and others. Moreover, the coverage of the industrial output series is limited (in the revised index entirely and in the official index through 1937) to the production of large-scale industry. But small-scale industry typically has been a haven for the output of consumers' goods of the craft type. Therefore, the trends displayed may not fully represent variations in total production of industrial consumers' goods. This is a double-edged conclusion which cuts both ways.

Both the official and revised indices may increase more rapidly than total production of consumers' goods during the years 1928–1937 due to the consolidation and reclassification of numerous enterprises from small-scale to large-scale production in these years. There are no clear indications of changes in the relative importance of small-scale and large-scale industrial establishments as suppliers of consumers' goods in later years, although it appears to have been official policy to encourage (at least by exhortation) an increase in small-scale production of consumers' goods in the immediate postwar years.[13]

TABLE 25

Indices of the Production of Industrial Consumers' Goods Per Capita in the Soviet Union, 1928–1950 (per cent of 1928)

Year	Revised Index	Official Index	Year	Revised Index	Official Index
1928	100	100	1940	194	468
1932	119	181	1946	84	279
1937	217	372	1950	188–194	488–502

SOURCE — Revised and official indices of the production of industrial consumers' goods by large-scale industry from Table 23, p. 123, divided by the index of population from Table 24, p. 124. The revised index value for 1928 has been obtained by dividing output for the *fiscal* year 1927–28 by population for January 1, 1928.

Finally, in assessing the importance to consumers of the indicated increase in per capita production of industrial consumers' goods, the nature of the comparison must be kept in mind. The increase is measured in relative rather than in absolute terms. Even a doubling of the available supply of industrial consumers' goods per capita measured in relative terms could be consistent with absolute quantities sufficient to provide for, say, only two-thirds of the population.

For these various reasons, the index of production of industrial consumers' goods per capita provides no guide to changes in living standards of Soviet citizens during the Five Year Plans. It does, however, indicate an increase in the volume of production by large-scale industry of industrial consumers' goods per capita of some 88 to 94 per cent from 1928 to 1950 and points to 1937 as the year marked by the highest production of industrial consumers' goods per capita during the period of the Five Year Plans. When allowance is made for the low level of per capita output of industrial consumers' goods in 1928, it is apparent that industrialization has brought but modest increases in supplies of consumers' goods to the average Soviet citizen.

International Comparisons of Industrial Growth

An assessment of Soviet industrial development by means of international comparisons is fraught with conceptual and statistical hazards. International comparisons of industrial growth may be made in terms of relative rates of growth or in terms of absolute increases. Common practice has been to compare *relative* rates of growth. The reasons for this choice are readily apparent.

Whenever two or more different products are concerned, comparisons of absolute increases involve the investigator in the complex question of appropriate value weighting.[14] If international comparisons of industrial growth are to be made on an absolute scale, equal absolute changes in physical quantities should produce equal absolute changes in value aggregates for both economies. This means that identical value weights must be assigned to identical physical quantities. But production values usually are computed by official government agencies, using the monetary unit and structure of the relative prices of an individual country. Therefore, the investigator must undertake a more or less comprehensive recomputation of production values for all countries but one which enter into the comparison. The magnitude of this undertaking is huge, and the obstacles to its successful completion are grave.

One embarrassing aspect of the index-number problem remains, moreover, even should the revaluation of industrial production in various countries be carried out successfully. Absolute changes in the value of industrial output in different countries will vary with the particular structure of relative prices underlying the value weights.[15] Thus, no unique solution to the problem of international comparisons of industrial growth is provided by the method of comparing absolute value magnitudes.

International comparisons more commonly made in terms of *relative* rates of growth in industrial production may be misleading for two reasons. The relative value weights applied to commodity series vary from country to country. Thus, identical changes in physical output in two countries will cause unlike changes in their production indices. Moreover, the absolute volumes of production which serve as a base for the calculation of subsequent percentage increases in output may be of quite different orders of magnitude in various countries. Here again identical absolute changes in output may produce markedly different percentage changes in the production indices of the various nations.

On theoretical grounds, the choice between making international comparisons of industrial growth in terms of absolute increases or percentage rates should be determined by the purpose of the comparison. If the emphasis is on the success with which individual economies have utilized the advantages and overcome the handicaps of their respective initial situations, it is appropriate to conduct the measurements in terms of values derived from scarcity relationships specific to each economy. If, instead, the purpose is to obtain some generalized measure of economic abundance or industrial strength, identical value weights should be assigned to identical physical products in all countries. In neither case, however, does the comparison provide a unique and unequivocal guide either to the past achievements or comparative industrial strength of the various economies.

The revised index of Soviet industrial production prepared in this study is compared to indices of industrial production for selected other countries in Table 26. *Relative* rather than absolute changes in industrial production are reflected in this table. Indices for countries other than the Soviet Union are from the United Nations *Statistical Yearbook 1951* and have been computed by national statistical offices in terms of their respective national monetary units and price systems. All indices include both manufacturing and mining. In addition, some indices include public utilities and some include construction.

The year 1932 has been chosen as the base year for the comparison to emphasize the similarity in the relative increases in industrial output in the Soviet Union, the United States, and Germany. The expansion in industrial output in these three countries far exceeds that of other world powers.

The achievement of the Soviet Union is underemphasized, of course, by measuring the increase in industrial output of other countries from the nadir of the Great Depression. Had 1929 served as the base year, the relative expansion in Soviet industrial output would have surpassed considerably that of either Germany or the United States. Allowance must be made, also, for the handicap which wartime destruction placed on Soviet industrial expansion relative to that of the United States. In 1946 Soviet industrial production had been reduced almost to the level of 1935, and it did not regain the level of the prewar year 1940 until 1948. Thus, the war may have set back the growth of Soviet industry nearly a decade or the equivalent of two five year plans. On the other hand, it hardly needs to be stressed that equal percentage increases in industrial output reflect far greater absolute increases in the United States than in the Soviet Union.

Reflections on Soviet Industrial Development

In the short span of thirty years the Soviet Union has risen from the ranks to become the second most powerful industrial nation in the world. The Soviet economic system, closely controlled and directed by a tightly knit and ruthless political organization, has proved itself a magnificent

TABLE 26
Indices of Industrial Production for Selected Countries, 1929–1950 [a]
(per cent of 1932)

Year	Soviet Union	United States [b]	Western Germany [c]	Japan [d]	France	Italy [e]
1929	70	190	172	—	140	149
1932	100	100	100	100	100	100
1937	216	197	200	182	123	148
1940	250	217	—	208	—	—
1946	177	297	—	62	89	—
1950	376	347	378	142	139	175

Sources — Data for Soviet Union from revised index for large-scale industry, Table 15, p. 89; for all other countries from *Statistical Yearbook 1951* (New York: United Nations Statistical Office, Department of Economic Affairs, 1951), United States, p. 122; Western Germany, p. 128; Japan, p. 124; France, p. 128; Italy, p. 130.

[a] Including mining, manufacturing, and public utilities; excluding construction unless otherwise stated.
[b] Excluding electricity and gas.
[c] Including building.
[d] Excluding electricity and gas.
[e] 1929–1937 include public works; 1929–1934 exclude mining.

instrument of forced draft industrialization for a nation which, save for technical assistance, has had to rely primarily upon its own, internal resources. The record of Soviet achievement in industrial development remains impressive even after allowance has been made for much overstatement in official claims. Recovery of Soviet industry from the devastation of World War II has been more rapid than many would have thought possible. It is an accolade to Soviet achievement that only the United

States remains to challenge its industrial supremacy. The force of the Soviet example cannot fail to exert a compelling attraction on backward nations who desire to set forth on the road to industrialization.

Amidst these encomiums, however, there is the danger that the essential nature of the Soviet achievement will be misinterpreted. Basically, Soviet success inheres in the application of technical and organizational methods, primarily borrowed from abroad and pioneered by other economic systems, to the vast human and natural resources of the Soviet state. To date, what has been unique in Soviet experience has been the *speed* with which previously mapped routes have been traveled with relatively little outside assistance other than the map itself. Few would deny that the costs of this achievement, above all the human costs, have been high. Regardless of costs, however, the record stands. Precisely in this aspect lies the strong appeal of the Soviet model of industrialization to other backward areas.

When current levels of industrial output, labor productivity, and standards of living in the United States replace those of backward areas as a gauge of Soviet industrial development, however, Soviet achievement is viewed in a different perspective. On the basis of studies of selected industries, Walter Galenson recently estimated comparative Soviet labor productivity per man year in all industry at roughly 40 per cent of that in the United States in the late 1930's.[16] According to findings in the present study, productivity per man year in Soviet industry increased 30 per cent from 1937 to 1950. Although comparable statistics are not available for changes in man-year productivity in American industry, it appears unlikely, on the basis of past experience, that the increase in the United States would have been less than, say, 1 per cent annually. Thus, as a rough approximation to an industry-wide average, productivity of labor per man year in Soviet industry is unlikely to have been more than about 47 per cent of that in American industry in 1950 and may have been much less. Moreover, much of this increase in Soviet productivity per man year is assignable to an 18 per cent increase in average annual man hours worked between 1937 and 1950.

No comparisons of absolute levels of total industrial output in the United States and the Soviet Union are available. On the basis of comparisons of output of individual physical products, however, it is obvious that Soviet production still lags far behind that in the United States. Of the products compared in Table 27, in only two cases, coal and sugar, does

Soviet production exceed 50 per cent of American production. The range of the remaining percentage comparisons is from 5 to 44 per cent with a central tendency for the entire comparison somewhere around 35 per cent (calculated by the unweighted arithmetic average).

International comparisons of standards of living are hazardous in the extreme owing not only to statistical problems, but also to intangible differences in tastes and customs, and the difficulty of allowing for imponderables such as personal security and education. Here again no statistical measure comparing Soviet and American living standards can be presented. It is scarcely open to question, however, that in this respect the gap between Soviet and American standards is even wider than has been indicated for industrial production and labor productivity.

TABLE 27

Comparison of Output of Selected Industrial Commodities in the USSR and USA in 1950

Product	Unit	USSR Output	USA Output	Ratio of USSR to USA (per cent)
Coal	1000 m. t.	261,000	505,319	52
Pig iron	1000 m. t.	19,400	60,217	32
Steel	1000 m. t.	27,300	87,848	31
Electric power	mil. kwhr.	90,300	388,674	23
Cement	1000 m. t.	10,400	38,724	27
Tractors	units	118,000	698,031[a]	17
Motor vehicles	units	364,000	8,003,066	5
Woven cotton fabrics	mil. meters	3,976	9,156	44
Woven woolen fabrics	mil. meters	155	383	41
Beer	1000 hl	12,480	104,202	12
Sugar	1000 m. t.	2,520	2,334	110[b]
Cigarettes	bil. units	125	385	32

SOURCES — USSR output data from Appendix A; USA output data, unless otherwise noted, are from *Statistical Yearbook 1952* (New York: United Nations, 1952).

[a] U.S. Dept. of Commerce, *Statistical Abstract of the United States 1951*, p. 807.

[b] Much of U.S. sugar is not produced domestically but is imported.

Despite the absence of precise quantitative measures in comparing current levels of production, productivity, and living standards in the United States and the Soviet Union, there can be little doubt of substantial differences in their orders of magnitude. This observation, of itself, is neither novel nor derogatory to Soviet accomplishments. What is interesting about the gaps indicated, however, is that they remain large even after approximately thirty years of rapid economic development in the Soviet Union. This fact testifies in part to the very low level from which planned Soviet economic development began and the setback suffered by Soviet industry through wartime destruction, and in part to continued economic development in the United States. No attempt should be made to gloss over the magnitude of the Soviet achievement nor to deny that the past three decades have witnessed a perceptible closing of the gap between levels of economic performance in the Soviet Union and the United States.

From this it does not follow, however, that the gap will be narrowed further *in comparable degree* during the next three decades. Although such a result is possible, it does not appear probable if the hypothesis proposed earlier in this chapter is correct. The high rate of Soviet industrial development during the first two Five Year Plans relied to an important extent upon the introduction of modern production techniques from abroad and upon a multiple expansion of the industrial labor force to employ these techniques. In the main, the introduction of these modern techniques constituted a technological revolution for Soviet industry, the like of which will not soon be repeated in that country. Nor can Soviet industry rely in the future on further expansion of the industrial labor force by proportions comparable to those of the first two Five Year Plans. The conclusion seems unmistakable that further Soviet industrial expansion will occur at a declining rate.

Soviet industrial development should continue to profit from the pioneering experience of American industry. This fact, coupled with Soviet economic controls, should enable Soviet industry to advance more rapidly than American industry for some time to come. But some aspects of both the technical and human organization of industry, especially the latter, are likely to prove too subtle for import. Individually, these refinements may be of minor importance, but in the aggregate, they may bulk very large. Unless Soviet industry succeeds in developing substitute organizational methods and attitudes through its own experience, it may find the gap between Soviet and American industrial performance increasingly difficult to close, the narrower it becomes. Whether Soviet industry will prove able to meet this challenge will depend to an important extent upon the ability of Soviet society as a whole to assimilate and foster the necessary attitudes and methods.

ADDENDUM

Production of Soviet Large-Scale Industry 1950 to 1953

After this study was completed and had gone to press the Soviet government released the report of plan fulfillment for the calendar year 1953. Percentage figures for increases in the output of individual products contained therein and in the similar report for the year 1952 permit the further extrapolation of the revised index for these two years. Products included in the revised index for 1952 and 1953 are identical to those included in 1951. Physical output data for these eighteen product series are presented in Table Y. The revised index computed from these data is compared to the official Soviet index of industrial production for the years 1950 to 1953 in Table Z.

A comparison of the revised and official indices for the years since 1950 is of considerable interest not only for the relative currency of the comparison but also because the methods used to compute the official index for the years since 1950 were drastically overhauled. (See discussion at the end of Chapter I.) In essence the relative values which underlie the official index since 1950 are the wholesale prices in effect on January 1, 1952. Thus the particular distortions in the official index which were attributable to the use of real or artificial 1926–27 prices may be presumed to have been removed since 1950.

The revised and official indices for these years are markedly similar, with the official index in each year slightly above the revised index. Moreover, both agree in indicating considerably reduced rates of annual increase in Soviet industrial output in the years of the Fifth Five Year Plan, rates which are from one-fifth to one-third below those indicated by the revised index for the First, Second, and Fourth Five Year Plans and, of course,

TABLE Y

Soviet Industrial Production 1952–1953
Physical Output Series

Commodity	1952 [a]	1953 [b]
1. Coal (1000 m.t.)	301,000	319,000
2. Crude oil extracted (excludes natural gas) (1000 m.t)	47,800	53,500
5. Electric power output (mil. kw. hr.)	116,000	131,000
6. Ferrous metals		
a. Pig iron (1000 m.t.)	25,200	27,500
b. Steel (ingots and castings, 1000 m.t.)	34,500	38,000
c. Rolled steel (includes iron pipe, 1000 m.t.)	26,800	29,400
15. Paper (1000 m.t.)	1,460	1,600
16. Cement (1000 m.t.)	14,300	16,400
20. Textiles		
d. Cotton cloth (mil. meters)	5,140	5,400
e. Unbleached woolen cloth (mil. meters)	189	206
g. Silk woven goods (1000 meters)	232,000	413,000
22. Food industry		
a. Sugar (granulated, 1000 centners)	30,600	34,300
f. Vegetable oils (1000 m.t.)	972	1,100
h. Fish caught (1000 centners)	23,900 [c]	25,200 [c]
i–j. Canning (1000 conv. tins)	1,910	2,050 [d]
k. Confections (1000 m.t.)	1,150	1,260
m. Beer (1000 hl.)	15,300	17,300
o. Cigarettes (bil. units)	158	183

[a] Obtained, except as noted below, from output figures expressed as percentages of output in 1951 as given in *Pravda*, January 23, 1953. These percentage increases have been applied to physical output data from Appendix A to calculate physical output in 1952. The brevity of the description of units of measurement as given by *Pravda* makes it impossible to establish with complete certainty the exact comparability of the *Pravda* reports for 1952 with those of prior years.

[b] Obtained, except as noted below, by the same procedure as outlined in note *a* from percentage increases given in *Pravda*, January 31, 1954.

[c] Obtained by interpolating between actual output in 1951 and planned output in 1955 on the assumption of a constant rate of growth 1951–1955. Data from United Nations, Economic Commission for Europe, *Economic Survey of Europe Since the War* (Geneva: 1953), pp. 42–43.

[d] Obtained by extrapolation on assumption that growth rate in 1952–53 equals that in 1951–52.

even further below corresponding growth rates for those periods as indicated by the official index. Perhaps such similarity between two indices which differ so considerably in weighting principles and in base years has little positive significance. Nevertheless, the correspondence is somehow reassuring. Further, the reduced rates of growth which show up in both indices appear to confirm the expectations expressed in Chapter 7 that further expansion in Soviet industrial production will proceed at a slower, although still respectable, pace.

TABLE Z

Production of Soviet Large-Scale Industry 1950–1953
(per cent of 1950)

Year	Revised Index	Official Index
1950	100	100
1951	115	116
1952	125	129
1953	138	144

SOURCES — Revised index: Computed by revised index methodology from the quantity data in Table Y. Official index: Computed from annual percentage increases as given in *Pravda*.

June 1954

APPENDIX A

Production Indicators for Soviet Large-Scale Industry in Physical or Conventional Units, 1927–28 to 1951 *

Abbreviations for sources cited in the following notes

A.B.M.S.: *Year Book of the American Bureau of Metal Statistics.*

Bakulin: S. N. Bakulin and D. D. Mishustin, *Vneshniaia torgovlia SSSR za 20 let, 1918–1937 gg.*, Statisticheskii spravochnik, (Foreign Trade of the USSR for 20 Years, Statistical Handbook; Moscow, 1939).

Bergson: Abram Bergson, James Horton Blackman, and Alexander Erlich, "Postwar Economic Reconstruction and Development in the USSR," *The Annals of the American Academy of Political and Social Science*, May 1949.

B.S.E.: *Bol'shaia Sovetskaia entsiklopedia* (Large Soviet Encyclopedia; USSR Volume, State Scientific Institute "Soviet Encyclopedia," Moscow: OGIZ, 1947).

4th Plan: Zakon o piatiletnem plane vosstanovleniia i razvitiia narodnogo khoziaistva SSSR na 1946–1950 gg. (Law Concerning the Five Year Plan for the Reconstruction and Development of the Economy of the USSR for the Years 1946–1950; OGIZ, 1946).

Gosplan reports in *Pravda:* 1946 *Pravda*, January 21,1947; 1947 *Pravda*, January 18, 1948; 1948 *Pravda*, January 20, 1949; 1949 *Pravda*, January 18, 1950; 1950 *Pravda*, January 26, 1951 and April 17, 1951; 1951 *Pravda*, January 29, 1952.

Granovsky: E. L. Granovsky and B. L. Markus, *Ekonomika sotsialisticheskoi promyshlennosti* (The Economics of Socialist Industry; Academy of Science of the USSR, Institute of Economics; Moscow: State Social-Economic Press, 1940).

Ioffe: *SSSR i kapitalisticheskie strany*, Statisticheskii sbornik tekhnikoekonomicheskikh pokazatelei narodnogo khoziaistva SSSR i kapitalisticheskikh stran za 1913–1937 gg. (USSR and the Capitalist Countries, Statistical Handbook of technical-economic indices of the economy of the USSR and the capitalist countries; prepared by Ia. A. Ioffe under the editorship of L. Ia. Eventov Moscow-Leningrad: State Planning Commission Press, 1939).

* See Tables A(i),(ii),(iii), in Tabular Section, p. 189 below.

Itogi: Itogi vypolneniia pervogo piatiletnogo plana razvitiia narodnogo khoziaistva Soiuza SSR (Summary of the Fulfillment of the First Five Year Plan of the Development of the Economy of the USSR; Moscow: State Planning Commission of the USSR, 1933).

M.S.E.: Malaia Sovetskaia entsiklopedia, (Small Soviet Encyclopedia; Moscow: State Dictionary-Encyclopedia Press "Soviet Encyclopedia," 1933).

Mishustin: D. D. Mishustin, *Vneshnaia torgovlia i industrializatsiia SSSR* (Foreign Trade and the Industrialization of the USSR; Moscow: V/O Mezhdunarodnaia kniga, 1938).

1941 Plan: Gosudarstvennyi plan razvitiia narodnogo khoziaistva SSSR na 1941 god (State Plan for the Development of the Economy of the USSR in 1941).

Plan 1935: Narodno-khoziaistvennii plan na 1935 god (The Economic Plan for 1935; second edition, Moscow: State Planning Commission of the USSR, 1935).

Plan 1937: Narodno-khoziaistvennii plan Soiuza SSR na 1937 god (Economic Plan of the USSR for the Year 1937; Moscow: State Planning Commission for the USSR, 1937).

P. Kh.: Planovoe Khoziaistvo (Planned Economy; monthly political and economic journal of the State Planning Commission, published in Moscow).

Proizvoditel'nost' truda: Proizvoditel'nost' truda v promyshlennosti SSSR (The Productivity of Labor in the Industry of the USSR; ed. P. A. Khromov; Moscow: State Planning Commission Press, 1940).

SS 1935: Sotsialisticheskoe stroitel'stvo SSSR, statisticheskii ezhegodnik (Socialist Construction in the USSR, statistical yearbook; Moscow: Central Administration of Economic Accounting [Tsunkhu] of the State Planning Commission of the USSR, 1935).

SC 1936 (E): Socialist Construction in the USSR (Statistical Abstract; Moscow: Central Administration of Economic and Social Statistics of the State Planning Commission of the USSR, 1936).

SS 1936 (R): Sotsialisticheskoe stroitel'stvo SSSR, statisticheskii ezhegodnik (Socialist Construction in the USSR, statistical abstract; Moscow: Central Administration of Economic Accounting of the State Planning Commission of the USSR, 1936).

SS 1933–38: Sotsialisticheskoe stroitel'stvo Soiuza SSR (1933–1938 gg.), statisticheskii sbornik (Socialist Construction in the Union SSR [1933–1938], a statistical handbook; Moscow-Leningrad: Central Administration of Economic Accounting of the State Planning Commission of the USSR, 1939).

Tretii: Tretii piatiletnii plan razvitiia narodnogo khoziaistva Soiuza SSR (1938–1942 gg.) (The Third Five Year Plan for the Development of the Economy of the Union SSR [1938–1942]; Moscow: The State Planning Commission Press, 1939).

Voznesenski, Economic Results of the USSR in 1940: N. Voznesenski, *Economic Results of the USSR in 1940 and the Plan of National Economic*

Development for 1941 (Moscow: Foreign Languages Publishing House, 1941).

Voznesenski: N. A. Voznesenski, *Piatilentnii plan vosstanovleniia i razvitiia narodnogo khoziaistva SSSR na 1946–1950 gg.* (Five Year Plan for the Reconstruction and Development of the National Economy of the USSR for the Years 1946–1950; OGIZ, 1946).

Zatov: V. P. Zatov, *Razvitie pishchevoi promyshlennosti v novoi piatiletke* (Development of the Food Industry in the New Five Year Plan; Gospolitizdat, 1947).

1. *Coal*: Production of bituminous, anthracite, and lignite coal in 1000 metric tons. Sources: 1927–28 to 1934 from *SS 1936 (R)*, pp. 100–101; 1935–1937 from Ioffe, p. 150; 1940 from *4th Plan*, pp. 11, 17; 1941 from *1941 Plan*, p. 13; 1950 from *Pravda*, April 17, 1951; 1945–1949, 1951, from Gosplan reports in *Pravda*.

2. *Crude oil extracted*: Production of crude oil (exclusive of natural gas) in 1000 metric tons. Sources: 1927–28 to 1934 from *SS 1936 (R)*, p. 113; 1935–1936 from *Plan 1937*, pp. 66–67; 1937 from *Tretii*, p. 202; 1940 from *Voznesensky*, p. 15; 1941 from *1941 Plan*, p. 15; 1950 from *Pravda*, April 17, 1951; 1945–1949, 1951 from Gosplan reports in *Pravda*.

3. *Petroleum refined*: The consumption of crude oil in 1000 metric tons is taken as the production indicator for this industry. Sources: 1927–28 to 1934 from *SS 1936 (R)*, p. 129; 1935–1936 from *Plan 1937*, pp. 66–67; 1937 from *Tretii*, p. 203; 1941 from *1941 Plan*, p. 16.

4. *Peat extracted*: Production of peat in 1000 metric tons includes production of both large-scale and small-scale industry. Sources: 1928–1934 from *SS 1936 (R)*, p. 130; 1935–1936 from *Plan 1937*, pp. 66–67; 1937 from *Tretii*, p. 202; 1940 from *4th Plan*, p. 19; 1941 from *1941 Plan*, p. 14.

5. *Electric power output*: Production in millions of kilowatt hours. Includes the output of regional, municipal, communal, industrial, agricultural, and transport power stations. Sources: 1928–1934 from *SS 1936 (R)*, p. 83; 1935–1936 from *Plan 1937*, pp. 64–65; 1937 from *Tretii*, p. 202; 1940 from *4th Plan*, pp. 11, 21; 1941 from *1941 Plan*, p. 12; 1950 from *Pravda*, April 17, 1951; 1945–49, 1951 from Gosplan reports in *Pravda*.

6. *Ferrous metals*

a. *Pig iron*: Production of pig iron in 1000 metric tons. Sources: 1927–28 to 1934 from *SS 1936 (R)*, p. 133; 1935–1936 from *Plan 1937*, pp. 68–69; 1937 from *Tretii*, p. 203; 1940 from *B.S.E.*, p. 808; 1941 from *1941 Plan*, p. 17; 1950 from *Pravda*, April 17, 1951; 1945–49, 1951 from Gosplan reports in *Pravda*.

b. *Steel*: Production of ingots and castings in 1000 metric tons. Sources:

1927–28 to 1934 from *SS 1936* (*R*), p. 133; 1935–1936 from *Plan 1937*, pp. 68–69; 1937 from *Tretii*, p. 203; 1940 from *B.S.E.*, p. 808; 1941 from *1941 Plan*, p. 18; 1950 from *Pravda*, April 17, 1951; 1945–49, 1951 from Gosplan reports in *Pravda*.

c. *Rolled steel*: Production of ordinary rolled steel, quality rolled steel, and iron pipe in 1000 metric tons. Iron pipe is included to secure comparability over time since the only aggregate figure for rolled steel in 1937 contains iron pipe. Sources: 1927–28 to 1934 from *SS 1936 (R)*, p. 133; 1935–1936 from *Plan 1937*, pp. 68–69; 1937 from *Tretii*, p. 203; 1940 from *B.S.E.*, p. 808; 1941 from *1941 Plan*, p. 18; 1950 from *Pravda*, April 17, 1951; 1945–49, 1951 from Gosplan reports in *Pravda*.

7. *Nonferrous metals*

a. *Fireburned copper*: Production in 1000 metric tons. Includes production from scrap. Sources: 1927–28 to 1934 from *SS 1935*, p. 190; 1935–1936 from *Plan 1937*, pp. 70–71; 1937 estimated by taking the average of the figures for output in 1936 and 1938. Production in 1938 was 103.2 thousand metric tons, from *SS 1933–38*, p. 62.

b. *Lead*: Production in 1000 metric tons. Sources: 1927–28 to 1934 from *SS 1935*, p. 190; 1935 estimated as the average of the figures for 1934 and 1936; 1936 calculated from percentage figures in *M.S.E.*, vol. 6, pp. 850–51; 1937 calculated from information in *Industriia*, March 4, 1939, p. 3, in which lead output in 1937 is set at 333.9 per cent of output in 1932.

c. *Zinc*: Production in 1000 metric tons. Sources: 1927–28 to 1934 from *SS 1935*, p. 190; 1935 estimated as the average of the figures for 1934 and 1936; 1936 calculated from percentage figures in *M.S.E.*, vol. 6, pp. 850–51; 1937 from Demitri Shimkin, *Minerals, A Key to Soviet Power* (Harvard University Press, 1953), p. 138. This figure is further substantiated by the application of the zinc recovery percentage in Soviet zinc refining (57–60 per cent) to the figure for zinc content of ore mined in 1937, 108,000 metric tons, which yields a figure of 64,800 metric tons of refined zinc.

d. *Aluminum*: Production in metric tons. Sources: 1927–28 to 1934 from *SS 1935*, p. 190; 1935 from Mishustin, p. 196; 1936 from A.B.M.S., 1941, p. 95; 1937 from *Tretii*, p. 204. Includes primary and secondary metal.

8. *Ore mining*

a. *Iron ore*: Production in 1000 metric tons. Data shown as for fiscal years 1927–28 to 1929–30 are actually for calendar years 1928–1930. Sources: 1928–1934 from *SS 1936 (R)*, p. 152; 1935–1936 from *Plan 1937*, pp. 68–69; 1937 from *Tretii*, p. 203; 1941 from *1941 Plan*, p. 16.

b. *Manganese ore*: Production in 1000 metric tons. Data shown as for fiscal years 1927–28 to 1929–30 are actually for calendar years 1928–1930. Sources: 1928–1934 from *SS 1936 (R)*, p. 153; 1935–1936 from *Plan 1937*, pp. 68–69; 1937 from *Tretii*, p. 203; 1941 from *1941 Plan*, p. 17.

c. *Copper ore*: Production in 1000 metric tons. Data shown as for fiscal years 1927–28 to 1929–30 are actually for calendar years 1928–1930. Sources: 1928–1931 from *SS 1935*, p. 190; 1932–1935 from *SC 1936 (E)*, p. 224; 1936 from "The Copper Industry in the USSR," *Bulletin of the Imperial Institute*, vol. XXXVI, 1938, London, p. 56; 1937 estimated on the assumption that the production of copper in 1937 exceeded that in 1936 by the same percentage that the production of electrolitic copper in 1937 exceeded that in 1936. Production of electrolitic copper in 1936 was 86.3 thousand metric tons (from *Plan 1937*, p. 71) and in 1937 was 90.8 thousand metric tons (from Demitri Shimkin, *Minerals, A Key to Soviet Power* (Harvard University Press, 1953), p. 111.

9. *Chemicals*

a. *Basic chemicals*. (1) *Soda ash*: Production in 1000 metric tons. Sources: 1927–28 to 1935 from *SS 1936 (R)*, p. 175; 1936 from *Plan 1937*, p. 91; 1937 from *Tretii*, p. 204; 1941 from *1941 Plan*, p. 56. (2) *Superphosphate*: Production in 1000 metric tons. Sources: 1927–28 to 1935 from *SS 1936 (R)*, p. 176; 1936 from *Plan 1937*, p. 91; 1937 from Ioffe, p. 181. (3) *Sulphuric acid*: Production of 100 per cent sulphuric acid in 1000 metric tons. Sources: 1927–28 to 1935 from *SS 1936 (R)*, p. 175; 1936 and 1937 from Ioffe, p. 179. The figure for 1937 is "planned."

b. *Aniline dyes*: Production in metric tons. Sources: 1927–28 to 1935 from *SS 1936 (R)*, p. 177; 1936 from *P. Kh.* no. 8, 1937, p. 190; 1937 estimated as the average of the figures for 1936 and 1938. Production of 35,300 metric tons in 1938 from *SS 1933–1938*, p. 67.

c. *Plastic pulp*: Production in 1000 metric tons. Sources: 1927–28 from *P. Kh.* no. 3, 1939, p. 89; 1928–29, 1929–30 estimated by interpolating in two equal amounts between the figure for 1927–28 of 300 metric tons and the figure for 1931 of 3,473 metric tons; 1931–1934 from *SS 1936 (R)*, p. 177; 1935–1936 from *Plan 1937*, pp. 92–93; 1937 from *P. Kh.* no. 3, 1939, p. 89; 1941 from *1941 Plan*, p. 57.

d. *Iodine*: Production in metric tons. Sources: 1927–28 to 1934 from *SS 1936 (R)*, p. 178; 1935 estimated as the average of the production figures for 1934 and 1936; 1936 from *P. Kh.* no. 8, 1937, pp. 189–190; 1937 estimated on the assumption that the percentage increase from 1935 to 1936 was repeated from 1936 to 1937.

e. *Dry white mineral pigments*: Production in metric tons. The production of dry white mineral pigments is used as the output indicator for the paints and varnishes branch of the chemical industry. Dry white mineral pigments include white lead, white zinc, and lithopone. Sources: 1927–28 to 1935 from *SS 1936 (R)*, p. 178; 1936–1937 from *Plan 1937*, pp. 90–91. The figure for 1937 is "planned"; 1941 from *1941 Plan*, p. 57.

10. *Coke*: Production of coke in terms of coke of 6 per cent moisture, in 1000 metric tons. Sources: 1928–1934 from *SS 1936* (*R*), p. 153; 1935 from

Plan 1937, pp. 66–67; 1936 from Granovsky, p. 290; 1937 from Ioffe, p. 178; 1941 from *1941 Plan*, p. 17.

11. *Grease, tallow, soap, and perfume*

Soap (hand and toilet): Production of soap (hand and toilet) in 1000 metric tons is used as the output indicator for the grease, tallow, soap, and perfume industry. Sources: 1928–1929, 1932–1937 from Ioffe, p. 195; 1929–30 to 1931 from *SS 1936 (R)*, p. 229; 1941 from *1941 Plan*, p. 76.

12. *Rubber industry*: Crude rubber produced and imported is taken to represent the consumption of crude rubber by the rubber industry and this, in turn, to represent the output of the rubber industry. Production and import of crude rubber in metric tons. Sources: 1927–28 to 1935 from *SS 1936 (R)*, p. 179; 1936 estimated as the average of the production figures for 1935 and 1937. The figure for 1937 is calculated as follows: (1) import of crude rubber in 1937 accounted for 23.9 per cent of crude rubber consumed in that year (from *B.S.E.*, p. 804), (2) Crude rubber imported in 1937 was 30,900 metric tons (Mishustin, p. 200), (3) therefore total consumption equalled 30,900 divided by .239 or 129,289 metric tons.

13. *Matches*: Production in 1000 case units. Sources: 1928–1934 from *SS 1936 (R)*, p. 190; 1935–1936 from *Plan 1937*, pp. 98–99; 1937 from *SS 1933–38*, p. 70; 1940, 1945–48 from Bergson, p. 56; 1941 from *1941 Plan*, p. 69.

14. *Wood processing*

a. *Sawn lumber*: Production in 1000 cubic meters. Sources: 1928–1934 from *SS 1936 (R)*, p. 190; 1935–1936 from *Plan 1937*, pp. 94–95; 1937 from *SS 1933–38*, p. 70. *Tretii*, p. 208 gives a figure of 28,800,000 cubic meters for 1937. The figure of 33,800,000 is thought to be more comparable to data for preceding years. The larger figure includes 5 million cubic meters "produced by establishments engaged in construction, by village soviets and other." (See Granovsky, pp. 106–7, footnote 8.) 1940, 1945–48 from Bergson, p. 56; 1941 from *1941 Plan*, p. 68.

b. *Plywood*: Production in 1000 cubic meters. Sources: 1928–1934 from *SS 1936 (R)*, p. 190; 1935–1936 from *Plan 1937*, pp. 94–95; 1937 from *SS 1933–38*, p. 70; 1941 from *1941 Plan*, p. 69.

15. *Paper*: Production of all types of paper in 1000 metric tons. Includes printing paper, newsprint, writing paper, album paper, book cover paper, wall paper, wrapping paper, cigarette mouthpiece paper and others. Sources: 1927–28 to 1935 from *SS 1936 (R)*, p. 192; 1936 from *Plan 1937*, pp. 96–97; 1937 from *SS 1933–38*, p. 71; 1940 from Voznesensky, p. 16; 1941 from *1941 Plan*, p. 69; 1950 from *Pravda*, April 17, 1951; 1945–49, 1951 from Gosplan reports in *Pravda*.

16. *Cement*: Production of all types of cement in 1000 metric tons. Sources: 1927–28 to 1934 from *SS 1936 (R)*, p. 183; 1935–1936 from *Plan 1937*, pp. 92–93; 1937 from *SS 1933–38*, p. 68; 1940 from Voznesensky, p. 16; 1941 from *1941 Plan*, p. 61; 1950 from *Pravda*, April 17, 1951; 1945–49, 1951 from Gosplan reports in *Pravda*.

17. *Building bricks*: Production in million units. Sources: 1927–28 from *Itogi*, p. 143; 1928–29, 1937 from *SS 1933–38*, p. 67; the figures for 1929–30 and 1931 are estimated by interpolating between the figures for 1928–29 and 1932 in equal annual increments; 1932–1934 from *SS 1936 (R)*, p. 183; 1935–1936 from *Plan 1937*, pp. 94–95; 1941 from *1941 Plan*, p. 63.

18. *Glass*

a. *Glass (all types)*: Production in 1000 metric tons. Includes sheet glass, containers, technical glass, domestic vessels, and lamp glass. Source: 1927–28 to 1934 from *SS 1936 (R)*, p. 180; 1935–1937 no data available.

b. *Window glass*: Production in 1000 square meters. Sources: 1933 from *SS 1933–38*, p. 67; 1934 from *SS 1936 (R)*, p. 180; 1935–1936 from *Plan 1937*, pp. 100–101; the figure for 1937 is an average of the figures for 1936 and 1938; production of 59,550 thousand square meters in 1938 from *SS 1933–38*, p. 67; 1927–28 to 1932, no data available; 1940 from Voznesensky, pp. 16–17; 1941 from *1941 Plan*, p. 67; 1950 from *Pravda*, April 17, 1951; 1945–49 from Gosplan reports in *Pravda*.

19. *Leather tanning*

a. *Large hides*: Production in 1000 units. Sources: 1928–29 to 1934 from *SS 1936 (R)*, p. 205; 1937 from A. Kurskii, "Narodno-khoziaistvennye sviazi v tret'em piatiletnym plane," *P. Kh.*, 1939, no. 3, p. 46 (figures refer to hides procured); the figure for 1927–28 is calculated on the assumption that the same percentage increase occurred from 1927–28 to 1928–29 as from 1928–29 to 1929–30; production of large hides in 1935 and 1936 is estimated by interpolating between the figures for 1934 and 1937 in equal annual increments.

b. *Small hides*: Production in 1000 units. Sources: identical with the sources for large hides.

20. *Textile industry*

a. *Ginned cotton fiber*: Production in 1000 metric tons. Sources: the figure for 1927–28 is estimated by calculating the relationship of the output of cotton gins in 1000 metric tons to the consumption of fiber of domestic origin in 1000 metric tons in the year 1928–29 (i.e. output of gins [237.9 thousand metric tons] divided by consumption of fiber of domestic origin [253.4 thousand metric tons] equals 93.9 per cent) and then applying this percentage to the figure (209.0 thousand metric tons) for consumption of fiber of domestic origin for 1927–28. All data for this estimate from *SS 1936 (R)*, p. 193; 1928–29 to 1934 from *SS 1936 (R)*, p. 193; 1935–1936 from *Plan 1937*, pp. 98–99; 1937 from *Tretii*, p. 209; 1941 from *1941 Plan*, p. 71.

b. *Raw silk*: Production in metric tons. Sources: 1927–28 to 1934 from *SS 1936 (R)*, p. 202; 1935–1936 from *Plan 1937*, pp. 98–99; 1937 from *Tretii*, p. 209; 1941 from *1941 Plan*, p. 71.

c. *Cottonized fiber*: Production in metric tons. Sources: 1927–28, 1928–29, no data available; 1929–30 to 1934 from *SS 1936 (R)*, p. 202; 1935–1937 from *Plan 1937*, pp. 98–99. The figure for 1937 is "planned."

d. (1) *Consumption of cotton*: The consumption of cotton in industry in 1000 metric tons is the production indicator for the cotton goods branch of the textile industry. The writer had originally chosen cotton woven goods produced measured in millions of linear meters as the production indicator for cotton textiles. The linear meters measure did not take into account changes in widths and weight of cotton cloth produced, however, and later evidence convinced the writer that changes in these dimensions had been sufficient during the period 1928–1934 at least to make the linear measure a poor indicator for changes in the value of cotton textile production. A glance at Table A(ii), below, of the production indicators for the cotton-goods industry will assure the reader that the linear meters measure of cotton-goods production displays a markedly individual pattern over the decade 1928–1937 in relation to the other series which might be taken to represent the production of cotton textiles. The only other series which covers the entire decade is that for the consumption of cotton in industry. This series has been used. Sources: 1927–28 to 1934 from *SS 1936 (R)*, p. 193; 1935–1937 from Ioffe, p. 190.

d. (2) *Cotton cloth*: Production in million meters. 1934 from *SS 1936 (R)*, p. 195; 1940 from *Bergson*, p. 56; 1941 from *1941 Plan*, p. 71; 1945–1948 from *Bergson*, p. 56; 1949–51 from Gosplan reports in *Pravda*.

e. *Unbleached woolen cloth*: Production in million meters, presumably linear. Sources: 1927–28 to 1931 from *SS 1935*, p. 254; 1932–1934 from *SS 1936 (R)*, p. 198; 1935–1936 from *Plan 1937*, pp. 98–99; 1937 from *Tretii*, p. 209; 1940 from *Bergson*, p. 56; 1941 from *1941 Plan*, p. 71; 1945–48 from *Bergson*, p. 56; 1949–51 from Gosplan reports in *Pravda*.

f. *Linen*: Production 1927–28 to 1934 in million square meters; 1935–1937 in million linear meters. Sources: 1927–28 to 1931 from *SS 1935*, p. 256; 1932–1934 from *SS 1936 (R)*, p. 201; 1935–1936 from *Plan 1937*, pp. 98–99; 1937 from *P. Kh.* no. 5, 1939, p. 161. *Tretii*, p. 209 gives a figure of 278.4 million meters which is net of the production of collective farms and "other" organizations. 1940 from *Bergson*, p. 56; 1941 from *1941 Plan*, p. 71.

g. *Silk woven goods*: Production in 1000 meters. Sources: 1927–28 to 1934 from *SS 1936 (R)*, p. 202; 1935–1936 from *Plan 1937*, pp. 98–99; 1937 from *Tretii*, p. 209; 1940 from *Bergson*, p. 56; 1941 from *1941 Plan*, p. 71; 1945–48 from *Bergson*, p. 56; 1949–51 from Gosplan reports in *Pravda*.

h. *Knitted wear*: Production of socks and stockings in million pairs, knit underwear in million pieces, knit outerwear in million pieces. Sources: 1927–28 to 1931 no data available; 1932–1934 from *SS 1936 (R)*, p. 204; 1935–1936 from *Plan 1937*, pp. 98–99; 1937 from *P. Kh.* no. 5, 1939, p. 161; 1941 from *1941 Plan*, p. 71.

21. *Leather footwear*: Factory production in 1000 pairs. Sources: 1927–28 to 1934 from *SS 1936 (R)*, p. 206; 1935, 1937 from Ioffe, p. 195; 1936 from *Plan 1937*, pp. 100–101; 1940 from Voznesensky, *Economic Results of the USSR in 1940*, p. 14; 1941 from *1941 Plan*, p. 72.

22. *Food industry*

a. *Sugar (granulated)*: Production in 1000 centners. Sources: 1927–28 to 1934 from *SS 1936 (R)*, p. 226; 1935–1936 from *Plan 1937*, pp. 102–103; 1937 from *P. Kh.* no. 5, 1939, p. 161; 1940 from Zatov, p. 10; 1941 from *1941 Plan*, p. 73; 1950 from *Pravda*, April 17, 1951; 1945–49, 1951 from Gosplan reports in *Pravda*.

b. *Macaroni*: Production in metric tons. Sources: 1927–28 to 1931 no data available; 1932–1934 from *SS 1936 (R)*, p. 214; 1935–1936 from *Plan 1937*, pp. 104–105; 1937 from *P. Kh.* no. 5, 1939, p. 161; 1941 from *1941 Plan*, p. 74.

c. *Bread*: Bread baked, 1000 metric tons. Two series are presented. Series one: bread baked only in large-scale bakeries. Sources: 1927–28 no data available; 1928–29 to 1934 from *SS 1936 (R)*, p. 214. Series two: includes in addition to bread produced in large-scale bakeries that baked in consumers' and industrial coöperatives, Workers' Supply Section, and "other" organizations (Cf. tables 189 and 190 in *SS 1936 (R)*, p. 214). Sources: 1933–1934 from *SS 1936 (R)*, p. 214; 1935–1936 from *Plan 1937*, pp. 102–103; 1937 from *P. Kh.* no. 5, 1939, p. 161; 1941 from *1941 Plan*, p. 75.

d. *Meat (slaughtering)*: Production in metric tons. Sources: 1927–28 to 1928–29 no data available; 1930–1934 from *SS 1936 (R)*, p. 215; 1935–1936 from *Plan 1937*, pp. 102–103; 1937 from *Tretii*, p. 210; 1941 from *1941 Plan*, p. 73.

e. *Butter (animal fats)*: Production in metric tons. Sources: 1928–1934 from *SS 1936 (R)*, 217; 1935–1936 from *Plan 1937*, pp. 104–105; 1937 from *Tretii*, p. 210; 1941 from *1941 Plan*, p. 73.

f. *Vegetable oils*: Production of oils from sunflowers, flaxseed, hempseed, cottonseed, and "other" in 1000 metric tons. Sources: 1927–28 to 1934 from *SS 1936 (R)*, p. 219; 1935–1936 from *Plan 1937*, pp. 102–103; 1937 from *Tretii*, p. 210; 1940 from *Zatov*, p. 13; 1941 from *1941 Plan*, p. 73; 1950 from *Pravda*, April 17, 1951; 1945–49, 1951 from Gosplan reports in *Pravda*.

g. *Margarine*: Production in metric tons. Sources: 1927–28 to 1934 from *SS 1936 (R)*, p. 222; 1935–1937 from *Plan 1937*, pp. 104–105. The figure for 1937 is "planned"; 1940 from *Zatov*, p. 13; 1941 from *1941 Plan*, p. 73; 1950 from *P. Kh.* no. 5, 1951, p. 40; 1945 from *Voprosy ekonomiki* no. 4, 1951, p. 10.

h. *Fish caught*: The catch of fish in 1000 centners is used as the production indicator for the fish processing industry. Sources: 1928 no data available; 1929–1934 from *SS 1936 (R)*, p. 223; 1935–1936 from *Plan 1937*, pp. 102–103; 1937 from *Tretii*, p. 209; 1940 from *4th Plan*, pp. 13, 33; 1941 from *1941 Plan*, p. 73; 1950 from *Pravda*, April 17, 1951; 1947 from statement in *Voprosy ekonomiki* no. 9, 1951, p. 25, that the catch of fish in 1947 "reached the prewar level"; 1945–1946, 1948–1951 from Gosplan reports in *Pravda*.

i. *Processing of fruits and vegetables*: Production in 1000 metric tons. Includes the production of both large-scale and small-scale industry as well as the fruit and vegetable processing sections of the confections, canning and wine industries. Therefore, it includes the canning series presented next below. Sources: 1928–1929, no data available; 1930–1934 from *SS 1936 (R)*, p. 222; 1935–1937, no data available.

j. *Canning*: Production in millions of conventional 400 gram cans. Includes the production of canned goods in canning factories as well as the production of canned goods in the canning sections of other branches of industry (meat, fish, fruit and vegetable processing, and confections). Sources: 1927–28 to 1931, no data available; 1932, 1937 from *P. Kh.* no. 5, 1939, p. 161; 1933–1934 from *SS 1936 (R)*, p. 225; 1935–1936 from *Plan 1937*, pp. 102–103; 1940 from Voznesensky, *Economic Results of the USSR in 1940*, p. 14; 1941 from *1941 Plan*, p. 74; 1945 from *Voprosy ekonomiki* no. 4, 1951, p. 10; 1950 from *Pravda*, April 17, 1951; 1948–49, 1951 from Gosplan reports in *Pravda*.

k. *Confections*: Production in 1000 metric tons. Sources: 1927–28 to 1934 from *SS 1936 (R)*, p. 228; 1935–1936 from *Plan 1937*, pp. 104–105; 1937 from *Tretii*, p. 210. Data for 1931 and earlier are less comprehensive than for 1932 and later. Establishments included in the figures for 1931 and earlier accounted for 83.2 per cent of the total output in 1932. The quantity *relatives* for 1927–28 to 1931 inclusive are adjusted upward to allow for the discrepancy in coverage by dividing them by .832; 1940 from *Zatov*, p. 11; 1941 from *1941 Plan*, p. 74; 1945 from *Voprosy ekonomiki* no. 4, 1951, p. 10; 1950 from *Pravda*, April 17, 1951; 1948–49, 1951 from Gosplan reports in *Pravda*.

l. *Yeast*: Production in metric tons. Sources: 1927–28, no data available; 1928–29 to 1934 from *SS 1936 (R)*, p. 228; 1935–1936 from *Plan 1937*, pp. 104–105; 1937 estimated by applying the quantity relative for the increase in beer production from 1936 to 1937 (119 per cent) to the output of yeast in 1936; 1941 from *1941 Plan*, p. 74.

m. *Beer*: Production in 1000 hectoliters. Sources: 1927–28 to 1934 from *SS 1936 (R)*, p. 228; 1935–1936 from *Plan 1937*, pp. 104–105; 1937 from *P. Kh.* no. 5, 1939, p. 161; 1940 from *Zatov*, p. 17; 1941 from *1941 Plan*, p. 74; 1945 from *Voprosy ekonomiki* no. 4, 1951, p. 10; 1950 from *P. Kh.* no. 5, 1951, p. 40; 1948–49, 1951 from Gosplan reports in *Pravda*.

n. *Starch and syrup*: Combined production in metric tons. Sources: 1927–

28 to 1934 from *SS 1936 (R)*, p. 227; 1935–1937 from *Plan 1937*, pp. 104–105; the figure for 1937 is "planned"; 1940 from *Zatov*, p. 41.

o. *Cigarettes*: The production indicator for the tobacco industry is cigarettes in units of one billion. Sources: 1928–1934 from *SS 1936 (R)*, p. 228; 1935–1936 from *Plan 1937*, pp. 104–105; 1937 from *P. Kh.* no. 5, 1939, p. 161. The figure for 1937 includes smoking tobacco converted into cigarettes. An alternative series for the production indicator for the tobacco industry is a series for coarse smoking tobacco. Since there was no way of assigning separate weights to the two series and thus using both, the cigarette series was arbitrarily chosen to represent the industry on the assumption that the value of cigarettes produced was the major portion of the value of product for the entire industry; 1940 from *Zatov*, p. 19; 1941 from *1941 Plan*, p. 74; 1945 from *Voprosy ekonomiki* no. 4, 1951, p. 10; 1950 from *P. Kh.* no. 5, 1951, p. 40; 1948–49, 1951 from Gosplan reports in *Pravda*.

p. *Salt*: Production in 1000 metric tons. Includes rock salt, pan salt, and salt from brine. Sources: 1927–28 to 1934 from *SS 1936 (R)*, p. 174; 1935–1937 from *Plan 1937*, pp. 104–105. The figure for 1937 is "planned"; 1940 from *Zatov*, p. 19; 1941 from *1941 Plan*, p. 74.

23. *Machinery*

a. *Electric power equipment*. (1) *Steam boilers*: Production measured in 1000 square meters of surface area. Sources: 1927–28 to 1935 from *SS 1936 (R)*, p. 154; 1936 from *Plan 1937*, pp. 70–71; 1937 from *Tretii*, p. 206; 1941 from *1941 Plan*, p. 27. (2) *Total prime movers*: Production measured in terms of aggregate capacity in 1000 kilowatts of steam and water turbines, steam machines and locomobiles, stationary and marine diesels, other oil-powered engines, and motor vehicle and tractor engines. Sources: 1927–28 to 1935 from *SS 1936 (R)*, p. 154; 1936–1937 comparable data not available; 1941 from *1941 Plan*, pp. 28–29. The 1941 figure is the sum of capacity of steam turbines (stationary) water turbines, small turbines, diesels (stationary and marine), oil-powered engines, and locomobiles.

b. *Power transformers*: Production in terms of aggregate KVA capacity. Sources: 1927–28 to 1935 from *SS 1936 (R)*, p. 155; 1936 from *Plan 1937*, pp. 70–71; 1937 from *Tretii*, p. 206; 1941 from *1941 Plan*, p. 30.

c. *Agricultural equipment and implements*. (1) *Tractors*. (a) *Wheeled*: Production in physical units. Sources: 1927–28 to 1935 from *SS 1936 (R)*, p. 160; 1936 from *Plan 1937*, pp. 82–83; 1937 estimated, see (c) below; 1940–41 none produced. (b) *Tracklaying*: Production in physical units. Sources: are the same as for wheeled tractors. (c) The classification of tractor output in 1937 into wheeled and track-laying tractors is estimated. Soviet sources provide only a figure for the total number of tractors of all types produced. Since 29,059 track-laying tractors were produced in 1936 and 32,200 in 1938 (*SS 1933–38*, p. 64) a figure of 30,000 track-laying tractors has been assumed for 1937. The remaining 21,000 tractors are assumed to be wheeled tractors. The output of wheeled tractors in 1936 was 83,366 (of which 18,486 were Universal cultivator tractors and 64,800 were STZ and KhTZ). A drop of the magnitude indicated in the production of wheeled tractors is reasonable since the year 1936 marked the conversion of the Stalingrad and Kharkov tractor plants producing the wheeled STZ and KhTZ models to the production of track-laying tractors. Furthermore, according to *Plan 1937*, pp. 82–83, the *planned* output of STZ and KhTZ wheeled tractors in 1937 was only 11,000 and that of the wheeled Universal cultivator type tractor 18,000 units. (d) *Total tractors*: 1950 from *Pravda*, April 17, 1951; 1945–49 from Gosplan reports in *Pravda*. (2) *Agricultural machinery*: Production of tilling implements, seeding and planting machinery, harvesting machinery, and threshing and sorting machinery in units. Sources: 1927–28 to 1935 from *SS 1936 (R)*, pp. 161–162; 1936–1937, only very scattered data not presented. 1941 data from *1941 Plan*, p. 41. For grain harvesters and threshers: 1940 from *Pravda*, April 17, 1951; 1949 from statement in *Voprosy ekonomiki* no. 5, 1950, p. 42, that "in 1949 agriculture received 29,000 combines"; 1947–48, 1950 from Gosplan reports in *Pravda*.

d. *Transportation equipment*. (1) *Railroad equipment*: Production of main line freight and passenger locomotives in physical units, of main line freight and flat cars in 2-axle units, and of main line passenger coaches in 2-axle units. Sources: 1927–28 to 1935 from *SS 1936 (R)*, pp. 163–164; 1936 from *Plan 1937*, pp. 80–81; 1937 from *Tretii*, p. 207. The sources for passenger coaches for 1936–1937 give production in physical units rather than 2-axle units. Since the production of passenger coaches in 1935 is given as 1774 2-axle units (*SS 1936* [*R*], p. 164) and as 890 physical units (*Plan 1937*, pp. 80–81) a conversion coefficient of two 2-axle units to one physical unit was used to convert production of passenger coaches in 1936–1937 to 2-axle units. Data for locomotive production in 1937 from *B.S.E.*, vol. 44, p. 239. 1941 data from *1941 Plan*, pp. 42–44. Freight cars given in 4-axle units in the *1941 Plan* have been expressed in 2-axle units. Total steam locomotives for 1940 from Voznesensky, *Economic Results of the USSR in 1940*, p. 14, or from *4th Plan*, p. 12, and Voznesensky, p. 16; freight cars in 2-axle units for 1940 from P. V. Nikitin, *Mashinostroenie SSSR v poslevoennoi stalinskoi piatiletke* (Moscow: Izd. "Pravda," 1949), *passim*. (2) *Motor vehicles*: Production of three major groups of motor vehicles in physical units: (1) passenger cars and 1½-ton trucks, (2) trucks from 2½ to 4 tons inclusive, (3) trucks of 5 tons and larger. Sources: 1927–28 to 1935 from *SS 1936 (R)*, p. 165; 1936–1937 from tables in article by A. Kirov in *Avtotraktornoe delo*, no. 2, 1938, pp. 6–9. Total passenger cars and trucks: 1940 from Voznesensky, p. 16; 1941 from *1941 Plan*, p. 45; 1945–48 from Bergson, p. 56; 1949–50 from Gosplan reports in *Pravda*. The data for 1945–50 are approximate since they have been calculated by applying percentage figures for trucks only to Bergson's *estimate* for output of *trucks and passenger cars* for 1947.

e. *Construction and roadbuilding machinery*. (1) *Power shovels*: Production of all types of power shovels in physical units. Sources: 1927–28 to 1934 from *SS 1936 (R)*, p. 166; 1935 from *Plan 1937*, pp. 76–78; 1936 from *P. Kh.* no. 8, 1937, p. 188; 1937 from *Tretii*, p. 207; 1941 from *1941 Plan*, p. 40. (2) *Stone crushers*: Production in physical units. Sources: 1927–28 to 1934 from *SS 1936 (R)*, p. 166; 1935 estimated as the average of the figures for 1934 and 1936; 1936–1937 from *Plan 1937*, pp. 76–77. The figure for 1937 is "planned"; 1941 from *1941 Plan*, p. 40. (3) *Concrete mixers*: Production in physical units. Sources: 1927–28 to 1934 from *SS 1936 (R)*, p. 166; 1935–1937 from *Plan 1937*, pp. 76–77. The figure for 1937 is "planned." (4) *Road graders (heavy, medium, and light)*: Production of all types in physical units. Sources: 1927–28 to 1935 from *SS 1936 (R)*, p. 166; 1936 estimated as the average of the production in 1935 and 1937; 1937 from *Tretii*, p. 41; 1941 from *1941 Plan*, p. 39. (5) *Ditch-digging machines*: Production in physical units. Sources: 1927–28 to 1935 from *SS 1936 (R)*, p. 166; 1936–1937, no data available. (6) *Road rollers*. (a) *Trailing, 4-ton*: Production in physical units. Sources: 1927–28 to 1935 from *SS 1936 (R)*, p. 166; 1936–1937, no data available; 1941 from *1941 Plan*, p. 39. (b) *Self-propelled, 9–11 tons*: Production in physical units. Sources: 1927–28 to 1935 from *SS 1936 (R)*, p. 166; 1936 from *Plan 1937*, pp. 78–79; 1937 from *Tretii*, p. 41; 1941 from *1941 Plan*, p. 39.

f. *Electric light bulbs*: Production in 1000 units. Sources: 1927–28 to 1934 from *SS 1936 (R)*, p. 167; 1935–1936 from *Plan 1937*, pp. 72–73; 1937 estimated on the assumption that the same percentage increase prevailed from 1936 to 1937 as from 1935 to 1936; 1941 from *1941 Plan*, p. 31.

g. *Telephone apparatus*: Production of telephone apparatus for hand-operated and automatic exchanges in physical units. Sources: 1927–28 to 1934 from *SS 1936 (R)*, p. 165; 1935–1936 from *Plan 1937*, pp. 84–85; 1937 estimated on the assumption that the same percentage increase prevailed from 1936 to 1937 as from 1935 to 1936; 1941 from *1941 Plan*, p. 46.

h. *Hoisting and handling equipment*. (1) *Overhead traveling cranes, electric; overhead traveling cranes, hand-operated; railway cranes, steam-operated*: Production in physical units. Sources: 1927–28 to 1934 from *SS 1936 (R)*, p. 166; 1935–1937 estimated by the following method. *Plan 1937*, pp. 84–85 gives the total number of cranes produced (exclusive of electric hoisting cranes, freight and passenger) in 1935 as 743, and in 1936 as 960. *Tretii*, p. 207 gives the total number of cranes produced in 1937 as 1120. It is assumed that the latter figure also excludes electric hoisting cranes, freight and passenger. These total output figures for cranes, therefore, include output of electric and hand-operated overhead traveling cranes, portal cranes, bracket cranes, steam-operated railroad cranes, and derricks. The ouput of these various types of cranes for the years 1932–1934 as given in *SS 1936 (R)*, p. 166 is totaled by type for these three years. The percentage of the production of each type to total production during this three year period is then calculated and applied to the totals for 1935–1937 to estimate the production by type in each of these latter three years. There can be little question that the resulting figures are inaccurate. However, the writer feels that they are the best estimate that can be obtained from the available data. The figures for 1941 are taken from *1941 Plan*, p. 46. (2) *Electric hoisting cranes, freight and passenger*: Production in physical units. Sources: 1927–28 to 1934 from *SS 1936 (R)*, p. 166; 1935–1937 from *Plan 1937*, pp. 84–85; 1937 is a "planned" figure; 1941 from *1941 Plan*, p. 46.

i. *Metal-cutting machine tools*: Production in physical units. Total production (all types) from *1941 Plan*, p. 46. (1) *Turning lathes*: Sources: 1927–28 to 1934 from *SS 1936 (R)*, p. 156; 1935–1936 from *Plan 1937*, pp. 72–73; 1937 estimated from the following data. *Tretii*, p. 207 gives 36,120 as the total number of metal-cutting machine tools produced in 1937. Ioffe, p. 170, indicates that turning lathes were 34.8 per cent, turret lathes 8.5 per cent, and milling machines 13.0 per cent of the total number of metal-cutting machine tools produced in 1937. Applying these percentages to the figure for total output of metal-cutting machine tools in 1937 yields the following absolute figures for production by type: turning lathes 12,350, turret lathes 3,250, milling machines 2,640. (2) *Turret lathes*: Sources: same as for turning lathes. (3) *Drilling machines*: Sources: 1927–28 to 1934 from *SS 1936 (R)*, p. 156; 1935–1937 no data available. (4) *Planers, vertical and horizontal*: Sources: 1927–28 to 1934 from *SS 1936* (*R*); 1935–1936 estimated by simple interpolation on the assumption of equal annual increments between the output figure of 1148 in 1934 and the estimated output figure of 2060 in 1937; 1937 estimated from the percentage of output of planers to total output as given in Ioffe, p. 170 and total output of metal-cutting machine tools as given in *Tretii*, p. 207. Ioffe gives no percentage figure for 1937 for planers, so, since the percentage figure of planers to total output had been fairly constant (varying from 5.2 per cent to 5.9 per cent over the years 1932–1935, the per cent 5.7 given for 1935 was assumed to hold also for 1937. (5) *Slotters*: Sources: 1927–28 to 1934 from *SS 1936 (R)*, p. 156; 1935–1937, no data available. (6) *Milling machines*: Sources: 1927–28 to 1934 from *SS 1936 (R)*, p. 156; 1935–1936 from *Plan 1937*, pp. 72–73; 1937 see discussion of estimates under *turning lathes*, above. (7) *Boring machines*: Sources: 1927–28 to 1934 from *SS 1936 (R)*, p. 156; 1935–1937 from *Plan 1937*, pp. 72–73; the figure for 1937 is "planned." (8) *Threading machines*: Sources: 1927–28 to 1934 from *SS 1936 (R)*, p. 156; 1935–1937, no data available. (9) *Grinding machines*: Sources: 1927–28 to 1934 from *SS 1936* (*R*), p. 156; 1935–1936 from *Plan 1937*, pp. 72–73; 1937 same as for *turning lathes*, above.

j. *Rolling-mill equipment*: Production of all types of rolling-mill equipment in metric tons. Sources: 1927–28 to 1935 from *SS 1936 (R)*, p. 156; 1936 from *P. Kh.* no. 8, 1937, p. 188; 1937 estimated as the average of the output figures for 1936 and 1938; according to *B.S.E.*, USSR, p. 816, output of rolling-mill equipment in 1938 was 17,200 tons; 1941 from *1941 Plan*, p. 34.

k. *Textile machinery*: Production in physical units of carding machines (all types), spinning water frames, doubling water frames, looms (all types), and knitting machines. Total water frames as given in *SS 1936 (R)*, p. 159

for the year 1935 are divided between spinning and doubling water frames according to the average percentage of each of the two types to the total production of water frames for the years 1932–1934 inclusive. Sources: 1927–28 to 1931, 1936–1937, no data available; 1932–1934 from *SS 1936 (R)*, p. 159; 1941 from *1941 Plan*, pp. 36–37.

l. *Articles for home and general use*: Production in physical units. (1) *Typewriters*: Sources: 1927–28 to 1934 from *SS 1936 (R)*, p. 168; 1935–1936 from *Plan 1937*, pp. 86–87; 1937 from Ioffe, p. 177; 1941 from *1941 Plan*, p. 50. (2) *Sewing machines*. (a) *Home type* and (b) *factory type*: Sources: 1927–28 to 1935 from *SS 1936 (R)*, p. 168; 1936 from *Plan 1937*, pp. 88–89; 1937 from *Tretii*, p. 208. The division of the total production of sewing machines into home and factory types in the years 1936 and 1937 is based on the percentage division of total production of sewing machines into these two types in the year 1935. (b) Factory type: 1941 from *1941 Plan*, p. 37. (3) *Bicycles*: Sources: 1927–28 to 1935 from *SS 1936 (R)*, p. 165; 1935–1936 from *Plan 1937*, pp. 88–89; 1937 from Ioffe, p. 175. (4) *Motorcycles*: Sources: 1927–28 to 1935 from *SS 1936 (R)*, p. 165; 1936–1937 from *Plan 1937*, pp. 88–89. The figure for production in 1937 is "planned."

APPENDIX B

Derivation of Weights

The following notes apply to Table B, below.* Each of the five columns in this table is discussed below in a general statement of the method used to obtain the data presented in the column with specific comments on particular industries or processes when needed. Specific comments are numbered to correspond with the item number in the table. Figures have been rounded to the limit of accuracy permitted by the original data, and do not in every case add exactly to the totals shown in the table. The difference in such cases is usually only a fraction of 1 per cent.

Column 1

The pay-roll figures shown in column 1 have been calculated from employment and wage data in *Trud v SSSR* (Labor in the USSR, 1934; Moscow: Central Administration of National Economic Accounting, State Planning Commission USSR, 1935). Employment data are either annual average employment for 1934 (from Tables 12–15, pp. 62–72 in *Trud*, 1934) or employment on July 1, 1934 (from Table 17, pp. 74–83 in *Trud*, 1934). Those pay-roll figures in column 1 which are based on July 1, 1934 employment data are marked with an asterisk. Wage data are average monthly wages (from Tables 30–35, pp. 144–167 in *Trud*, 1934). Both employment and wage data in *Trud*, 1934 are classified by five main categories of industrial personnel in each industry, so that each pay-roll figure in column 1 is the sum of the pay rolls for these five subdivisions of industrial personnel (workers, apprentices, engineers and technical personnel, administrative personnel, and minor service personnel). Monthly wages have *not* been converted to annual wages before calculating pay rolls, since the only effect of this would have been to multiply all succeeding computations by a factor of twelve.

7. *Nonferrous metals*: Wage figures used in calculating this pay roll are borrowed from data for ferrous metals since none are available for non-ferrous metals.

9. *Chemicals*: This pay roll was calculated by multiplying July 1 employment data for basic chemicals, aniline dyes, artificial fibers, other chemicals, pharmaceutical chemicals, wood chemistry, and paints and varnishes by the average monthly wage for each category of industrial personnel for the *chemi-*

* See Tabular Section, p. 189.

cal industry as a whole. These separate pay rolls were then summed to obtain the aggregate pay roll for the chemical industry.

10. *Coke*: The wage rates used in calculating this pay roll are the average wages in the chemical industry under which coke is classified in *Trud*, 1934. No specific average wage rates are available for coke.

18. *Glass*: The unadjusted pay roll for the glass industry is the sum of three subpay rolls as follows: (1) a pay roll for "glass for home and other use" calculated from July 1, 1934 employment data for that kind of glass and average wages for the category "production of articles for domestic use," (2) a pay roll for "window and mirror glass" calculated from July 1, 1934 employment data for that kind of glass and average wages for the category "production of building materials," and (3) a pay roll for "electrotechnical glass" calculated from July 1, 1934 employment data for that kind of glass and average wages for the category "electrotechnical" industry.

20. *Textile industry*: The unadjusted pay roll for this industry is the sum of the subpay rolls shown in column 1. Subpay rolls "d" through "h" were calculated as indicated in the general comment to column 1 above. The subpay rolls for cotton ginning, silk reeling, and cottonized fiber were calculated by multiplying the average wage *for the textile industry as a whole* by the employment in each of these processes on July 1, 1934.

22. *Food industry*: Unadjusted pay rolls marked with an asterisk were calculated by multiplying employment in the indicated division of the food industry on July 1, 1934 by average wages *for the food industry as a whole.*

The pay roll for the meat industry is the sum of the pay rolls for bacon, sausages, and meat slaughtering.

The pay roll for "liquors, vinous and distilled" is the sum of the pay rolls for vodka and for raw spirits and refining.

23. *Machinery*: All unadjusted pay rolls for the machinery industry were calculated by multiplying employment in the indicated division of the machinery industry on July 1, 1934 by average wages *for the machinery industry as a whole.* The unadjusted pay roll for miscellaneous machinery (Items "i" through "p" in column 1) is the sum of the unadjusted pay rolls calculated from *Trud*, 1934 for "production of equipment for all branches of the economy," "production of equipment for heavy industry," and "production of equipment for light industry."

Column 2

The adjustment coefficient for employment coverage is calculated by comparing the annual average number of workers in each industry as given in *Socialist Construction in the USSR* (Moscow: Central Administration of Economic and Social Statistics of the State Planning Commission of the USSR, 1936), pp. 42–47 with the data in *Trud*, 1934 showing annual average number of workers (pp. 62–72) or number of workers on July 1, 1934 (pp. 74–83). If the employment figure from *Socialist Construction* is larger than that from

Trud 1934 the pay roll from column 1 is made proportionately larger and vice versa. To the extent that differences between the annual average number of workers given in *Socialist Construction* and the number of workers on July 1, 1934 given in *Trud*, 1934 are seasonal, the adjustment coefficient may be considered an adjustment for seasonal factors as well as for differences in coverage.

2. *Crude oil extracted*: The pay roll for this industry was not adjusted for employment coverage. The *Socialist Construction* data on the average annual number of workers in this industry exclude those engaged in the drilling of new wells, while the *Trud*, 1934 data include these workers. Application of the employment coefficient would have reduced the pay-roll figure by the estimated amount of the wages of personnel engaged in drilling. Since the writer thought it appropriate to include the wages of these personnel in the weights, he made no adjustment in this instance.

9. *Chemicals*: The adjustment for employment coverage was made for five separate groups in the chemical industry: (1) basic chemicals, (2) pharmaceutical chemicals, (3) wood chemistry, (4) paints and varnishes, (5) aniline dyes, artificial fibers and "other chemicals." The employment adjustment for the fifth group, a reduction, was allowed to fall entirely on the category "other chemicals." These five group pay rolls were then summed to obtain an aggregate pay roll for the entire chemical industry.

23. *Machinery*: The employment coverage adjustment for items "i–p" in the machinery industry was made as follows: (1) the *sum* of the annual average number of workers in these branches of machinery from *Socialist Construction* was compared to the *sum* of the number of workers on July 1, 1934 as given by *Trud*, 1934 for the categories "production of equipment for all branches of the economy," "production of equipment for heavy industry," and "production of equipment for light industry." Matching of these two general categories was done by a process of elimination in comparing the tables in *Socialist Construction* and *Trud*, 1934. The resulting employment coverage coefficient, 116.2 was applied to the unadjusted pay roll for these branches calculated as indicated in column 1 (23). Pay rolls adjusted for employment coverage for each of the machinery items "i–p" in the table were then calculated by apportioning their aggregate adjusted pay roll according to the percentage share of each in the sum total of annual average number of workers employed in these branches of machinery (from *Socialist Construction*).

Column 3

The adjustment coefficient used to increase pay rolls so as to include the estimated amount of the pay-roll tax is calculated by comparing pay rolls as a per cent of total factory costs of production with the *pay-roll tax* as a per cent of total factory costs of production. Thus, if pay rolls are 10 per cent of factory costs of production and pay-roll taxes are 2.5 per cent of costs of production, pay-roll taxes are 25 per cent of pay rolls, and the pay-roll figure is multiplied by an adjustment coefficient of 125 per cent to estimate pay rolls inclusive of the pay-roll tax. The pay-roll tax coefficients are calculated from data in *Sotsialisticheskoe stroitel'stvo SSSR* (Socialist Construction in the USSR; Moscow: Central Administration of National Economic Accounting of the State Planning Commission USSR, 1936), pp. 32–34.

8. *Ore mining*: The pay-roll tax coefficient for ore mining is calculated from data for iron ore mining alone.

14. *Wood processing*: Adjustments for the pay-roll tax are made separately for lumber and plywood. The combined pay roll for lumber and plywood, already adjusted for employment coverage, is divided between the two products according to the relative size of their separate pay rolls calculated with July 1, 1934 employment figures. Then the individual pay-roll tax coefficients are applied to obtain final adjusted pay rolls for lumber and plywood.

20. *Textile industry*: The adjustment for pay-roll tax for the textile industry was made as follows: (1) the total pay roll for the textile industry shown in column 1 was multiplied by the pay-roll tax coefficient for the textile industry as a whole, 124.9 per cent, (2) the subpay rolls "d" through "h" were each multiplied by the appropriate specific pay-roll tax coefficient and their sum subtracted from the adjusted pay roll for all textiles leaving the adjusted pay roll for items "a" through "c" for which no specific pay-roll tax coefficients could be calculated, (3) it was assumed that the pay-roll tax adjustment affected each of the items "a" through "c" equally, and the residual adjusted pay roll for textiles was subdivided among these three items in proportion to the relative size of the unadjusted pay rolls for these three items.

22. *Food industry*: The adjustment for pay-roll tax in the food industry was made as follows: (1) the items for which specific pay-roll tax coefficients could be calculated were adjusted according to these individual coefficients, (2) the sum of individual pay rolls adjusted for employment coverage (but not for pay-roll tax) was taken, and this sum (115,800 thousand rubles), representing the aggregate pay roll for the food industry adjusted for employment coverage, was multiplied by the pay-roll tax coefficient for the food industry as a whole resulting in an aggregate pay roll of 145,900 thousand rubles (correct to four figures), for the food industry as a whole adjusted for both employment coverage and the pay-roll tax, (3) the sum of those individual pay rolls for which specific individual pay-roll tax adjustments had been made was then deducted from the adjusted pay roll for the food industry as a whole, (4) the residual adjusted pay roll so obtained was then divided among those subdivisions of the food industry for which specific individual pay-roll tax adjustments had not been possible, according to the relative size of the unadjusted pay roll of each subdivision. Minor discrepancies between totals and sum of subtotals are the result of rounding.

23. *Machinery*: The pay-roll tax coefficient for *machinery as a whole* is the only available pay-roll tax coefficient for machinery items. Accordingly, all

pay rolls for branches of the machinery industry are adjusted by the same pay-roll tax coefficient, 116.5 per cent. No entries are made for item "p" (other equipment) since the weight for this item is ignored entirely in the final weighting of machinery quantity series. Item "p" is included in the table, since a part of the total unadjusted pay roll of 74,831 thousand rubles is ascribable to it. The writer decided to exclude the pay roll for item "p" from final weights for the machinery quantity series for two reasons: (1) no quantity series was available for item "p," and (2) lack of information regarding the machinery content of item "p" argued against an easy assumption that production in that category moved with the general machinery index.

Column 4

The net value-added weights shown in column 4 in most cases are the products of the first three columns in the table. Thus they are pay rolls adjusted for employment coverage and expanded to include pay-roll taxes. For some items in the food and machinery industries, the adjusted pay rolls shown in column 4 were obtained in a more complicated manner than simply multiplying the first three columns together. These special cases have already been discussed in the notes to the first three columns.

22(f & g). The joint payroll for vegetable oils and margarine has been divided between them in proportion to the average annual number of workers employed by each in 1934.

Column 5

The final adjusted weights shown in column 5 are those actually applied to the quantity series in constructing the production index. Some of the weights in column 5 are identical to those in column 4, since, in these particular cases, no further adjustment was required. Those weights in column 5 which differ from the corresponding entries in column 4 either have been further subdivided among individual production series or have been increased by having been assigned a proportionate share in pay-roll weights within their particular industry for which there were no quantity series.

6. *Ferrous metals*: The total weight for the ferrous metals industry has been divided among the three constituent series for pig iron, steel, and rolled steel on the basis of unit wage costs (including pay-roll taxes) per ton for each of these types of products as given by S. G. Strumilin in *Chernaia metallurgia v Rossii i v SSSR* (Ferrous Metallurgy in Russia and the USSR; Moscow-Leningrad: Academy of Sciences of the USSR, 1935), p. 320. Data are for the Southern Metallurgical Trust in the year 1930. Production of pig iron, steel, and rolled steel in tons in 1934 was multiplied by the wage cost per ton of each product. Then total wage costs of each product were expressed as a percentage of aggregate wage costs for the three products. The total adjusted pay roll for ferrous metals was then divided in accordance with these per-

centages to obtain the weights shown in column 5. Details of these computations are reproduced in the accompanying table.

TABLE B1

Subdivision of Weights for Ferrous Metals

Product	1000 Metric Tons Produced in 1934	Wage Cost per Ton (rubles)	Total Wage Cost (1000 rubles)	Per Cent of Total Wage Cost
Pig iron	10,428	4.07	42,442	26.7
Steel	9,693	5.90	57,189	35.9
Rolled steel	7,204	8.25	59,433	37.4
			159,064	100.0

7. *Nonferrous metals*: The total pay-roll weight for nonferrous metals was divided among the constituent series for copper, aluminum, zinc and lead according to the share of each in the total annual average number of workers engaged in producing these four products in 1934 (from *Socialist Construction in the USSR*, p. 43). Since the number of workers in zinc and lead smelting and refining is reported jointly, it is arbitrarily assumed that one-half of the workers reported are engaged in the production of zinc, the other half in lead production.

8. *Ore mining*: The total pay-roll weight for ore mining was divided among iron ore, manganese ore, and copper ore according to the share of each in the total number of workers engaged in these three lines in 1934. For iron ore and manganese ore the annual average number of workers is given in *Socialist Construction in the USSR*, p. 42. For copper ore the number of workers on July 1, 1934 as given in *Trud*, 1934, p. 76 was used. These figures are shown in the accompanying table.

TABLE B2

Subdivision of Weights for Ore Mining

Product	Number of Workers	Per Cent of Workers
Iron ore	38.8	64.78
Manganese ore	9.4	15.69
Copper ore	11.7	19.53
	59.9	100.00

9. *Chemicals*: Total pay-roll weights for the chemical industry were divided among five branches of that industry, (1) basic chemicals, (2) aniline dyes, (3) artificial fibers, (4) pharmaceutical chemicals, (5) paints and varnishes,

according to the share of each branch in the aggregate pay roll for these five branches. In other words, weights for wood chemistry and "other" chemicals were imputed to the above branches in the above stated proportion.

The weight for basic chemicals was further subdivided among soda ash, superphosphate, and sulphuric acid by the following method. *Proizvoditel'-nost' truda v promyshlennosti SSSR* (The Productivity of Labor in the USSR; ed. P. A. Khromov; Moscow: State Planning Commission Press, 1946), p. 248 gives the annual output per worker in tons in 1936 for superphosphate (1,569.5 metric tons), sulphuric acid (314.0 metric tons) and soda ash (393.0 metric tons). For soda ash the figures are based on all the producing enterprises; for sulphuric acid and superphosphate, on data for 50–70 per cent of the total volume of output. These data for annual production per worker in 1936 were then used to divide the annual output in 1934 of each of these chemicals in metric tons to obtain an estimate of the number of man years required to produce the stated quantity of each chemical in 1934. These estimated man years were then summed and the share of the man years required to produce each chemical to the total number of man years required to produce the three chemicals was calculated. The total weight for basic chemicals was then assigned to the series for soda ash (24.97 per cent), superphosphate (13.29 per cent) and sulphuric acid (61.74 per cent) on the basis of these percentages.

22. *Food industry*: For milling, factory kitchens, tea and coffee, wines, and liquors vinous and distilled no production indicators were available. Therefore, the assumption was made that these series moved in accordance with the general index for the food industry. Accordingly, the aggregate pay-roll weights for these subdivisions of the food industry were reassigned to the quantity series which were available for the food industry in proportion to the existing weight carried by each of these series. This had the effect of increasing the weight for each of the quantity series in the food industry by 22.8 per cent.

Taking the number of workers employed on July 1, 1934 as an approximate guide, beer was given nine-tenths and yeast one-tenth of the jointly derived weight for the production of beer and yeast.

23. *Machinery*: All adjusted pay-roll weights in column 5 are larger than weights for the same machinery items shown in column 4 by 12.4 per cent. This percentage increase results from the spreading of the weights for "pumps and compressors," "control and measuring instruments," "equipment for the food industry," and "other industrial machinery" (items m,n,o,q) over the other items for machinery in proportion to the size of the weights for these items as shown in column 4. While no production indicators were available for items m,n,o,q, the writer deemed it not unreasonable to assume that their production moved in harmony with the general index of machinery output. This asumption was not made for item "p" (other equipment). In the absence of more information regarding item "p," its weight was entirely excluded from the final weights for the general machinery index.

a. *Power equipment*: The final weight for power equipment was divided between "steam boilers" and "total prime movers" in proportion to the annual average number of workers engaged in each of these two branches of machinery production.

c. *Agricultural machinery and implements*: (1) *Tractors*: The final weight for tractors includes the final weight for spare parts and is divided between "wheeled" and "track-laying" as follows: (a) In the year 1934, 157 man hours of the production workers' time were required to produce a wheeled tractor (models STZ or KhTZ) and 540 man hours of the production workers' time were required to produce a track-laying tractor (model ChTZ).[1] (b) On this basis the production of 83,360 wheeled tractors in 1934 required 13,087,520 man hours and the production of 10,605 track-laying tractors required 5,726,700 man hours. Thus, 70 per cent of total man hours were required in the production of wheeled tractors and 30 per cent in the production of track-laying tractors. (c) These percentages were then assumed to apply also to the pay rolls paid in the production of tractors, so that 70 per cent of the final pay-roll weight was assigned to wheeled tractors and 30 per cent to track-laying tractors.

d. (1) *Railroad equipment*: The division of the total pay-roll weight for railroad equipment among the constituent equipment series was based on the accompanying data for man hours of work required in the production of each type of equipment.

TABLE B3

Man Hours Required to Produce Railroad Rolling Stock

Type of Equipment	Man Hours Required in Production	
	1935	1940
Locomotive E and EM	13,906	—
Locomotive FD	25,668	13,783
Locomotive SU	29,878 [a]	16,046
Locomotive IS	29,881 [a]	16,048
Two-axle, 20-ton freight car	435	—
Passenger coach (4-axle)	4,070	—

[a] These figures are based on the assumption that the percentage change in man hours for locomotive FD from 1935 to 1940 was indicative of a similar percentage change for locomotives SU and IS.

SOURCES — 1935: *Proizvoditel'nost' truda v promyshlennosti SSSR*, p. 185; 1940 I. Iunovich, "Voprosy organizatsii truda v mashinostroenii", *Planovoe khoziaistvo* no. 6, 1940, p. 31.

Next it was assumed that relative man-hour requirements for the different types of equipment included in the above table did not change significantly between 1934 and 1935. Then the production in 1934 of each type of railroad equipment included in the index was multiplied by the appropriate number of man hours from the above table to estimate total man hours required in the production of that type of equipment. The total pay-roll weight for railroad equipment was then divided among the items of equipment in proportion to total man hours required for their production. The man-hour requirements for a freight locomotive type FD were taken to be appropriate also for a freight locomotive type SO for which it was not possible to establish independent man-hour requirements. For the same reason the man-hour requirements for a passenger locomotive type SU were assumed to be appropriate also for passenger locomotive type M.

Since only 4-axle passenger coaches were produced in 1935,[2] the man-hour requirements for passenger coaches obviously refer to 4-axle coaches. Therefore, before estimating total man-hour requirements for the production of passenger coaches in 1934, the output of passenger coaches in that year, shown in Table A in 2-axle units, was reëxpressed in 4-axle units by dividing the Soviet figure by two.

d. (2) *Motor vehicles*: The total pay-roll weight for motor vehicles was divided among the three categories (1) passenger cars and 1½-ton trucks, (2) trucks from 2½ to 4 tons inclusive, and (3) trucks 5 tons and larger according to the annual average number of production workers in each category in the year 1934.

The GAZ plant accounted for the entire production of passenger automobiles and 1½-ton trucks in 1934 and produced no other models.[3] The annual average number of production workers employed by the GAZ plant in 1934 was 22,851.[4] The ZIS plant accounted for the entire production of 3- and 4-ton trucks in 1934 (no 2½-ton trucks were produced in 1934) and produced no other models. The annual average number of production workers employed by the ZIS plant in 1934 was 13,867. The IaAZ plant, which specialized in trucks of 5 tons and larger and was their sole producer, employed 2,375 production workers on the average in 1934. Therefore, the total pay-roll weight for motor vehicles was divided among these three categories of vehicles on the basis of these employment data.

TABLE B4

Subdivision of Weights for Motor Vehicles

Vehicle Category	Per Cent of Weights
1. Passenger cars and 1½-ton trucks	58.45
2. Trucks from 2½ to 4 tons, inclusive	35.47
3. Trucks 5 tons and larger	6.08
	100.00

APPENDIX C

The Machinery Index

Not only does the machinery index illustrate most of the procedures followed in the construction of the indices for other industries, but, in addition, its construction involves some methods not used in any other industry. Moreover, the machinery industry is the most important single industry in the Soviet industrial economy. For these reasons, it appears advisable to discuss in somewhat greater detail the statistical procedures involved in the construction of the machinery index.

(a) Weights for the Machinery Index

Weights for group and individual product quantity relatives in the machinery industry were obtained as the result of the following five statistical steps: (1) the calculation of unadjusted pay rolls from employment and wage data in *Trud v SSSR*, (2) adjustment of these payrolls for employment coverage on the basis of data on the average annual number of workers employed in different branches of the machinery industry taken from *Socialist Construction in the USSR*, (3) the further adjustment of these pay rolls to allow for the pay-roll tax, (4) the splitting up of group weights and their assignment to subseries on the basis of employment data, unit labor cost and unit labor time requirements, and (5) the imputing of weights for which no production indicators could be obtained to the other product series in the machinery industry in proportion to the size of the weights already assigned to these series.

All unadjusted payrolls for the machinery industry were calculated by multiplying employment in the various divisions of the machinery industry on July 1, 1934 by the average wage for the machinery industry as a whole. A separate, specific wage rate was used for each of the five different categories of industrial personnel, but no allowance was made for variation in the wage for a specific category, for example, workers, or apprentices, among the different branches of the machinery industry. Thus, for example, it was assumed that workers engaged in the production of agricultural machinery, railroad rolling stock, metal-cutting machine tools, and textile machinery all earned the same average wage. This is not an assumption which one would wish to make if the existing data permitted a differentiation of average wage rates by specific types of machinery and equipment. In fact, however, the available data leave no alternative but that which has been pursued.

In adjusting the machinery weights for employment coverage, some difficulty was encountered in matching properly the designations for divisions of the machinery industry used by the labor division of the Central Statistical Administration with those used by the industrial division. Not only was the terminology employed by the two divisions different in some instances, but the labor division did not give as detailed a classification of employment by types of machinery and equipment as did the industrial division. Therefore, the following procedure in making adjustments for employment coverage in the machinery industry was adopted.

The writer matched as many individual categories as possible and for these categories made individual adjustments for differences in employment coverage. The *sum* of the number of workers on July 1, 1934 as given by *Trud*, 1934, for the categories "production of equipment for all branches of the economy," "production of equipment for heavy industry," and "production of equipment for light industry," was then compared to the *sum* of the annual average number of workers for eight subdivisions of the machinery industry as shown in *Socialist Construction in the USSR* which were judged to be the equivalent categories in the industrial division classification system. Comparison of these two sums permitted the calculation of a general employment coverage coefficient which was applied to the aggregate unadjusted pay roll for the categories "production of equipment for all branches of the economy," "production of equipment for heavy industry," and "production of equipment for light industry" from *Trud v SSSR*. The aggregate adjusted pay roll thus obtained was apportioned among the eight equipment categories from *Socialist Construction in the USSR* according to the percentage share of each in the sum total of annual average number of workers employed in these branches of machinery.

It will be remembered (see Chapter 3) that the adjustment of pay rolls to include the pay-roll tax was accomplished by the application of coefficients calculated from the relationship of pay rolls as a per cent of total factory costs of production to pay-roll taxes as a per cent of total factory costs of production of the output of a given industry. Data on the structure of costs of production of machinery are available only for the machinery industry as a whole. Accordingly, all pay rolls for branches of the machinery industry are adjusted by the same pay-roll tax coefficient. As was mentioned earlier, this is not likely to introduce important distortions in the weighting system, since the factors which affect the size of the pay-roll tax, such as working conditions and composition of the labor force, are less variable within an industry than among industries.

Certain branches of the Soviet machinery industry have no representation at all in the present index of machinery output. Among the branches omitted, the two most important are repair plants and shipbuilding. These two branches were omitted because nothing approaching satisfactory data on the physical output of either branch was available. Moreover, since there was no apparent reason to assume that the physical output of these branches had moved in harmony with the general index of machinery output calculated for other branches, the net value-added weights for these branches, estimated from pay-roll data, were excluded from the aggregate weight for the machinery industry in the general index of industrial output. Several other branches of the machinery industry for which adequate physical output series were lacking were included in the aggregate weight for the machinery index. While no adequate production indicators were available for "pumps and compressors," "control and measuring instruments," "equipment for the food industry," and a relatively small category labeled "other industrial equipment," the writer deemed it not unreasonable to assume that their production had moved in accord with the general index of machinery output. The net value-added weights calculated for these branches of machinery were imputed, therefore, to the other branches of machinery output represented in the index in proportion to the existing weights carried by these other branches.

The machinery industry provides several interesting examples of the assignment of weights to physical series on the basis of man hours required in the production of the several products. One such case is the division of the weight for the production of tractors between wheeled and track-laying tractors. It was possible to compute the group weight for tractors directly from employment and wage data in *Trud v SSSR*, but the data from this source did not permit the splitting of the group weight among the different types of tractors. Fortunately, another source, ***Proizvoditel'nost' truda v promyshlennosti SSSR*** (The Productivity of Labor in the Industry of the USSR), contained the information that in 1934 an average of 157 man hours of production workers' time were required to produce a wheeled tractor and 540 man hours of production workers' time were required to produce a track-laying tractor.[1] Table C1, showing man-hour requirements for the production of tractors, is of additional interest as an indication of the decline in costs of production of new products with the increase in productive efficiency over time.

This has bearing on the Soviet practice in constructing the official production index of valuing new products at current-year prices of the first year during which the new products were produced. Note that the labor time requirements of the wheeled model STZ declined by about 60 per cent from the first to the second year (see Table C1) and at the end of eight years were approximately one-tenth of what they were in the first year. While not so severe, the reductions in labor requirements for the models KHTZ and CHTZ are likewise pronounced. Thus, it is clear that the costs of new products in their first year of production were often very high with respect to the costs in succeeding years, so that the practice of entering new products in the official index of industrial production at current-year prices, even if these prices were adjusted downward by a correction coefficient calculated from current versus constant price relation-

TABLE C1

Labor Time Required to Produce One Tractor (in man hours of production workers)

Year	Wheeled Models		Tracklaying Model
	STZ	KHTZ	CHTZ
1930	1,023	—	—
1931	386	—	—
1932	329	442	—
1933	185	205	738
1934	155	159	540
1935	140	143	426
1936	105	105	336
1937	105	105	336

SOURCES — *Proizvoditel'nost' truda v promyshlennosti SSSR* (The Productivity of Labor in the Industry of the USSR; ed. P. A. Khromov; Moscow: State Planning Commission Press, 1940), p. 213.

ships of *established* products, must have resulted in a substantial exaggeration of the relative value of new goods and thus in an unwarranted inflation in the official production index. The table is evidence, too, that shifting the base-weight year of the production index from 1926–27 to 1934 by no means frees the revised index from all such bias. To establish this point, one has only to compare the relative man-hour costs of track-laying and wheeled tractors in 1934 and again in 1937. In four years, the ratio of man-hour requirements for track-laying tractors to those for wheeled tractors declines from about 350 per cent to about 320 per cent.

Soviet production of wheeled tractors during the years 1928–1937 included the wheeled models STZ and KHTZ for which man-hour requirements are shown in the table above and the Universal, Models 1 and 2, wheeled tractors especially designed for cultivating and, therefore, built higher off the ground than the other wheeled models. Both the STZ and KHTZ have the same design and dimensions; a thirty horsepower engine and a drawbar capacity of 15 horsepower. The Universal has a 20 horsepower engine and a 15 horsepower drawbar capacity. A Soviet source states that the Universal models are quite similar to the STZ and KHTZ models in the mechanical details of their construction (for example, the engine) and differ only slightly in dimensions.[2] Therefore, the writer felt justified in lumping the output of these types of wheeled tractors in a single series to be assigned a single weight in the index.

The basic model for the Soviet track-laying tractors during the years covered by the index was the Stalinets 60 or CHTZ.[3] This tractor has a 60 horsepower engine and a drawbar capacity of 50 horsepower. A small number of other heavy track-laying tractors were produced in these years, but for practical purposes their effect on the aggregate of track-laying tractors can be ignored, and they can be lumped with the Stalinets 60. This position can be supported by the following evidence. If the aggregate engine capacity and aggregate drawbar capacity of track-laying tractors produced in 1934 are divided by the number of track-laying tractors produced in that year, the average engine capacity obtained is 61.4 horsepower and the average drawbar capacity is 48.1 horsepower.[4] There is no great difference between these figures and the 60/50 specifications for the Stalinets 60.

On the basis of the foregoing considerations, the writer felt justified in dividing the total production of tractors in Soviet industry into two basic series, wheeled and track-laying. Since, in the base year 1934, 540 man hours of production workers were required to produce a track-laying tractor, the production of 10,605 track-laying tractors in that year required 5,726,700 man hours. The production of 83,360 wheeled tractors at 157 man hours per tractor required 13,087,520 man hours. Thus, 70 per cent of total man hours were required in the production of wheeled tractors and 30 per cent in the production of track-laying tractors. These percentages were then assumed to apply also to the pay rolls paid in the production of tractors, so that 70 per cent of the final pay-roll weight was assigned to the quantity relative for wheeled tractors and 30 per cent to the quantity relative for track-laying tractors.

Other examples of this general approach to the problem of assigning group weights to individual product subseries are discussed in Appendix B, to which the interested reader is referred for more complete details.

(b) Physical Quantity Series for Machinery

The machinery index is the arithmetic mean of weighted quantity relatives for 23 individually weighted output series. In a few cases, the series are for one single standard type of equipment in physical units (for example, freight locomotives, series E) to which the full assigned weight actually belongs. Other series either are less homogeneous (for example, trucks from 2½ to 4 tons) or obtain an artificial homogeneity by adopting a conventional unit of measure (such as kilowatt capacity of prime movers or of power transformers), and in this way attain comprehensive coverage of the products of the particular branch of machinery concerned.

Still other quantity series carry the imputed weight for a much more comprehensive list of products than they actually include. Thus, the quantity relative for electric light bulbs produced receives the weight for electric appliances in addition to that for light bulbs, and the total weight for communications equipment is assigned to the series for the output of hand and automatic telephone exchanges (in itself not a homogeneous series). All these are familiar devices in the construction of production indices employing imputed weights, and the writer does not propose to argue their merits and defects. It is his judgment that the procedures followed give a reasonably accurate picture of production movements in the branches of the machinery industry concerned and that within the framework of the present weighting system and the limitations of published Soviet production statistics, no better picture is to be obtained. There is another feature of the machinery index, however, which is unusual enough to require special comment, namely, the use of unit values from the United States *Census of Manufactures* as price weights in the construction of some subindices in the machinery industry.

(c) Census Unit Values as Weights for Subindices in the Machinery Industry

For six branches of the machinery industry: agricultural implements and equipment, textile machinery, construction and road-building machinery, hoisting and handling machinery, metal-cutting machine tools, and a miscellaneous group consisting of sewing machines, typewriters, motorcycles, and bicycles, it was possible to calculate net value-added weights for the entire branch, but the detailed employment and wage data needed to calculate net value-added weights for the many individual products were lacking. There was no single dominant or representative series in any of the subgroups, and in no instance was there a measure of output in conventional units to serve as a common denominator for the physically diverse collection of products. Thus, there was a choice between omitting these important products from the production index or finding a method to construct a subindex for each group to which the net value-added weights for each group could then be assigned. Each subindex once constructed could be reweighted with Russian pay-roll weights and thus assimilated to the general methodology of the index. Therefore, the writer concluded that the final machinery index (and the general index of industrial output as well) would come closer to portraying the actual movements in the physical volume of Soviet production if the output of the several problem branches of the machinery industry were included in this manner than if they were omitted entirely.

American prices for identical or similar equipment suggested themselves as the most readily obtainable weights for this undertaking. After a few preliminary explorations of the problem, the writer settled on unit values derived from the United States *Census of Manufactures* as the best organized and most broadly representative body of data from which prices could be obtained without lengthy correspondence with individual machinery producers in this country or special technical knowledge of the equipment involved. Once this decision had been taken, it was a matter of selecting the appropriate volumes of the *Census of Manufactures*, matching Soviet and U. S. Census product designations, abstracting quantity and aggregate value statistics, and dividing value by quantity to obtain unit values. The details of this work are set forth in Tables C(i) to C(vi), in the Tabular Section (see p. 189, below). Some general comments on the theoretical and practical aspects of this procedure are now in order.

The basic assumption involved in the use of U. S. unit values as price weights for Soviet industrial products is that relative prices for identical products in the two economies bear at least an approximate relationship to each other. Thus, if a combined harvester-thresher costs approximately fourteen times as much as a grain drill in the United States, it is assumed that the Soviet prices (f.o.b. factory and net of the turnover tax) stand in somewhat the same approximate relationship to each other.

The factors that influence the general structure of relative prices in an economy are many and complex. Some of the more fundamental are the pattern of natural resources, the size and composition of the labor force, the pattern of consumer and state demand, the development and structure of industry, the influence of foreign trade, the development and application of technology, the technical coefficients of production for different products, the length of time different products have been in production, the relation of quantity demanded to the most efficient level of production, and the cyclical state of business conditions.

It is obvious that the writer cannot have made any serious attempt to weigh the influence of these many factors in coming to his decision to use American price weights. Such considerations as the effect of resource patterns, the pattern of demand, and the structure of industry on relative prices are too broad and complex to serve as more than cautions to be duly noted when making such assumptions. An attempt was made, however, in choosing the year from which U. S. Census unit values were to be taken, to allow for technical and technological factors and short-run fluctuations in demand. The writer sought to find a year in which there was at least a good possibility that equipment design and production techniques were fairly similar in the Soviet and American machinery industries and a year in which business conditions in the United States might be described as "normal." Nevertheless, on theoretical grounds the use of U. S. Census unit values as price weights for Soviet machinery is clearly a risky procedure. The most that can be hoped is that despite undoubted and important discrepancies between the two price systems, significant similarities are also to be found.

Some exceedingly rough evidence on possible similarities in the relative structure of Soviet and American machinery prices is available. At one stage in the development of this study, consideration was given to the use of Soviet prices, preferably for the late 1930's after the removal of subsidies, as weights for these subindices in the machinery industry. While Soviet price quotations undoubtedly are available in greater detail than has been generally realized, those available did not provide sufficient product coverage, especially for agricultural machinery, to warrant their use. However, there were enough prices available for two product groups, namely, metal-cutting machine tools, and construction and road-building machinery, to permit of a very rough check on the assumption that relative prices for identical products in the Soviet and American economies bear at least an approximate relationship to each other.

The method used was to calculate and compare the percentage relationship of the price of individual products in each of these groups to the unweighted arithmetic mean price for the group. The calculations were made separately for each economy. For American prices, the Census unit values actually used as weights in constructing the subindices were taken. These unit values, of course, reflect the composition of American output in each product class. For Soviet prices, the simple unweighted arithmetic mean of ruble prices for each class of product was taken. Thus, the Soviet prices do *not* reflect the actual composition of Soviet output. The results of these calculations are contained in Tables C2 and C3.

TABLE C2

Soviet and American Price Relatives for Metal-cutting Machine Tools

Product Designation	Soviet Price Relative	American Price Relative
1. Turning lathes	0.82	0.27
2. Turret lathes	0.53	0.80
3. Drilling machines	0.15	0.12
4. Planers (vertical and horizontal)	1.75	2.63
5. Slotters	0.34	1.40
6. Milling machines (all types)	0.49	0.42
7. Boring machines	2.42	1.55
8. Grinding machines	0.75	0.80

SOURCE — Soviet prices from *Tsennik dlia sostavleniia smet na stroitel'stvo* (v tsenakh 1945 god; Chast' IV, tseny na oborudovanie, Gosplanizdat, 1947).

TABLE C3

Soviet and American Price Relatives for Construction and Road-building Machinery

Product Designation	Soviet Price Relative	American Price Relative
1. Power shovels	3.00	2.03
2. Stone crushers	1.32	2.08
3. Concrete mixers	0.13	0.01
4. Road graders	0.20	0.15
5. Ditch diggers	1.99	2.03
6. Road rollers		
trailing	0.04	0.19
self-propelled	0.32	0.52

SOURCE — Soviet prices from Planovaia komissiia Mosoblispolkoma, *Spravochnik tsen na stroitel'nye materialy, oborudovanie, i transportnye sredstva po Moskovskoi oblasti na 1937 g.*, 1937.

The two tables reveal a tendency for high and low price relatives to be associated, with "slotters" the main exception. Since each of the product classes is fairly broad, a great deal depends on the actual composition of Soviet and American output in the product class. More detailed information on the composition of Soviet output is lacking, so that it seems questionable whether the substitution of Soviet prices for U. S. Census unit values would reduce significantly the arbitrariness of the present procedure.

In addition to the theoretical shortcomings of U. S. unit value weights, certain practical problems were encountered in their use. First, the *Census of Manufactures* has never appeared annually, so that the years when it did not appear were automatically ruled out. Second, the *Census of Manufactures* varies from time to time and from industry to industry in the scope of its reporting of data on different products. It was necessary to survey the volumes which appeared acceptable on other grounds to select the one which provided the most complete reporting of the products for which unit values were desired.

Taking the several theoretical and practical requirements together, it appeared, to the writer that Census unit values for some year in the decade of the 1920's would prove most satisfactory. A survey of the available Censuses for the 1920's revealed that there was no single Census from which unit values for all the necessary types of machinery and equipment could be derived. In the end, although unit values for all the products in any given product group entering into a single subindex were computed from the same census year, it was necessary to draw on three Censuses to obtain unit values for all the groups desired.

Unit values for agricultural machinery and equipment, metal-cutting machine tools, and the group consisting of sewing machines, typewriters, motorcycles, and bicycles were taken from the *Biennial Census of Manufactures 1927*; unit values for textile machinery were taken from the *Biennial Census of Manufactures 1925*. Business conditions were "normal" in both of these years, and it is unlikely that price relatives changed appreciably within any one product group. No census prior to the *Census of Manufactures 1947* published data from which unit values for an adequate number of items of construction and road-building equipment and hoisting and handling equipment could be derived. This was unfortunate both because unusual demand conditions may have distorted price relationships in 1947 and because equipment design and production techniques undoubtedly changed a great deal in the 20 years from 1927 to 1947. The writer's decision to use unit values from 1947 was based on the hope that, granted the hazards, gross price differences among basic types of equipment would remain, although quite possibly considerably modified. It was likewise felt that to include the production of construction and road-building equipment and hoisting and handling equipment in the machinery index, even under these conditions, was preferable to omitting it altogether.

The problem of matching Soviet and American products deserves special comment. The writer can claim no more than a layman's familiarity with many of the more specialized types of equipment concerned. While identical nomenclature was employed in the Soviet and U. S. sources for many items, for many others, designations differed, and the writer was forced to exercise discretion in the pairing of products from the two sources. Although the writer proceeded with caution in this regard and referred frequently to various engineering and technical handbooks, equipment catalogues, and encyclopedia articles explaining the intricacies of machinery of various types to the layman, he has no doubt that he has committed blunders which an investigator having an adequate knowledge of engineering could have avoided. The reader who has this knowledge can test the writer's pairing of items by referring to the detailed tables C(i) to C(vi), below.

There are some cases, however, where no amount of engineering information could improve the matching of items. These are the cases in which the product designation used in the Soviet or U. S. source refers not to a single item of equipment but to a type of equipment within which there may be a considerable range with respect to size and specialized function. Thus, for example, while Soviet production statistics for power shovels distinguish only single and multiple bucket shovels, the *Census of Manufactures* for 1947 lists the following subdivisions under the general heading "power cranes, draglines, and shovels": (1) "crawlers mounted" under which there are seven subdivisions by capacity of the bucket in cubic yards, (2) "truck or wheel mounted" with two subdivisions for bucket capacity under and over ¾ cubic yards, (3) "walking draglines and walking cranes," (4) "ditchers and trenchers" divided into "ladder type," "wheel and blade type," and "type not specified," in addition to (5) a general miscellaneous category. In the absence of more detailed specifications for Soviet equipment, matching of Soviet equipment types with those given in the *Census of Manufactures* clearly was a fairly arbitrary procedure. Moreover, even when the classification of types of equipment was fairly detailed so that the problem of dealing with a range of equipment was negligible, in the absence of technical specifications, one could not be sure that identical Soviet and U. S. Census nomenclature referred to identical pieces of machinery and equipment so far as design, capacity, and motive power were concerned. Unless there were specific indications to the contrary, the writer usually assumed that Soviet equipment approximated the less complex U. S. equipment of the type in question.

What can be said of the possible effects of introducing these subindices weighted with American unit values into the production index for Soviet machinery? The effect depends on variations in the relative weights assigned to different products with the substitution of U. S. unit values for Soviet pay-roll weights. It is quite possible that some definite bias has been introduced by this substitution of weights. Whether the resulting machinery index increases more or less rapidly than would have been the case had Soviet pay-roll weights been used is conjectural.

One view has been expressed by Professor Alexander Gerschenkron. According to this view, a lower rate of growth for Soviet machinery output should be obtained when U. S. values are used than when Soviet values are used as weights. Professor Gerschenkron writes: "Applying 1939 machinery prices of the advanced American economy as weights to Soviet machinery output over a period of years should result *in a rate of growth lower than the one that would be shown by any index of Soviet machinery output based on Russian prices.*"[5]

This conclusion rests on a concept of industrialization as a process at the beginning of which "highly fabricated" goods are both scarce and expensive compared to "low fabricated" goods, but during which the quantity of "highly fabricated" goods increases and their prices decline relative to "low fabricated" goods.[6] Thus, the spread between prices of low and highly fabricated goods may be expected to be greater, the less mature industrially a country is. Since highly fabricated goods increase more rapidly than low fabricated goods in the process of industrialization, the use of preindustrialization (that is, Russian) value weights for machinery output will result in a higher rate of growth for the machinery industry than if postindustialization (that is, American) price weights are used.

The Soviet economy may well have been backward relative to the United States in the 1930's and may still be today. Whether the structure of its system of industrial prices, especially machinery prices, was during the 1930's or is now backward (or preindustrialization) relative to the price structure of the United States is quite another matter.

In the early stages of industrialization, a backward country can scarcely avoid having a preindustrialization price structure. But for how long after embarking on an industrialization program does a backward country retain a preindustrialization price structure? If the prices of "highly fabricated" goods may be expected to decline relative to prices of "low fabricated" goods during the process of industrialization, there would appear to be no inherent limitation to this process to cause it to stop short of achieving a structure of relative prices comparable to that of an advanced country. Given proper conditions of differential changes in productive efficiency in different product lines, a backward country might even achieve an internal price structure more "advanced" than that of the more modern and more productive economy of an advanced country. Such a structure of internal price relatives would be perfectly consistent with higher absolute prices for all products produced in the backward country than in the advanced country.

Thus, no *a priori* statement with respect to the effect of substitution of American for Soviet value weights in the Soviet machinery index appears to be possible. Whatever the effect, its importance should not be exaggerated. First, its influence is diminished by the reweighting of the subindices by Russian value weights before they are included in the index for the machinery industry as a whole. Second, only 27 per cent of the entire net value-added weight of the machinery index as a whole (or about five per cent of the total net value-added weight for all industry) is assigned to the six subindices constructed with American unit value weights. Moreover, any judgment as to the degree of upward or downward bias in the machinery index as a whole relative to an ideal index would have to take into account numerous other factors. Among these may be mentioned the comprehensiveness of product coverage, representativeness of product series included in the index, relation of conventional units of measure to physical units, and others. The problem of coverage is discussed in Chapter 4.

For the presentation of the *Census of Manufactures* data from which unit values were derived along with the machinery subindices which were computed using U. S. unit value weights, see Tables C(i) to C(vi), below.

APPENDIX D

Revised Production Indices for Soviet Large-Scale Industry, 1927–28 to 1937

The following notes apply to Table D, below.* To obtain the industry indices shown in Table D, the physical product series of Table A were converted into quantity relatives as a percentage of the output of each in 1934, and these quantity relatives were then weighted by values from Table B and their arithmetic mean value calculated industry by industry. In the process of obtaining quantity relatives there were some cases in which lack of data made certain statistical expedients necessary. The purpose of these notes is to explain such expedients as were required. Item *numbers* refer to the major industrial classifications used throughout the appendices. Item *letters* refer to the industrial subgroups distinguished in Tables A and B.

18. *Glass*: The quantity relatives for the glass industry for the years 1927–28 to 1934 are based on the total tonnage of glass articles of all types produced; for the years 1935–1951 on the production of window glass in 1000 square meters using production of window glass in 1000 square meters as the base for 1934. In 1934 window glass accounted for 96 per cent of sheet glass measured in square meters, while sheet glass in turn accounted for 54 per cent of the production of all glass articles in 1934 measured in metric tons.

19. *Leather tanning*: To obtain a single quantity relative for the leather-tanning industry the quantity series for large hides and that for small hides were each expressed as quantity relatives and a single arithmetic mean of these two quantity relatives calculated giving equal weight to each of the two series. Since in most years there were between two and three times as many small hides produced as large hides, this equal weight is equivalent to setting one large hide equal to between two and three small hides.

20 (h). *Knitted wear*: To obtain a single quantity relative for knitted wear each of the three constituent series, namely socks and stockings in million pairs, knitted underwear in million pieces, knitted outerwear in million pieces, was expressed as a quantity relative and an arithmetic mean of quantity relatives was calculated giving equal weight to each of the three series.

22 (i & j). *Processing of fruits and vegetables and canning*: No data for the processing of fruits and vegetables were available after 1934 while for canning

* See Tabular Section following p. 189.

no data were available prior to 1932. Therefore, to obtain a more extended quantity series the quantity series for the two separate sets of data were linked and the resulting single quantity series was assigned the joint value-added weight of the two separate industrial processes. The writer feels that this operation is justified since the series for the processing of fruits and vegetables

TABLE D1

Quantity Relative to Base Year 1934 (per cent)

	1932	1933	1934
Processing of fruits and vegetables	80.1	77.0	100.0
Canning	80.8	80.3	100.0

includes the canning series, and since the two series move quite closely together during the three years, 1932–1934, when their simultaneous movement can be observed. The final series of quantity relatives for processing of fruits and vegetables and canning consists of the quantity relatives for processing of fruits and vegetables for the years 1929–30 to 1934 and the quantity relatives for canning for the years 1935–1951.

23. *Machinery*: Quantity relatives for textile machinery, construction and road-building machinery, hoisting and handling equipment, metal-cutting machine tools, and the group consisting of sewing machines, typewriters, bicycles and motorcycles are actually subindices constructed from production data in physical units taken from Soviet statistical sources and then weighted by unit values computed from data in the *Census of Manufactures* compiled and published by the Bureau of the Census of the United States Department of Commerce. Details of these computations are contained in Appendix C. The quantity relative for metal-cutting machine tools for 1941 is based simply on a comparison of total numbers of such tools produced in 1934 and 1941.

23 C2. *Agricultural machinery*: Quantity relatives for agricultural machinery for the years 1927–28 to 1935 inclusive were obtained by constructing an index based on production data in physical units taken from Soviet statistical sources and unit value weights taken from the *Census of Manufactures*. Details of this computation are presented in Appendix C. Lack of sufficient production data for agricultural equipment for the years 1936–1937 made it necessary to devise a different method to obtain quantity relatives for those two years. The projection was finally made on the basis of a series giving the annual consumption of ferrous metals in the agricultural machinery industry for the years 1932–1938. The writer constructed this series from data given by L. R. Shulkin in *Potreblenie chernykh metallov v SSSR* (Consumption of Ferrous Metals in the USSR; statistical handbook; Moscow, 1940), tables 1–5, pp. 20–28. The tables show the consumption of ordinary rolled steel, quality rolled steel, pig iron,

and ferro-alloys in thousands of metric tons by different branches of the machinery industry. There is a separate entry in the tables for agricultural machinery and for tractors, so that the coverage of the statistics on the consumption of ferrous metals may reasonably be assumed to correspond to that of the production series for agricultural machinery. Table D2 below presents the statistics for consumption of ferrous metals by the agricultural machinery branch of the machinery industry.

Table D3 compares the quantity relatives for the consumption of ferrous metals by the agricultural machinery branch of the machinery industry with the subindex for agricultural machinery computed from Soviet production data in physical units and census unit values.

For the years 1933–1935 the two series of quantity relatives move in close harmony. On the assumption that this close relationship continued in 1936 and 1937 the index of ferrous metals consumption in the production of agricultural machinery has been substituted for the output of agricultural machinery in

TABLE D2

Consumption of Ferrous Metals in Agricultural Machinery

(1000 metric tons)

	1932	1933	1934	1935	1936	1937	1938
Rolled steel							
Ordinary	225.7	234.6	241.6	347.3	534.3	519.6	447.2
Quality	12.3	16.3	13.0	27.2	38.2	52.7	31.7
Pig iron and ferro-alloys	127.2	139.2	164.8	211.0	187.8	181.2	141.0
Total	365.2	390.1	419.4	585.5	760.3	753.5	619.9
per cent of 1934	87.0	93.0	100.0	139.6	181.3	179.7	147.8

TABLE D3

Indices for Agricultural Machinery

(per cent of 1934)

	1932	1933	1934	1935	1936	1937	1938
(1) Production index	96.5	90.1	100.0	139.7	—	—	—
(2) Index of ferrous metals consumption	87.0	93.0	100.0	139.6	181.3	179.7	147.8
(3) Ratio of (1) to (2)	110.9	96.9	100.0	100.0	—	—	—

these two years. Table D4 presents the subindex for the production of agricultural machinery which is the result of these computations.

These are the quantity relatives which receive the weight for agricultural machinery in the computation of the general production index.

TABLE D4

Subindex for the Production of Agricultural Machinery
(per cent of 1934)

1927–28	143.8	1933	90.1
1928–29	188.8	1934	100.0
1929–30	198.2	1935	139.7
1931	128.0	1936	181.3
1932	96.5	1937	179.7

Notes

Chapter 1: Official Measures of Soviet Industrial Production

1. TsUNKhU, *Socialist Construction in the USSR* (Moscow, 1936), p. 23.

2. As defined in Soviet practice, large-scale industry includes mining, fishing, and lumbering in addition to manufacturing. Primarily, large-scale industry is composed of all basic industrial enterprises of the industrial ministries regardless of the number of workers employed or the use of mechanical power in them with the exception of subsidiary (by-product) establishments and establishments subject to the supervision of regional industrial administrations. In addition, large-scale industry includes those establishments of an industrial nature within the industrial ministries or subject to regional industrial administrations which are engaged in construction, marketing, scientific experimental work, or education, and also those establishments of nonindustrial ministries, of central institutes, of industrial coöperatives, and of collective farms which employ sixteen workers and use mechanical power or employ thirty workers without mechanical power. See *Slovar'-spravochnik po sotsial'no-ekonomicheskoi statistike* (Dictionary Handbook for Social-Economic Statistics; 2nd ed.; Central Statistical Administration of the State Planning Commission: Moscow, 1948), p. 108.

3. A. I. Rotshtein, *Problemy promyshlennoi statistiki SSSR* (Problems of Industrial Statistics in the USSR; State Social-Economic Press: Leningrad Division, 1936), I, 325.

4. Rotshtein, *loc. cit.*, pp. 324–25.

5. R. Riz, "Ob ischislenii valovoi produktsii promyshlennosti," (Calculating Gross Output of Industry), *Plan*, no. 12, 1934.

6. The following discussion of valuation procedure in theory and in practice is based on Rotshtein, *Problemy promyshlennoi statistiki SSSR*, I, 238–252.

7. Three main classes of goods are recognized in Soviet industrial statistics: finished goods, semi-fabricates, and unfinished goods. *Finished goods* are those which are to undergo no further processing within a given enterprise, which are complete in every detail, and have been accepted by technical control or by the representative of the purchaser. *Semi-fabricates* are goods which have been completely processed by a given shop or process within an enterprise but which are intended for further processing within a different production division or shop of the same enterprise. For example, yarn is a semi-fabricate in a textile mill, and pig iron in a steel mill. *Unfinished goods* are those which have not been completely processed within a given shop or those which, although completely processed, have not yet been accepted by technical control or by the representative of the purchaser. Work still set up in machine tools is an example of unfinished goods. Central Statistical Administration of Gosplan USSR, *Slovar'-spravochnik po sotsial'no-ekonomicheskoi statistike* (Gosplanizdat: Moscow, 1944), pp. 59–60.

8. A. Zelonovskii, "Tsenniki neizmennykh tsen 1926–27 g." (Price Lists of Constant 1926–27 Prices), *Plan*, no. 8, 1935, pp. 30–32; "Kak primeniat' unifitsirovannye tsenniki neizmennykh tsen 1926–27 g." (How to Use the Unified Lists of Constant Prices of 1926–27), *Plan*, no. 19, 1935, pp. 57–58.

9. The major discrepancies in the two systems of prices were expected in products of local industries and the wood and light (textiles, etc.) industries. The article which discusses this problem gives a purely theoretical example in which the value of output in the revised 1926–27 prices is 8 per cent above that in the unrevised 1926–27 prices. (See "Kak primeniat' unifitsirovannye tsenniki neizmennykh tsen 1926–27 g.," *Plan*, no. 19, 1935, pp. 57–58.) It

was expected that replacement of 1932 prices by 1926–27 prices in calculating output totals for producers' coöperatives, local industry and other branches of industry which had used 1932 prices or current prices previous to the 1936 reform would reduce the value of output in these branches. However, as late as 1937 output of the industrial coöperatives was still planned in 1932 prices and then converted to 1926–27 prices by means of a general coefficient. (See "Ukazaniia i formy k sostavleniiu narodnokhoziaistvennogo plana na 1937 g." [Instructions and Forms for the Preparation of the National Economic Plan for 1937], *Plan*, no. 18, 1936, p. 29.) Revised 1926–27 prices were used in planning and reporting the output of local industry for the first time in 1937. (See "Unifitsirovannye neizmennye tseny 1926–27 g. v mestnoi promyshlennosti" [Unified Constant Prices of 1926–27 for Local Industry], *Plan*, no. 5, 1937, pp. 58–59.) Thus any deflating of output totals on this account was postponed to 1937.

10. Rotshtein, *op. cit.*, I, 247.
11. *Ibid.*, I, 253.
12. *Ibid.*, I, 246.
13. The following figures are in billions of rubles and at 1926–27 prices. Figures for large-scale industry are taken from *Sotsialisticheskoe stroitel'stvo SSSR*, 1936 TsUNKhU (Moscow, 1936), p. 3.

Output Leningrad Industry		*Total Industrial Output*	*Per Cent*
1932	4.520	38.800	11.6
1934	5.065	50.600	10.0

14. The production of important types of industrial commodities in the Leningrad oblast in 1935 and their share in the total output in the USSR, taken from the *Narodnokhoziaistvennyi plan na 1936 god*, Tom vtoroi, *Plan razvitiia raionov* [The Economic Plan for 1936, vol. II, Plan for the Development of Regions]; Moscow: Gosplan, 1936), p. 292, are as follows:

Commodity	*Unit of Measurement*	*Output*	*Per Cent of Total Output*
Production of electric energy by regional power stations	mil. kw	2446.6	13.51
Peat	1000 tons	2037.8	11.02
Oil shale	1000 tons	177.0	42.55
Steel	1000 tons	463.2	3.70
Rolled steel	1000 tons	339.6	3.78
Metalworking	mil. roubles	2785.0	21.13
Cement	1000 tons	156.7	3.49
Bricks	mil. units	378.0	6.63
Sawn lumber	mil. cu. meters	2033.0	8.16
Paper	1000 tons	197.4	30.93
Cotton cloth	mil. meters	149.2	5.99
Woolen cloth	mil. meters	3.8	5.05
Leather footwear	mil. pairs	18.9	24.64
Fish caught	1000 tons	203.5	16.25

15. Gosplan, *Vtoroi piatiletnyi plan razvitiia narodnogo khoziaistva SSSR* (1933–1937) tom vtoroi, plan razvitiia raionov [Second Five Year Plan for the Development of the National Economy of the USSR, Plan for Regional Development]; Moscow, 1934), I, 348.
16. Ia. A. Ioffe as quoted by Alexander Gerschenkron, *A Dollar Index of Soviet Machinery Output, 1927–28 to 1937* (The Rand Corporation, 1951), p. 5.

17. Gerschenkron, *op. cit.*, pp. 5–6.

Naum Jasny, *The Soviet Price System* (Stanford University Press: November 1951), p. 170.

18. Jasny, *The Socialized Agriculture of the USSR* (Stanford University Press: 1949), pp. 784–785.

19. Jasny, *Soviet Prices of Producers' Goods* (Stanford University Press, 1952).

20. *Ibid.*, footnote to table, p. 15.

21. *Ibid.*

22. See, for example, Maurice Dobb, "Comment on Soviet Statistics," *Soviet Studies* (University of Glasgow, June 1949), vol. I:1, pp. 21–22.

23. Sh. Turetskii, "Dlia chego planiruetsia produktsiia v neizmennykh tsenakh 1926–27 g." ("Why Plan Production in the Constant Prices of 1926–27?"), *Plan*, no. 11, 1935, pp. 62–63.

24. Sh. Turetskii, "K probleme tsenovykh pokazatelei v plane" (The Problem of Value Indices in the Plan), *Plan*, no. 5, 1934, p. 39. Italics added.

25. A. Kurskii, Review of *Narodnyi dokhod SSSR, ego obrazovanie i uchet* (National Income of the USSR, Its Formation and Computation; ed. D. I. Chernomordik) *Planovoe khoziaistvo*, no. 1, 1940. Italics added.

26. G. V. Teplov, *Planirovanie na mashinostroitel'nykh zavodakh* (Planning in Machinery Plants; State Scientific Press for Literature for the Machinery Industry: Moscow, 1949), p. 216.

27. For a description of current practice in the valuation of Soviet industrial production see S. A. Shchenkov, *Otchetnost' promyshlennykh predpriiatii* (Accounts of Industrial Enterprises, Moscow: State Statistical Press, 1952), pp. 40–49.

Chapter 2: Value-Added Weights for Soviet Industry

1. Naum Jasny, *Soviet Prices of Producers' Goods*, 1952.

2. See, for example, Alexander Gerschenkron, *A Dollar Index of Soviet Machinery Output, 1927–28 to 1937*, April 6, 1951.

3. The difference between valuing output in prices of a different economy and in prices of a different year, however, is merely one of degree.

4. See Edwin Frickey, *Production in the United States, 1860–1914* (Harvard University Press, 1947), chap. II; Solomon Fabricant, *The Output of Manufacturing Industries 1899–1937* (National Bureau of Economic Research, Inc., 1940), appendix C.

5. Fabricant, *op. cit.*, p. 348.

6. *Ibid.*

7. For example, see *National Income Supplement to the Survey of Current Business*, July 1947, p. 27, footnote 1.

8. U. S. Department of Commerce, Office of Business Economics, *National Income and Product of the United States 1929–1950* (Washington, 1951), p. 26. In a subsequent paragraph the publication adds "The classification of business taxes in this report is dictated by the belief that the above assumptions about tax shifting are the most realistic summary ones that can be made. It may be noted, however, that the entire subject of tax shifting and incidence is a rather controversial one and that definitive and final conclusions are not available."

9. Note, however, that American workers have a third source of income not available to Soviet workers, namely, income from property and investments, which reduces the relative importance of salaries and wages in determining their real income. A Soviet worker, however, may invest in government bonds upon which interest is paid.

10. Abram Bergson, *The Structure of Soviet Wages* (Harvard University Press, 1946), p. 35.

11. This statement is based on a comparison of the relation of the director's fund (of which such profits are *a part*) per employee to the average annual wage in a number of industries in 1936. According to L. Vilenskii, "Finansovye voprosy promyshlennosti" (Financial Questions of Industry), *Planovoe khoziaistvo*, no. 10, 1938, p. 63.

"On the average for the five industrial commissariats the director's fund per employee came to 6.3% of the average annual wage. However, for several branches this per cent is considerably higher and reaches 21.5% for lumber and wood-working, about 25% for the fur industry and the leather footwear industry, and up to 55% for the liquor, macaroni, and feed (*kombikormovoi*) industries."

Since a large per cent of profits in excess of plan (approximately 50 per cent during the mid-1930's) was assigned to the director's fund, an unusually large director's fund per employee implies unusually large profits in excess of plan.

12. With the exception of interest paid to individuals for savings deposits and on government loans.

13. The writer is indebted to his colleague, Professor Franklyn D. Holzman, of the University of Washington, for assistance in distinguishing between the functions of the turnover and profits taxes as instruments of financial and fiscal policy. A more detailed discussion of these taxes and related matters will be found in Professor Holzman's forthcoming book, *Taxation in the Soviet Union*, to be published by the Harvard University Press.

14. See A. K. Suchkov, *Gosudarstvennye dokhody SSSR* (State Income of the USSR; Gosfinizdat, 1949), pp. 68–71, 136–139.

15. Compare the treatment of indirect taxes by the U. S. Department of Commerce as indicated by the quotation on p. 21 above.

16. During the period of the 1930's at least, apparently not even the Central Statistical Office of the Soviet State Planning Commission knew the exact composition of the cost category "other money outlays." According to A. I. Pashkov, the annual reports submitted by industrial enterprises in these years did not require any breakdown of the cost category "other money outlays." In 1938 the Central Statistical Office conducted a sampling survey of industrial enterprises in the Moscow area to determine the content of the "other money outlays" item. The survey, of limited applicability because of the nonrepresentatives of the sample, revealed that 26 per cent of the costs entered in this category were material costs and the remaining 74 per cent were assignable to net value-added. See A. I. Pashkov in *Narodnyi dokhod SSSR* (National Income of the USSR) ed. Professor D. I. Chernomordik Moscow-Leningrad: State Planning Commission Press, 1939), pp. 59–60.

17. This formulation was suggested to the writer by his colleague, Alexander Erlich, of the Russian Research Center, Harvard University.

18. Abram Bergson, *The Structure of Soviet Wages*.

19. *Ibid.*, p. 207. The statistical measure used is the quartile ratio of the earnings frequency distribution for each industry.

20. *Ibid.*, p. 209.

21. *Ibid.*, p. 147.

22. *Ibid.*, pp. 152–53.

23. *Ibid.*

Chapter 3: Statistical Procedures in Constructing the Production Index

1. It may be in order to comment briefly on the difference between imputed and earned weights. In an index which employs earned weights, each physical quantity series or quantity relative is given a weight in proportion to the value or value-added in production of that particular product alone. Such a value in any year is usually determined by multiplying the quantity of the product produced by a price or unit value from the base period or year. If the earned weight is being applied to a quantity relative for the particular product, the weight is the total value or value-added in production in the base period rather than the unit value. The total weight for an industry is the sum of the earned weights for the various products produced within the industry which are physically represented in the index. The value of products produced within the industry for which either no specific quantity data or specific value weights are available is excluded from the production index.

When imputed weights are employed, the procedure is to establish the general value or value-added weight for the entire industry in question and to subdivide this general weight on the basis of relevant criteria among the available quantity relatives for the products produced by that industry. In this system of weighting, the full base-period weight for the industry is assigned to the available quantity relatives for products of the industry regardless of whether or not these represent the full variety of individual products produced by the industry. This procedure assumes that the production of the missing products moves in accordance with the weighted mean of the products physically included in the index. Exceptions may be made and the general weight for the industry correspondingly reduced when there are reasons to believe that the movement in the production of certain of the missing products has been erratic in relation to the production of those products which are included.

Earned weights require more detailed and comprehensive weighting and quantity data for individual products than do imputed weights. On theoretical grounds there is no clear case for preferring either earned or imputed weights. Which system is preferable depends largely on the coverage of individual products which it is possible to obtain with the available data, that system of weights being preferable which permits of the most complete coverage in the given instance.

2. *Socialist Construction in the USSR*, 1936, pp. 4, 5.

3. Official statistics as quoted in Abram Bergson, *The Structure of Soviet Wages*, p. 147.

4. See "O dvukh krugakh ucheta promyshlennoi statistiki i statistiki truda" (The Two Spheres of Recording of Industrial and Labor Statistics) *Planovoe khoziaistvo*, no. 3, 1938, p. 173; and *Socialist Construction in the USSR*, 1936, p. 394.

5. *Trud v SSSR* (1934 god), ezhegodnik, (Labor in the USSR, 1934 yearbook; Central Administration of National-Economic Accounting of the State Planning Commission, Moscow, 1935), pp. 62–72.

6. *Ibid.* pp. 74–83.

7. *Ibid.* pp. 144–167.

8. *Socialist Construction in the USSR* (Central Administration of Economic and Social Statistics of the State Planning Commission of the USSR, Moscow, 1936), pp. 42–47.

9. The workers' pay roll as per cent of total pay roll for major industrial groups is calculated from *Trud v SSSR*, 1934, pp. 62–72, 74–83, 144–167 and is as follows:

Industry	*Per Cent*	*Industry*	*Per Cent*
Coal	80	Chemicals	67
Crude oil extraction	72	Rubber goods	75
Petroleum refining	66	Publishing	71
Peat	79	Wood processing	78
Electric power	65	Cement	75
Ferrous metals	76	Textiles	81
Nonferrous metals	67	Food	63
Ore mining	72	Machinery	69

10. See the tables showing the breakdown of costs of production in industry on pages 32–34 of *Sotsialisticheskoe stroitel'stvo* (Socialist Construction; Central Administration of National-Economic Accounting of the State Planning Commission: Moscow, 1936).

11. *Narodnokhoziaistvennyi plan na 1936 god* (National-Economic Plan for the Year 1936; 2nd ed.; State Planning Commission Press: Moscow, 1936), pp. 392–393.

Chapter 4: Production of Soviet Large-Scale Industry, 1927–28 to 1937

1. *Socialist Construction in the USSR* (Moscow, 1936), p. 42.

2. See pp. 35–42 above for a discussion of estimates of net value-added in Soviet industry.

3. *Trud v SSSR*, 1936, pp. 20–21.

4. *Trud v SSSR* (1934 god), ezhegodnik (Labor in the USSR, 1934 yearbook; TsUNKhU: Moscow, 1935), p. 63.

5. *Sotsialisticheskoe stroitel'stvo SSSR,* 1936, (TsUNKhU: Moscow, 1936), p. 32.

6. See p. 39 above.

7. *Socialist Construction in the USSR* (Moscow, 1936), p. 42.

8. According to *Trud v SSSR* (Moscow, 1936), p. 21, the pay roll in lumbering in 1934 was 1,662.5 million rubles. If this sum is adjusted upward by an arbitrary 10 per cent to allow for the pay-roll tax and divided by 12 to put it on a basis comparable to the weights used in the revised index, a figure of 152 million rubles is obtained as the net value-added weight for the lumbering industry. This is approximately 13 per cent of the sum of the weights for large-scale industry including lumbering.

9. Gerschenkron, "The Soviet Indices of Industrial Production," *The Review of Economic Statistics,* November, 1947, p. 219, footnote 8.

10. See above, p. 7.

11. See p. 4 above.

12. See *Socialist Construction in the USSR,* p. 49, footnote 6.

13. Note, however, that in 1927–28 both of the revised indices excluded fisheries, since no data on fish caught were available for that year.

14. The reader may compare the revised index with other official indices of Soviet industrial production by referring to Table 1, p. 2.

15. See the discussion of this reform on pp. 6–8 above.

16. "From April 1936, the coal-, peat-, and iron-mining industries, heavy and non-ferrous metal industries, a number of chemical and certain machine-building industries, and the cement and timber industries were deprived of State subsidies . . ." Alexander Baykov, *The Development of the Soviet Economic System* (New York: The Macmillan Company, 1947), p. 295.

Chapter 5: Production of Soviet Large-Scale Industry, 1937–1951

1. The first published work of this kind was an article by Abram Bergson, James H. Blackman, and Alexander Erlich, "Postwar Economic Reconstruction and Development in the U.S.S.R." in *The Annals of the American Academy of Political and Social Science,* May, 1949. Materials presented by these authors have been utilized in the present study along with additional and more recent materials from Soviet sources. See Appendix A.

2. *Gosudarstvennyi plan razvitiia narodnogo khoziaistva SSSR na 1941 god.* (State Plan for the development of the National Economy of the USSR in 1941.)

3. See the discussion in Chapter 1.

4. See the discussion in Chapter 4, pp. 79–80.

5. A Soviet journal, *Soviet Finance,* contains evidence of the inflation of production values occasioned by the introduction of war-time substitutes. The table below compares the physical and value indices of production of perfume and eau de cologne and of powder by a cosmetics factory in the years 1940–1944. It will be observed that the production index in constant prices exceeds that in physical units for all years, in some cases, by more than 100 per cent.

The authors explain that wartime conversion and the introduction of substitutes in the cosmetics industry posed the problem of calculating "constant 1926–27 prices" for the substitute products. Current wholesale prices were converted to "constant 1926–27 prices" by applying the old, average coefficient of price change for prewar (1940) products. Since wartime conditions had caused wholesale prices of the war years to be even higher relative to 1926–27 prices than the prices of 1940, use of the 1940 conversion coefficient resulted in a similar inflation of "constant 1926–27 prices" relative to 1940. Actually, the unit costs of production for wartime substitutes were below those of the peacetime article. Thus, while costs of production fell, the value of output at "constant 1926–27 prices" actually rose.

Production Data for a Cosmetics Factory

Year	Perfume and Eau de Cologne: Physical Output	Perfume and Eau de Cologne: Output in Constant Prices	Powder: Physical Output	Powder: Output in Constant Prices
1940	100.0	100.0	100.0	100.0
1941	40.4	57.8	52.4	48.2
1942	20.2	43.4	35.5	150.0
1943	16.7	64.8	26.1	122.4
1944 (Plan)	18.6	79.3	34.3	148.0

These data are taken from N. Zaimova, N. Rochko, "O metodakh otsenki produktsii v neizmennykh tsenakh," *Sovetskie finansy* 6–7, 1944, ("Methods of Valuing Products in Constant Prices," *Soviet Finance* 6–7, 1944; State Planning Commission Press), pp. 30–32.

6. Computed output of the Soviet machinery and metalworking industry in 1941 is 61.0 billion 1926–27 rubles. (See Table 15 in the text.) The *1941 Plan*, p. 9, gives the value of output of the heavy, medium, and light machinery commissariats and the electrical industry commissariat as 19.5 billion 1926–27 rubles and the output of the four defense industry commissariats as 31.9 billion 1926–27 rubles. Total production of these commissariats is 51.4 billion 1926–27 rubles compared to total planned output of the machinery and metalworking industry of 61.0 billion 1926–27 rubles. Unless the production of the Defense Commissariats is classified as machinery and metalworking production, it is difficult to see how Voznesensky's total for machinery and metalworking production is to be obtained. The remaining 10 billion 1926–27 rubles of machinery and metalworking output presumably was scheduled for production in other branches of heavy industry and in the industrial coöperatives.

Chapter 6: Other Measures of Soviet Industrial Growth

1. See sources to Table 16 for references to the work of these authors.

2. For statistics and discussion of the covariation of industrial production and freight transportation indices, see James H. Blackman, "Transportation," in Abram Bergson (ed.), *Soviet Economic Growth* (Evanston: Row, Peterson and Co., 1953); Thor Hultgren, *American Transportation in Prosperity and Depression* (National Bureau of Economic Research, Inc., 1948); and U. N., Economic Commission for Europe, Transport Division, *Annual Bulletin of Transport Statistics 1950*.

3. Demitri B. Shimkin, *Minerals: A Key to Soviet Power* (Harvard Universtiy Press, 1953), pp. 24–26.

4. Gregory Grossman and D. B. Shimkin, *Mineral Consumption and Economic Development in the United States and the Soviet Union*, April 1952. A mimeographed manuscript obtainable on request from the Russian Research Center, Harvard University, Cambridge 38, Massachusetts.

5. *Ibid.*

6. However, some of the production estimates used by Shimkin and Grossman, i.e., Colin Clark's, Naum Jasny's, and that of the Institut für Konjunkturforschung, are discussed later in this chapter.

7. *Ibid.*

8. Thor Hultgren, *American Transportation in Prosperity and Depression* (National Bureau

of Economic Research, Inc., 1948); Gregory Grossman and D. B. Shimkin, *Mineral Consumption and Economic Development in the United States and the Soviet Union.*

9. U.N. Economic Commission for Europe, Transport Division, *Annual Bulletin of Transport Statistics 1950*, p. 9.

10. See sources to Table 16.

11. *Ibid.*

12. Colin Clark, *The Conditions of Economic Progress*, 2d ed., (London: Macmillan and Co., 1951), pp. 185–86.

13. See sources to Table 16.

14. Naum Jasny, *The Soviet Economy During the Plan Era*, pp. 21–22.

15. See Table 1, p. 2.

16. An estimate of the maximum effect of shifting the base for the revised index from fiscal year 1927–28 to calendar year 1928 indicates that the value for 1937 might be reduced from 371 to 354. See pp. 46–47 above.

17. Naum Jasny, *Soviet Prices of Producers' Goods*, appendix tables.

18. Jasny, *Soviet Prices of Producers' Goods*, p. 15, footnotes to table.

19. *Ibid.*

20. Jasny, *The Soviet Economy During the Plan Era*, p. 18.

21. If it is correct to assume that weights for Jasny's index of industrial prices are taken from output of state industry in the year 1926–27, it follows that the production index (obtained by deflating industrial output in current prices by Jasny's price index) is implicitly weighted by prices not of the base year 1926–27 but of the other year involved in the comparison (i.e. the given year). Thus Jasny's index of industrial production appears to be characterized by a changing regimen of weights which vary from one given year to the next. This somewhat surprising conclusion follows from the simple algebra of Jasny's procedure. Let $\Sigma\, pq$ represent the value of industrial production in any year where the p's stand for prices and the q's for quantities. Let the subscript "o" indicate the base year and the subscript "l" indicate the given year. Then Jasny's production index is derived as follows:

$$(1)\qquad \frac{\dfrac{\Sigma\, p_1q_1}{\dfrac{\Sigma\, p_1q_o}{\Sigma\, p_oq_o}}}{\Sigma\, p_oq_o} = \frac{\Sigma\, p_1q_1}{\Sigma\, p_1q_o},$$

that is, the price weights for the production index are taken from the given year. Had Jasny desired to obtain a production index with base-year weights, it would have been necessary for him to employ changing given year weights in constructing his price index.

Since Jasny's purpose was to obtain the value of Soviet industrial output in "real 1926–27 prices" what he needed was a production index weighted by base year (1926–27) price weights. What his production values in fact appear to be is the rather curious value obtained from the following expression:

$$(2)\qquad \frac{\Sigma\, p_1q_1}{\dfrac{\Sigma\, p_1q_o}{\Sigma\, p_oq_o}}$$

in which the price index deflator is computed with base-year rather than given-year quantity weights. Clearly, the value of industrial production obtained from expression (2) is not in "1926–27 prices" in any sense and may not properly be aggregated, gross or net, with other values actually expressed in 1926–27 prices (e.g. as in computing national income in the given year). If Jasny actually followed this procedure, it provides further grounds for questioning the validity of his findings.

The fact that Jasny's production index implicitly uses given-year weights need not provide any further explanation of the discrepancies between Jasny's index and that developed in this study, since the difference between base- and given-year weighted indices turns on weight correlation bias and this is not *a priori* predictable. (See Edwin Frickey, "The Theory of Index-Number Bias," *The Review of Economic Statistics*, November, 1937, pp. 161–173.) Nevertheless, in the historical circumstances of the Soviet economy, it appears likely that given-year price weights would assign less relative importance than base-year price weights to the rapidly expanding output of new products whose production costs may be presumed to have declined relative to established products. If this is so, then Jasny's production index should register smaller increases than the production index developed in this study. Moreover, the discrepancy between the two production indices probably should increase with each successive year.

22. See *Slovar'-spravochnik po sotsial'no-ekonomicheskoi statistike* (Dictionary-Handbook of Social-Economic Statistics; Gosplanizdat: Moscow, 1948), pp. 130–132.

23. A partial indication of Jasny's procedure in removing turnover taxes from retail prices of final products may be provided by the following statement: "If computation of the wholesale prices of consumers' goods is to be made on the basis of prices free of turnover tax, the taxes must obviously be deducted. Yet no full series of turnover taxes during the entire period is available. Since the level of prices for all industrial goods is vastly important, a discussion is ventured below (Chapter 6) of the wholesale prices of *two important consumers' goods (calico and shoes) in one year, free of tax. These are used in chapter I in computing rough indexes of wholesale prices of all industrial goods, free of tax.*" Jasny, *Soviet Prices of Producers' Goods*, p. 4. Italics added.

24. A. I. Rotshtein, *Problemy promyshlennoi statistiki SSSR* (Problems of Industrial Statistics USSR; State Social-Economic Press: Leningrad Division, 1936), I 254.

25. See, for example, Jasny, *Soviet Prices of Producers' Goods*, p. 3.

26. Jasny, *The Soviet Price System*, p. 114.

27. Jasny, *Soviet Prices of Producers' Goods*, p. 15.

28. *Ibid.*, p. 19.

29. Alexander Gerschenkron, *A Dollar Index of Soviet Machinery Output, 1927–28 to 1937.*

30. Gerschenkron, *A Dollar Index*, p. 49. Italics in original.

31. See the discussion of earned and imputed weights in note 1, Chapter 3 above.

Chapter 7: Aspects of Soviet Industrial Development

1. For a discussion of Soviet labor productivity concepts, see Walter Galenson, "Industrial Labor Productivity," in Abram Bergson (ed.), *Soviet Economic Growth*, pp. 190–194.

2. See p. 42 above.

3. TsUNKhU, *Sotsialisticheskoe stroitel'stvo* (Moscow, 1936), p. 704, footnote 5.

4. See pp. 35–37 above.

5. Output indices for large-scale and census industry may be compared in Table 1, p. 2. above.

6. Ia. A. Ioffe, *SSSR i kapitalisticheskie strany* (USSR and the Capitalist Countries; Gosplanizdat: Moscow, 1939), p. 75.

7. *Ibid.*, footnote 1.

8. *Izvestiia TSIK*, June 27, 1940.

9. Rates calculated from data in Solomon Fabricant, *Employment in Manufacturing 1899–1939* (National Bureau of Economic Research, Inc., New York, 1942), p. 331.

10. Norman M. Kaplan, "Capital Formation and Allocation," in Abram Bergson (ed.), *Soviet Economic Growth*, pp. 48–50.

11. *Ibid.*, pp. 40, 59.

12. The question of a labor shortage in the Soviet economy turns mainly upon whether or not the labor surplus which existed in Soviet agriculture in 1928 has now been completely absorbed. For an affirmative view, see Joseph A. Kershaw, "Agricultural Output and Employment," in Abram Bergson (ed.), *Soviet Economic Growth*, pp. 294–308; and Naum Jasny, *The Socialized Agriculture of the USSR*, passim, and especially chap. XVIII, pp. 415–446. For an argument that surplus labor remains in Soviet agriculture, see I. M. Finegood, "A Critical Analysis of Some Prevailing Concepts Concerning Soviet Agriculture," in *Soviet Studies*, July, 1952.

13. P. Evseev, "Rezervy uvelicheniia vypuska tovarov shirokogo potrebleniia v mestnoi i kooperativnoi promyshlennosti" (Reserves for Increasing the Production of Consumers' Goods in Local and Coöperative Industry; *Planovoe khoziaistvo*, no. 4, 1948).

14. For a discussion of some aspects of this problem, see Alexander Gerschenkron, *A Dollar Index of Soviet Machinery Output, 1927–28 to 1937*, pp. 47–57.

15. *Ibid.*

16. Walter Galenson, "Industrial Labor Productivity," in Abram Bergson (ed.), *Soviet Economic Growth*, pp. 207–214.

Appendix B: Derivation of Weights

1. *Proizvoditel'nost' truda v promyshlennosti SSSR* (The Productivity of Labor in the Industry of the USSR; ed. P. A. Khromov; Moscow: State Planning Commission Press, 1940), p. 213.

2. See *Sostialisticheskoe stroitel'stvo* 1936, p. 164.

3. Identification of plants and models of vehicles from A. Kogan, "Automobile Types in the Third 5 Year Plan," *Avto-Traktornoe delo* no. 6, 1937, pp. 205–210. Output of vehicles from *Sotsialisticheskoe stroitel'stvo* 1936, p. 165.

4. Number of production workers in the respective plants taken from *Problemy ekonomiki*, no. 6, 1935, p. 79.

Appendix C: The Machinery Index

1. *Proizvoditel'nost' truda v promyshlennosti SSSR* (The Productivity of Labor in the Industry of the USSR; ed. P. A. Khromov; Moscow: State Planning Commission Press, 1940), p. 213.

2. B. I. Anokhin and V. G. Rozanov, *Kolesnye traktory* (Wheel Tractors; Moscow: State Publishing House for Agricultural Literature, 1946), pp. 3–6.

3. *Malaia Sovetskaia entsiklopediia* (State Institute "Soviet Encyclopedia"; Moscow: 1940), X, 807.

4. Data from *Socialist Construction in the USSR*, 1936, p. 76.

5. Alexander Gerschenkron, *A Dollar Index of Soviet Machinery Output, 1927–28 to 1937* (The RAND Corporation, 1951), p. 49.

6. *Ibid.*, pp. 47–50.

Bibliography

I. OFFICIAL GOVERNMENT PUBLICATIONS

A. *Russian*

Gosudarstvennaia planovaia komissiia Soiuza SSR (State Planning Commission of the Union SSR), abbr. as Gosplan, *Itogi vypolneniia pervogo piatiletnogo plana razvitiia narodnogo khoziaistva Soiuza SSR* (Summary of the Fulfillment of the First Five Year Plan of the Development of the Economy of the USSR), Moscow: Gosplanizdat, 1933.

—— *Narodnokhoziaistvennyi plan na 1935 god* (The Economic Plan for 1935), 2d. ed., Moscow: Gosplanizdat, 1935.

—— *Narodnokhoziaistvennyi plan na 1936 god* (The Economic Plan for 1936), 2d. ed., Moscow: Gosplanizdat, 1936.

—— *Narodnokhoziaistvennyi plan na 1936*, tom vtoroi, *Plan razvitiia raionov* (The Economic Plan for 1936, vol. II, Plan for the Development of Regions), Moscow: Gosplan, 1936.

—— *Narodno-khoziaistvennyi Plan Soiuza SSR na 1937 god* (Economic Plan of the Union SSR for the Year 1937), Moscow: Gosplanizdat, 1937.

—— *SSSR i kapitalisticheskie strany* (USSR and the Capitalist Countries), ed. by Ia. A. Ioffe, Moscow-Leningrad: Gosplanizdat, 1939.

—— *Tretii piatiletnyi plan razvitiia narodnogo khoziaistva Soiuza SSR* (1938–1942 gg.) (Third Five Year Plan for the Development of the Economy of the Union SSR [1938–1942]), Moscow: Gosplanizdat, 1939.

—— *Vtoroi piatiletnyi plan razvitiia narodnogo khoziaistva SSSR* (1933–1937) tom vtoroi, *plan razvitiia raionov* (Second Five Year Plan for the Development of the National Economy of the USSR [1933–1937], Vol. II, Plan for Regional Development), Moscow, 1934.

Gosudarstvennyi plan razvitiia narodnogo khoziaistva SSSR na 1941 god (Prilozheniia k Postanovleniiu SNK SSSR i TsK VKP [b] no. 127 ot 17 Ianvaria 1941 g.) (State Plan for the Development of the Economy of the USSR in 1941 [Appendix to the Decree of the SNK USSR and CC of the All-Union Communist Party, (Bolshevik) no. 127, January 17, 1941.])

Tsentral'noe upravlenie narodnokhoziaistvennogo ucheta Gosplana SSSR (Central Administration of Social-Economic Accounting of Gosplan USSR), abbr. as TsUNKhU, *Narodnoe Khoziaistvo SSSR* (The Economy of the USSR), Moscow-Leningrad, 1932.

—— *Slovar'-spravochnik po sotsialno-ekonomicheskoi statistiki* (Dictionary-Handbook for Social-Economic Statistics), Moscow: Gosplanizdat, 1944.

—— *Slovar'-spravochnik po sotsialno-ekonomicheskoi statistiki* (Dictionary-Handbook for Social-Economic Statistics) 2d. ed., Moscow, 1948.

—— *Socialist Construction in the USSR*, Moscow, 1936.

—— *Sotsialisticheskoe stroitel'stvo SSSR* (Socialist Construction in the USSR), Moscow, 1934.

—— *Sotsialisticheskoe stroitel'stvo SSSR* (Socialist Construction in the USSR), Moscow, 1935.

—— *Sotsialisticheskoe stroitel'stvo SSSR* (Socialist Construction USSR), Moscow, 1936.

—— *Sotsialisticheskoe stroitel'stvo Soiuza SSR* (1933–1938 gg.), statisticheskii sbornik (Socialist Construction of the Union SSR [1933–1938], statistical abstract), Moscow-Leningrad: Gosplanizdat, 1939.

—— *Trud v SSSR* (Labor in the USSR), Moscow, 1935.

—— *Trud v SSSR* (Labor in the USSR), Moscow, 1936.

Zakon o piatiletnem plane vosstanovleniia i razvitiia narodnogo khoziaistva SSSR na 1946–1950 gg. (Law Concerning the Five Year Plan for the Reconstruction and Development of the Economy of the USSR for the Years 1946–1950), OGIZ, 1946.

B. *United Nations*

United Nations, Statistical Office, Department of Economic Affairs, *Statistical Yearbook 1951*, New York, 1951.

C. *United States*

United States, Department of Commerce, Bureau of the Census, *Biennial Census of Manufactures, 1925*, Washington, 1928.

—— *Biennial Census of Manufactures, 1927*, Washington, 1930.

—— *Census of Manufactures, 1947*, Washington, 1948.

—— *Statistical Abstract of the United States 1951*, Washington, 1951.

U.S. Department of Commerce, Office of Business Economics, *National Income and Product of the United States 1929–1950*, Washington, 1951.

—— *National Income Supplement to the Survey of Current Business*, July, 1947.

II. BOOKS AND PAMPHLETS

Bakulin, S. N., and Mishustin, D. D. *Vneshnaia torgovlia SSSR za 20 let 1918–1937 gg.*, statisticheskii spravochnik (Foreign Trade of the USSR for 20 Years, statistical handbook), Moscow, 1939.

Baykov, Alexander. *The Development of the Soviet Economic System*, New York: The Macmillan Company, 1947.

Bergson, Abram, (ed.). *Soviet Economic Growth*, Row, Peterson & Co., 1953.

—— *The Structure of Soviet Wages*, Cambridge: Harvard University Press, 1946.

Bergson, Abram; Blackman, James H.; and Erlich, Alexander. "Postwar Economic Reconstruction and Development in the U.S.S.R.," in *The Annals of the American Academy of Political and Social Science*, May, 1949.

Blackman, James H. "Transportation" in *Soviet Economic Growth* (ed. A. Bergson), Row, Peterson & Co., Evanston, Ill., 1953.

Bol'shaia Sovetskaia entsiklopedia (Large Soviet Encyclopedia), USSR Volume, State Scientific Institute "Soviet Encyclopedia," OGIZ, Moscow, 1947.

Chernomordik, D. I. (ed.). *Narodnyi dokhod SSSR* (National Income of the USSR), Moscow-Leningrad: Gosplanizdat, 1939.

Clark, Colin. *The Conditions of Economic Progress*, 2d. ed., London: Macmillan and Co., 1951.

Eason, Warren W. *Trends and Prospects of the Soviet Population and Labor Force*, Santa Monica, California: The RAND Corporation, March 1952, a multilithed manuscript.

Fabricant, Solomon. *Employment in Manufacturing 1899–1939*, New York: National Bureau of Economic Research, Inc., 1942.

—— *The Output of Manufacturing Industries 1899–1937*, New York: National Bureau of Economic Research, Inc., 1940.

Finegood, I. M. "A Critical Analysis of Some Prevailing Concepts Concerning Soviet Agriculture," *Soviet Studies*, July, 1952.

Frickey, Edwin. *Production in the United States, 1860–1914*, Cambridge: Harvard University Press, 1947.

Galenson, Walter. "Trends in Soviet Labor Productivity," in *Soviet Economic Growth* (ed. A. Bergson), Row, Peterson & Co., 1953.

Gerschenkron, Alexander. *A Dollar Index of Soviet Machinery Output, 1927–28 to 1937*, Santa Monica, California: The RAND Corporation, 1951.

Granovsky, E. L. and Markus, B. L. *Ekonomika sotsialisticheskoi promyshlennosti* (The Economics of Socialist Industry), Academy of Sciences of the USSR, Institute of Economics, Moscow: State Social-Economic Press, 1940.

Hultgren, Thor. *American Transportation in Prosperity and Depression*, New York: National Bureau of Economic Research, Inc., 1948.

Jasny, Naum. *The Socialized Agriculture of the USSR*, Stanford: Stanford University Press, 1949.

—— *The Soviet Economy During the Plan Era*, Stanford: Stanford University Press, 1951.

—— *The Soviet Price System*, Stanford: Stanford University Press, 1951.

—— *Soviet Prices of Producers' Goods*, Stanford: Stanford University Press, 1952.

Kaplan, Norman. "Capital Formation and Allocation," in *Soviet Economic Growth* (ed. A. Bergson), Row, Peterson and Co., Evanston, Ill., 1953.

Khromov, P. A. (ed.). *Proizvoditel'nost' truda v promyshlennosti SSSR* (The Productivity of Labor in the Industry of the USSR), Moscow: Gosplanizdat, 1940.

Lorimer, Frank. *The Population of the Soviet Union: History and Prospects*, Geneva: League of Nations, 1946.

Malaia Sovetskaia entsiklopedia (Small Soviet Encyclopedia), Moscow.

Mishustin, D. D. *Vneshnaia torgovlia i industrializatsiia SSSR* (Foreign Trade and the Industrialization of the USSR), V/O Mezhdunarodnaia kniga, Moscow, 1938.

Nikitin, V. P. *Mashinostroenie v poslevoennoi stalinskoi piatiletke* (The Machinery Industry in the Postwar Stalin Five Year Plan), Izd. "Pravda," Moscow, 1949.

Rotshtein, A. I. *Problemy promyshlennoi statistiki SSSR* (Problems of Industrial Statistics in the USSR), 3 vols.: vol. I, Gosudarstvennoe sotsialno-ekonomicheskoe izdatel'stvo (State Social-Economic Press), Leningrad Division, 1936; vol. II, State Social-Economic Press, Leningrad Division, 1938: vol. III, Gosudarstvennoe izdatel'stvo politicheskoi literatury (State Press for Political Literature), Leningrad, 1947.

Shimkin, Demitri B., and Grossman, Gregory. *Mineral Consumption and Economic Development in the United States and the Soviet Union*, an unpublished manuscript available from the Russian Research Center, Harvard University.

Shimkin, Demitri B. *Minerals — A Key to Soviet Power*, Cambridge: Harvard University Press, 1953.

Suchkov, A. K. *Gosudarstvennye dokhody SSSR* (State Incomes of the USSR), Gosfinizdat, 1949.

Teplov, G. V. *Planirovanie na mashinostroitel'nykh zavodakh* (Planning in Machinery Plants), Moscow: State Scientific Press for Literature for the Machinery Industry, 1949.

Varga, E. *Kapitalizm i sotsializm za 20 let* (Capitalism and Socialism During 20 Years), Partizdat Ts.K.V.K.P. (b), 1938.

Voznesenskii, N. *Economic Results of the USSR in 1940 and the Plan of National Economic Development for 1941*, Moscow: Foreign Language Publishing House, 1941.

Voznesensky, N. *The Growing Prosperity of the Soviet Union*, New York: Workers Library Publishers.

Voznesenskii, N. *Piatiletnii plan vosstanovleniia i razvitiia narodnogo khoziaistva SSSR na 1946–1950 gg.* (Five Year Plan for the Reconstruction and Development of the National Economy of the USSR for the Years 1946–1950), OGIZ, 1946.

Zatov, V. P. *Razvitie pishchevoi promyshlennosti v novoi piatiletke* (Development of the Food Industry in the New Five Year Plan), Gospolitizdat, 1947.

III. PERIODICALS

"The Copper Industry in the USSR," *Bulletin of the Imperial Institute*, vol. XXXVI, 1938, London.

Deutsches Institut für Konjunkturforschung, *Weekly Report*, Berlin, March 30, 1940.

Dobb, Maurice. "Comment on Soviet Statistics," *Soviet Studies*, University of Glasgow, June 1949.

Evseev, P. "Rezervy uvelicheniia vypuska tovarov shirokogo potrebleniia v mestnoi i kooperativnoi promyshlennosti" (Reserves for Increasing the Production of Consumers' Goods in Local and Coöperative Industry), *Planovoe khoziaistvo* no. 4, 1948.

Gerschenkron, Alexander. "Review of N. Voznesenski, Voyennaya ekonomika SSSR v period otechestvennoy voyny" (The War Economy of the USSR in the Period of the Patriotic War), *The American Economic Review*, September, 1948.
—— "The Soviet Indices of Industrial Production," *The Review of Economic Statistics*, November, 1947.
Izvestiia (News). Official Organ of the Presidium of the Supreme Soviet of the USSR.
Jasny, Naum. "A Close-up of the Soviet Fourth Five-Year Plan," *Quarterly Journal of Economics*, May, 1952.
"Kak primeniat' unifitsirovannye tsenniki neizmennykh tsen 1926–27 g." (How to Use the Unified Lists of Constant Prices of 1926–27), *Plan* no. 19, 1935.
Kurskii, A. Review of *Narodnyi dokhod SSSR, ego obrazovanie i uchet*, (National Income of the USSR, Its Formation and Computation), ed. D. I. Chernomordik, *Planovoe khoziaistva* no. 1, 1940.
Kuz'minov, I. "Nepreryvnyi pod"em narodnogo khoziaistva SSSR — zakon sotsializma" (The Uninterrupted Rise of the Economy of the USSR — The Law of Socialism) in *Voprosy ekonomiki* (Questions of Economics), no. 6, 1951.
Malenkov, G. M. *Report to the Central Committee of C. P. S. U. (B) to XIX Congress of the Party.*
Miroshnichenko, B. "Planning Industrial Production," *Planovoe khoziaistvo*, no. 3, 1951.
Moskvin, P. "On Calculating the Index of the Physical Volume of the National Product," *Vestnik statistiki*, no. 2, 1951.
"O dvukh krugakh ucheta promyshlennoi statistiki truda" (The Two Spheres of Recording of Industrial and Labor Statistics) *Planovoe khoziaistvo*, No. 3, 1938.
Plan (Plan). A prewar planning journal. Organ of the State Planning Commission and the Central Administration of National-Economic Accounting.
Planovoe khoziaistvo (Planned Economy). Monthly political and economic journal of the State Planning Commission, published in Moscow.
Pravda (Truth). Organ of the Central Committee and Moscow Committee of All-Union Communist Party.
Problemy ekonomiki (Problems of Economics). A prewar monthly journal of the Institute of Economics of the Academy of Sciences, USSR.
Riz, R. "Ob ischislenii valovoi produktsii promyshlennosti" (Calculating Gross Output of Industry), *Plan*, no. 12, 1934.
Turetskii, Sh. "Dlia chego planiruetsia produktsiia v neizmennykh tsenakh 1926–27 g." (Why Plan Production in the Constant Prices of 1926–27?). *Plan*, no. 11, 1935.
—— "Ekonomicheskaia effektivnost' osvoeniia novoi tekhniki" (Economic Effectiveness of Mastering the New Technique), *Planovoe khoziaistvo*, no. 8, 1936.
—— "K probleme tsenovykh pokazatelei v plane," (The Problem of Value Indices in the Plan), *Plan*, no. 5, 1934.
"Ukazaniia i formy k sostavleniiu narodnokhoziaistvennogo plana na 1937 g." (Instructions and Forms for the Preparation of the National Economic Plan for 1937), *Plan*, no. 18, 1936.
"Unifitsirovannye neizmennye tseny 1926–27 g. v mestnoi promyshlennosti" (Unified Constant Prices of 1926–27 for Local Industry), *Plan*, no. 5, 1937.
United Nations, Economic Division for Europe, Transport Division, *Annual Bulletin of Transport Statistics 1950.*
Vilenskii, L. "Finansovye voprosy promyshlennosti" (Financial Questions of Industry), *Planovoe khoziaistva*, no. 10, 1938.
Voprosy ekonomiki (Questions of Economics). A postwar monthly or bimonthly journal issued by the Institute of Economics of the Academy of Sciences of the USSR.
Zaimova, N., Rochko, N. "O metodakh otsenki produktsii v neizmennykh tsenakh," *Sovetskie finansy* 6–7, 1944 (Methods of Valuing Products in Constant Prices, *Soviet Finance* 6–7, 1944).
Zelonovskii, A. "Tsenniki neizmennykh tsen 1926–27 g." (Price Lists of Constant 1926–27 Prices), *Plan*, no. 8, 1935.

TABULAR SECTION

& INDEX

Abbreviations used in tables

bil.	billion (10^9)
cent.	centner (one-tenth of a metric ton)
cu.	cubic
hl	hectoliter
kw	kilowatt
kw hr	kilowatt hour
lin.	linear
m. t.	metric ton
mil.	million
sq.	square
conv. gr.	conventional gram

TABLE 28

Official and Revised Production Indices for Specific Industries, 1928 - 1937

Industry		1928[a]	1929[a]	1930[a]	1931	1932	1933	1934	1935	1936	1937
Electric power stations	O[b]	16.1	21.6	32.5	45.6	60.5	75.9	100.0	-[c]	-	-
	N[b]	23.8	29.6	39.8	50.8	64.4	77.8	100.0	125.1	157.0	173.0
Coal mining	O	38.1	42.9	50.7	61.6	72.3	81.8	100.0	-	-	-
	N	37.8	42.6	50.9	60.4	68.8	81.1	100.0	115.9	134.5	135.3
Crude petroleum products	O	50.9	59.8	72.0	88.3	83.5	84.4	100.0	-	-	-
	N	47.4	55.8	76.2	92.5	88.4	88.7	100.0	103.8	112.9	117.7
Petroleum refining	O	35.6	46.4	66.2	83.4	90.0	88.5	100.0	-	-	-
	N	43.8	54.4	79.7	98.1	99.6	90.9	100.0	105.7	122.0	130.3
Peat industry	O	32.2	33.2	38.8	63.1	81.3	74.8	100.0	-	-	-
	N	29.1	37.9	44.2	67.7	81.0	75.8	100.0	101.3	122.6	130.0
Iron ore mining	O	27.9	35.7	48.6	49.2	56.4	67.9	100.0	-	-	-
	N	28.5	37.2	49.6	49.2	56.2	67.2	100.0	125.9	129.2	129.1
Manganese ore mining	O	40.0	96.0	80.0	64.0	56.0	64.0	100.0	-	-	-
	N	38.6	77.4	76.0	48.5	45.7	56.1	100.0	130.9	164.7	151.1

Chemical industry	O	18.4	24.6	39.1	53.8	58.8	74.0	100.0	-	-	-
	N	34.9	44.8	58.9	63.6	65.6	74.1	100.0	121.0	150.0	185.9
a. Basic chemicals	O	19.5	25.8	43.4	52.3	57.9	72.0	100.0	-	-	-
	N	32.5	38.7	54.0	62.0	71.3	80.9	100.0	123.2	146.8	186.7
b. Drugs medicines and compounds	O	35.9	45.0	68.7	65.0	85.5	97.7	100.0	-	-	-
	N	0.3	0.4	2.0	23.2	63.9	74.6	100.0	140.0	180.3	232.0
c. Paints and varnishes	O	27.0	40.0	73.6	78.6	79.6	78.1	100.0	-	-	-
	N	84.9	109.5	130.1	112.9	77.3	72.2	100.0	158.6	210.7	289.6
Cement industry	O	53.0	64.0	89.1	105.0	105.0	82.0	100.0	-	-	-
	N	52.4	63.2	85.1	94.4	98.5	76.7	100.0	127.0	165.6	154.5
Glass industry	O	37.0	48.3	60.1	64.2	80.3	74.6	100.0	-	-	-
	N	57.2	66.6	79.9	75.6	75.4	70.3	100.0	135.6	175.6	147.2
Ferrous metals	O	33.4	40.2	48.2	49.8	60.6	72.1	100.0	-	-	-
	N	42.7	49.5	58.7	56.4	61.6	70.9	100.0	127.7	162.1	170.2
Nonferrous metals	O	32.6	44.4	57.6	58.1	71.9	75.4	100.0	-	-	-
	N	31.0	38.4	49.5	55.8	62.1	65.0	100.0	151.2	207.7	230.0

[Table 28 continued]

		1928[a]	1929[a]	1930[a]	1931	1932	1933	1934	1935	1936	1937
Machinery industry	O	14.6	20.0	32.7	54.5	66.6	79.1	100.0	131.6	185.5	230.4
	N	27.5	39.1	48.3	64.6	70.9	89.5	100.0	156.7	172.4	172.0
a. Tractors	O	-	-	2.2	17.6	41.3	69.4	100.0	-	-	-
	N	1.4	3.2	8.6	32.8	41.7	65.7	100.0	136.4	153.2	104.0
b. Motor vehicles	O	2.9	5.2	11.4	22.2	41.5	69.9	100.0	-	-	-
	N	0.9	1.8	5.0	7.0	37.9	72.6	100.0	133.7	190.4	272.5
Rubber and asbestos industry	O	23.0	30.8	42.3	57.7	77.5	76.8	100.0	-	-	-
Rubber industry only	N	24.8	21.7	27.7	47.6	60.0	56.5	100.0	107.8	163.0	218.2
Saw mills and plywood	O	37.7	52.2	70.5	76.8	87.1	86.7	100.0	-	-	-
	N	43.9	53.8	71.3	77.9	80.3	88.9	100.0	93.5	109.8	112.6
Matches	O	71.2	93.2	122.0	101.7	81.4	86.4	100.0	-	-	-
	N	60.7	75.1	103.4	84.2	61.9	75.4	100.0	119.1	91.2	78.6
Paper industry	O	49.3	70.7	77.9	79.7	82.1	90.1	100.0	-	-	-
	N	50.3	68.0	87.5	89.3	84.6	89.5	100.0	113.3	134.9	147.0
Textile industry	O	61.4	72.5	71.9	75.1	84.8	89.6	100.0	-	-	-
	N	82.6	89.8	83.9	85.1	87.3	90.4	100.0	105.0	132.7	163.5

a. Cotton goods	O	78.4	88.3	75.3	75.8	87.2	91.1	100.0	-	-	-
	N	79.7	85.6	73.2	78.7	91.7	91.3	100.0	99.5	123.2	162.4
b. Linen goods	O	76.8	112.4	129.6	90.0	86.4	86.4	100.0	-	-	-
	N	110.9	112.4	116.3	87.9	84.9	89.3	100.0	132.0	179.7	178.5
c. Woolen goods	O	79.0	93.2	103.8	102.2	96.6	97.9	100.0	-	-	-
	N	112.7	127.1	143.3	130.6	112.8	112.9	100.0	97.7	118.6	127.1
d. Silk goods	O	26.6	36.5	60.6	64.5	70.6	83.3	100.0	-	-	-
	N	30.7	41.7	57.1	62.4	68.7	83.2	100.0	121.9	164.0	185.4
e. Knitted goods	O	20.1	30.2	46.1	60.1	65.5	80.8	100.0	-	-	-
	N	-	-	-	-	55.8	73.9	100.0	113.1	145.0	178.5
Leather industries	O	70.1	109.1	130.5	145.3	133.0	101.0	100.0	-	-	-
	N	98.5	116.4	137.6	143.7	135.0	101.7	100.0	101.0	101.9	102.9
Boot and shoe industry	O	36.0	60.4	105.0	110.6	114.2	108.4	100.0	-	-	-
Leather footwear	N	39.2	64.6	99.9	114.8	112.2	106.3	100.0	119.8	128.0	217.6
Grease, tallow, soap, and perfume	O	62.9	73.5	76.8	82.0	83.5	68.1	100.0	-	-	-
	N	64.5	73.6	69.3	70.4	84.5	57.7	100.0	112.0	123.3	147.1

[Table 28 continued]

		1928[a]	1929[a]	1930[a]	1931	1932	1933	1934	1935	1936	1937
Food industry (excluding fisheries)	O	42.2	46.8	54.7	67.2	76.1	82.6	100.0	-	-	-
	N	61.5	56.2	53.8	79.0	74.3	80.4	100.0	123.0	141.4	159.2
Including fisheries	N	61.5	57.9	60.4	82.2	77.0	81.3	100.0	117.6	133.7	147.5

Sources All official indices have been derived from gross value data in Socialist Construction in the USSR (Moscow: TsUNKhU, 1936), pp. 48-49, with the exception of: Machinery industry (1928-1934) from Socialist Construction in the USSR, 1936, p. 49; (1935-1937) from SSSR i kapitalisticheskie strany (Moscow, 1937), p. 166, and Sawmills-plywood and Matches from Socialist Construction in the USSR, 1936, p. 184.

[a] Revised indices shown as calendar years are actually fiscal years as follows: (1928-1930) Coal mining, Crude petroleum products, Petroleum refining, Cement industry, Glass industry, Ferrous metals, Non-ferrous metals, Machinery industry; (1928-1929) Chemical industry, Paper industry, Textile industry, Food industry; (1928 only) Rubber industry.

[b] O designates an index derived from official Soviet data for gross value of industrial output.
N designates an index derived in the present study.

[c] Dash (-) indicates no data.

TABLE A (i)

Production Indicators for Soviet Industry in Physical or Conventional Units, 1927-28 to 1937

Industry and Commodity	1927-28	1928-29	1929-30	1931	1932	1933	1934	1935	1936	1937
1. Coal (1,000 m.t.[a])	35,510	40,067	47,780	56,752	64,664	76,205	93,940	108,900	126,400	127,100
2. Crude oil extracted (excludes natural gas) (1,000 m.t.)	11,472.2	13,509.0	18,450.8	22,391.9	21,413.2	21,489.1	24,218.0	25,135.7	27,337.3[b]	28,501.1
3. Petroleum refined (consumption of crude oil) (1,000 m.t.)	8,882.2	11,034.0	16,172.5	19,919.9	20,214.5	18,455.5	20,300.4	21,450.7	24,774.4[b]	26,448.0
4. Peat extracted (1,000 m.t.)	5,319.9	6,913.7	8,076.1	12,357.2	14,788.6	13,845.8	18,253.7	18,496.6	22,385.0[b]	23,822
5. Electric power output (mil. kw hr)	5, 007	6,224	8,368	10,687	13,540	16,357	21,016	26,294	33,000[b]	36,400

6. Ferrous metals (1,000 m.t.)										
a. Pig iron	3,282.3	4,021.0	4,963.6	4,871.1	6,161.1	7,109.8	10,428.3	12,488.9	14,400.0[b]	14,487.4
b. Steel (ingots and castings)	4,250.9	4,854.3	5,760.7	5,619.7	5,927.1	6,889.1	9,693.2	12,588.2	16,330[b]	17,729.8
c. Rolled steel (includes iron pipe)	3,579.2	4,087.3	4,736.1	4,443.0	4,598.1	5,229.5	7,203.9	9,444.6	12,470[b]	12,992.9
7. Nonferrous metals (1,000 m.t.)										
a. Fireburned copper	30.0	35.5	44.5	44.3	45.0	44.3	53.3	76.0	100.75	102.0[c]
b. Lead	2.3	5.5	8.6	15.5	18.7	13.7	27.2	37.9[c]	48.6	62.5
c. Zinc	2.2	3.0	4.3	9.0	13.7	16.6	27.1	44.4[c]	62.1	65.0
d. Aluminum (m.t.)	0	0	0	0	855	4,434	14,391	25,000	37,900	46,800
8. Ore mining (1,000 m.t.)										
a. Iron ore	6,133.0	7,997.1	10,663.4	10,591.3	12,085.7	14,454.5	21,508.8	27,077.9	27,937.9[b]	27,770.0
b. Manganese ore	702.4	1,409.2	1,384.6	883.5	832.1	1,021.3	1,821.0	2,384.6	3,000.1[b]	2,752.0
c. Copper ore	641	800	919	1,106	1,187	1,333	2,083	2,791[b]	3,562	4,580[c]
9. Chemicals (1,000 m.t.)										
a. Basic Chemicals										
(1) Soda ash	215.2	231.4	260.8	273.4	284.9	324.5	396.1	415.7[b]	504.5[b]	517.0
(2) Superphosphate	149.1	203.5	400.7	518.8	615.6	690.2	841.8	1,167.5[b]	1,256.8[b]	1,435.0
(3) Sulphuric acid	210.6	264.9	395.7	464.1	552.1	627.2	782.4	995.6[b]	1,206.0	1,666.0[d]
b. Aniline dyes (m.t.)	10,252	13,302	16,789	16,262	13,542	15,999	24,022	25,343[b]	30,300	32,800[c]
c. Plastic pulp (m.t.)	300	1,358[c]	2,416[c]	3,473	3,875	4,193	5,556	6,139	10,664[b]	13,800
d. Iodine (m.t.)	0.3	0.4	1.8	21.0	57.8	66.9	90.4	126.7[c]	163	210.0[c]

[Table A (i) continued]

	1927-28	1928-29	1929-30	1931	1932	1933	1934	1935	1936	1937
e. Dry white mineral pigments (m.t.)	11,606	14,976	17,786	15,434	10,570	9,874	13,672	21,677 [b]	28,807 [b]	39,600 [d]
10. Coke (of 6 per cent moisture) (1,000 m.t.)	4,176	4,992	6,205	6,756	8,421	10,225	14,221	16,743	19,900	19,800
11. Grease, tallow, soap, and perfume										
a. Soap (hand and toilet) (1,000 m.t.)	217.1	247.8	233.3	236.8	284.3	194.3	336.6	377	415	495.2
12. Rubber industry (crude rubber produced and imported) (m.t.)	14,707	12,827	16,408	28,227	30,790	33,474	59,248	63,861 [b]	96,575 [c]	129,289
13. Matches (1,000 cases)	5,532	6,845	9,419	7,675	5,642	6,876	9,114	10,850	8,314 [b]	7,163
14. Wood processing (1,000 cu. meters)										
a. Sawn lumber	13,633	16,585	21,884	23,839	24,427	27,334	30,579	28,160	32,910 [b]	33,800
b. Plywood	185	247	339	385	423	424	497	543.7	663.7 [b]	672.3
15. Paper (1,000 m.t.)	284.5	384.9	495.3	505.2	478.5	506.1	565.8	641.0	763.3 [b]	831.6
16. Cement (1,000 m.t.)	1,850.1	2,232.4	3,005.7	3,336.2	3,481.2	2,710.3	3,532.8	4,488.6	5,849.7 [b]	5,459.0
17. Building bricks (mil. units)	1,780	3,755	4,137 [c]	4,519 [c]	4,900	3,823	4,941	5,612	8,304 [b]	8,666
18. Glass										
a. Glass (all types) (1,000 m.t.)	324.5	377.8	453.2	428.8	427.2	399.0	566.9	-	-	-
b. Window glass (1,000 sq. meters)	-	-	-	-	-	29,788	50,063	67,900	87,890 [b]	73,720 [c]
19. Leather tanning (1,000 units)										
a. Large hides	12,359 [c]	15,164	18,606	17,444	16,649	12,255	10,429	10,386 [c]	10,343 [c]	10,300
b. Small hides	22,927 [c]	25,474	28,235	35,051	32,219	25,072	29,173	29,849 [c]	30,525 [c]	31,200

20. Textile industry										
a. Ginned cotton fiber (1,000 m.t.)	196.2[c]	237.9	257.4	337.7	389.8	378.5	419.7	437.2	596.2[b]	716.7
b. Raw silk (m.t.)	397	619	762	810	837	774	901	1,210.1	1,509.6[b]	1,624.0
c. Cottonized fiber (m.t.)	-	-	3,658	9,236	16,031	19,140	20,588	18,500	26,700[b]	27,500[d]
d. (1) Consumption of cotton (1,000 m.t.)	354.0	380.2	325.1	349.4	407.3	405.3	444.1	442.0	547.0	721.0
(2) Cotton cloth (mil. meters)	-	-	-	-	-	-	2,673.0	-	-	-
e. Unbleached woolen cloth (mil. meters)	93.2	105.1	118.5	108.0	93.3	93.4	82.7	80.8	98.1[b]	105.1
f. Linen (mil. sq. meters)	177.2	179.6	185.9	140.4	135.7	142.7	159.8	210.9	287.2[b]	285.2
g. Silk woven goods (1,000 meters)	9,601	13,038	17,823	19,484	21,459	25,992	31,233	38,060	51,220[b]	57,900
h. Knitted wear										
(1) Socks and stockings (mil. pairs)	-	-	-	-	208.0	250.9	322.9	340.8	367.2[b]	409.1
(2) Knit underwear (mil. pieces)	-	-	-	-	27.3	36.1	53.7	63.4	90.1[b]	111.5
(3) Knit outerwear (mil. pieces)	-	-	-	-	11.7	17.2	22.4	25.9	34.4[b]	45.1
21. Leather footwear (factory production) (1,000 pairs)	29,588	48,780	75,447	86,685	84,749	80,267	75,514	90,500	96,640[b]	164,300
22. Food industry										
a. Sugar (granulated) (1,000 cent.)	13,331	12,826	8,230	14,862	8,268	9,953	14,035	20,316	19,990[b]	24,211

[Table A (i) continued]

	1927-28	1928-29	1929-30	1931	1932	1933	1934	1935	1936	1937
b. Macaroni products (m.t.)	-	-	-	-	185,447	148,922	181,118	180,300	263,100 [b]	263,800
c. Bread										
(1) Baked in large-scale bakeries (1,000 m.t.)	-	1,300	1,656	1,866	2,331	3,072	4,012	-	-	-
(2) Baked in large-scale bakeries, consumers' and industrial cooperatives Workers Supply Section, and "other" organizations (1,000 m.t.)	-	-	-	-	-	8,065	10,329	14,355.0	16,145.0 [b]	19,131
d. Meat (slaughtering) (m.t.)	-	-	550,000	691,800	458,343	410,507	496,185	585,600	773,100 [b]	797,200
e. Butter (m.t.)	82,130	77,784	41,040	82,835	71,588	124,350	138,035	154,800	187,800 [b]	185,200
f. Vegetable oils (1,000 m.t.)	282.2	363.3	317.7	321.0	409.7	287.1	372.1	425.7	450.9 [b]	495.3
g. Margarine (m.t.)	0	0	6,339	20,623	38,305	51,800	69,245	81,800	75,000 [b]	65,000 [d]
h. Fish caught (1,000 cent.)	-	9,564	12,794	14,316	13,261	12,905	15,261	15,023.7	16,201.0 [b]	16,089
i. Processing of fruits and vegetables (1,000 m.t.)	-	-	251.5	511.0	926.8	891.3	1,157.3	-	-	-
j. Canning (thous. of conv. 400-gram cans)	-	-	-	-	906.1	900.4	1,121.9	1,155.0	1,171.5 [b]	1,371.9
k. Confections (1,000 m.t.)	77.7	118.4	240.5	503.6	510.5	428.8	522.3	606.4	831.6 [b]	921.4
l. Yeast (m.t.)	-	18,243	19,505	21,107	24,291	24,090	27,664	35,300	47,600 [b]	56,644 [c]
m. Beer (1,000 hl)	-	2,723	3,383	3,920	4,143	4,315	4,568	5,185.5	7,436.1 [b]	8,864.1
n. Starch and syrup (m.t.)	69,106	68,587	97,533	99,354	106,996	150,419	193,573	249,200	292,200 [b]	285,500 [d]
o. Cigarettes (bil. units)	49.5	57.7	61.7	64.8	57.9	62.7	67.8	78.6	85.9 [b]	102.1

p. Salt (1,000 m.t.)	2,336.3	2,669.6	3,158.0	3,181.5	2,636.4	2,734.0	3,544.7	4,184.3	4,006.9 [b]	3,212.0 [d]
23. Machinery										
a. Electric power equipment										
(1) Steam boilers (1,000 sq. meters of area)	87.9	126.4	166.1	125.3	166.4	200.3	226.0	197.3	182.2 [b]	170.4
(2) Total prime movers (1,000 kw aggregate capacity)	133.5	233.6	280.0	564.3	750.7	1,529.5	1,294.7	2,264.0	-	-
b. Power transformers (1,000 kw)	403.2	791.1	1,525.3	3,182.5	3,426.0	3,330.0	2,874.0	3,461.3	3,203.0 [b]	2,743.0
c. Agricultural equipment and implements (units)										
(1) Tractors										
(a) Wheeled (units)	1,115	3,050	8,589	37,251	48,437	71,625	83,360	91,736	83,366 [b]	21,000 [c]
(b) Track laying (units)	157	231	508	618	488	2,103	10,605	20,830	29,059	30,000 [c]
(2) Agricultural machinery										
(a) Tilling implements										
Plows, tractor drawn Moldboard plows										
2 bottom	510	3,595	19,763	2,078	6	105	306	2	-	-
3 bottom	0	0	61	28,430	12,893	3,174	17,923	37,412	-	-
4 bottom	0	0	0	42,433	35,716	50,746	53,852	42,945	-	-
Disk plows										
4 disk	0	0	0	0	5	258	295	0	-	-
13 and 16 disk	0	0	0	9,055	11,416	10,330	302	0	-	-
Horse-drawn plows	1,146,490	1,683,013	1,999,108	226,930	36,612	80,305	93,429	99,062	-	-

[Table A (i) continued]

	1927-28	1928-29	1929-30	1931	1932	1933	1934	1935	1936	1937
Gang harrows, tractor-drawn, disk type	0	0	170	20,886	15,854	10,659	4,946	3,472	-	-
Harrows, horse-drawn	517,311	672,272	813,665	226,189	58,400	29,602	58,858	61,690	-	-
Cultivators for all-round plowing										
Horse-drawn	50,249	45,506	73,175	27,486	5,079	7,978	34,264	41,172	-	-
Tractor-drawn	0	0	0	16,455	15,105	16,224	8,528	13,698	-	-
Ridge plows, horse-drawn	15,869	50,660	201,153	143,511	11,357	19,417	24,233	-	-	-
Weeders	16,376	73,405	233,310	155,186	75,591	37,453	14,286	16,570	-	-
(b) Seeding and planting machinery (units)										
Drills, tractor-drawn	561	2,799	17,783	50,529	19,187	11,868	12,098	17,715	-	-
Drills, horse-drawn	57,152	99,031	149,382	43,095	19,816	19,185	27,101	33,492	-	-
Combined plows and drills, horse- and tractor-drawn	30,168	30,266	18,352	4,415	3,750	5,862	289	0	-	-
Corn and cotton planters	946	1,436	7,075	21,054	7,411	193	17	2,200	-	-
Vegetable planters, horse-drawn	0	4,493	17,077	18,518	10,364	2,594	945	1,161	-	-
Fertilizer distributors	0	0	0	16	1,720	554	735	584	-	-
(c) Harvesting machinery (units)										
Grain harvesters and threshers	0	0	104	3,549	10,006	8,578	8,239	20,169	-	-

Windrowers	0	0	0	950	2,374	1,847	2,045	504	-	-
Reapers, self-raking	54,671	68,076	78,651	23,771	13,760	25,621	31,733	37,068	-	-
Reapers, nonraking	62,264	165,816	90,845	24,298	11,600	17,486	46,441	50,209	-	-
Potato diggers										
Tractor-drawn	0	0	0	10	501	330	31	24	-	-
Horse-drawn	0	0	0	14,242	14,472	5,022	754	351	-	-
Corn pickers	0	0	0	171	2,022	2,723	2,341	774	-	-
Hay mowers, horse- and tractor-drawn	57,140	78,434	134,660	94,275	54,947	62,871	64,180	75,950	-	-
Rakes, horse-drawn	0	1,082	19,175	55,625	24,364	45,638	45,300	51,573	-	-
(d) Threshing and sorting machinery (units)										
Grain threshers, tractor- and horse-drawn	54,354	57,105	41,744	21,084	16,015	12,908	17,276	19,320	-	-
Grain-grading machines	0	7,038	26,897	16,750	3,289	0	1,153	2,861	-	-
d. Transportation equipment										
(1) Railroad equipment										
(a) Freight locomotives, series E (units)	308	437	564	809	678	727	758	560	0	0
(b) Freight locomotives, series FD and SO (units)	0	0	0	1	1	21	184	586	982[b]	887
(c) Passenger locomotives series M and SU	159	138	61	0	147	181	221	370	113[b]	179
(d) Passenger locomotives series IS	0	0	0	0	1	1	2	2	3[b]	105

[Table A (i) continued]

	1927-28	1928-29	1929-30	1931	1932	1933	1934	1935	1936	1937
(e) Main line freight and flat cars in 2-axle units	10,612	15,190	19,427	21,175	20,152	18,126	28,957	85,675	67,200 [b]	59,000
(f) Main line passenger coaches in 2-axle units	434	525	995	2,130	2,135	2,548	2,980	1,774	1,450 [b]	1,824
(2) Motor vehicles										
(a) Passenger cars and 1 1/2-ton trucks	580	1,242	2,313	1,268	7,511	26,736	49,296	63,580	86,278	137,016
(b) Trucks from 2 1/2 to 4 tons	0	0	416	1,623	15,149	20,916	20,635	30,750	47,858	60,261
(c) Trucks 5 tons and larger	91	148	646	1,114	1,219	2,072	2,541	2,290	2,447	2,730
e. Construction and roadbuilding machinery (units)										
(1) Power shovels, (excavators) total	0	0	0	2	85	116	276	458	573	522
(2) Stone crushers	63	392	793	1,309	1,642	1,351	1,196	934 [c]	673 [b]	750 [d]
(3) Concrete mixers	25	372	720	1,633	1,104	492	433	636	855 [b]	845 [d]
(4) Road graders (heavy, medium and light)	97	342	769	1,428	1,165	1,693	1,267	759	709 [c]	660
(5) Ditch-digging machines	39	105	416	489	444	397	255	199	-	-
(6) Road rollers										
(a) Trailing 4-ton	0	0	505	778	246	330	449	868	-	-
(b) Self-propelled 9-11 ton	0	0	0	40	69	133	224	350	318 [b]	394

f. Electric light bulbs (1,000 units)	13,725	19,099	33,162	44,003	54,199	69,526	83,637	101,030	113,250[b]	126,840[c]
g. Telephone apparatus (for hand and automatic exchanges) (units)	58,499	84,267	116,961	248,962	234,462	232,911	240,988	258,300	274,500[b]	291,595[c]
h. Hoisting and handling equipment (units)										
(1) Overhead traveling cranes, electric	46	94	107	129	460	518	312	411[c]	531[c]	620[c]
(2) Overhead traveling cranes, hand-operated	15	45	86	213	165	190	18	118[c]	154[c]	179[c]
(3) Railway cranes, steam-operated	0	1	0	12	122	151	83	114[c]	147[c]	171[c]
(4) Electric hoisting cranes, freight and passenger	155	166	219	245	389	373	256	252	280[b]	250[d]
i. Metal-cutting machine tools (units)										
(1) Turning lathes	830	1,495	3,295	7,059	7,115	7,816	9,076	6,841	8,253[b]	12,570[c]
(2) Turret lathes	0	0	0	26	512	1,049	1,677	1,919	1,912[b]	3,070[c]
(3) Drilling machines	546	963	2,167	6,951	6,838	5,204	4,971	-	-	-
(4) Planers, vertical and horizontal	181	397	633	892	1,068	1,033	1,148	1,452[c]	1,756[c]	2,060[c]
(5) Slotters	35	5	35	11	46	89	100	-	-	-
(6) Milling machines	53	205	189	730	1,071	1,581	1,608	2,076	2,859[b]	4,696[c]
(7) Boring machines	10	118	30	7	67	95	155	123	173[b]	250[c]
(8) Threading machines	110	540	521	464	861	807	851	-	-	-
(9) Grinding machines	18	75	155	530	475	619	1,111	895	1,883[b]	1,842[c]

[Table A (i) continued]

	1927-28	1928-29	1929-30	1931	1932	1933	1934	1935	1936	1937
j. Rolling-mill equipment (m.t.)	0	0	0	3,616.0	3,656.8	6,505 0	8,455.0	21,790.0	26,000	21,600[c]
k. Textile machinery (units)										
(1) Carding machines (all types)	-	-	-	-	105	279	589	932	-	-
(2) Water frames										
(a) Spinners	-	-	-	-	0	167	397	425[c]	-	-
(b) Doublers	-	-	-	-	39	163	91	221[c]	-	-
(3) Looms, total	-	-	-	-	300	1,928	2,118	3,687	-	-
(4) Knitting machines	-	-	-	-	1,806	2,555	2,761	-	-	-
1. Articles for home and general use (units)										
(1) Typewriters	0	0	0	139	1,442	4,021	6,450	9,693	17,094[b]	20,818
(2) Sewing machines										
(a) Home	285,604	425,241	538,458	500,850	318,814	265,834	260,864	402,828	469,540[c]	488,700[c]
(b) Factory	0	0	0	2,465	8,822	16,086	16,580	17,554	20,460[c]	21,300[c]
(3) Bicycles	10,847	20,960	35,370	80,899	128,415	132,429	274,533	324,200	557,500[b]	540,000
(4) Motorcycles	0	0	0	16	112	119	365	1,202	6,700[b]	15,000[d]

[a] Abbreviations used: bil., billion (10^9); cent., centner (one-tenth of a metric ton); cu., cubic; hl, hectoliter; kw, kilowatt; kw hr, kilowatt hour; lin., linear; m.t., metric ton; mil., million; sq., square; conv. gr., conventional gram.

[b] Preliminary data.
[c] Estimated.
[d] Planned production.

Table A (ii)
Production Indicators for Soviet Industry in Physical or Conventional Units, 1940 to 1951

Industry and Commodity	1940	1941	1945	1946	1947	1948	1949	1950	1951
1. Coal (1,000 m.t.) [a]	166,000	171,160	148,000	162,500	182,000	208,000	235,000	261,000	282,000
2. Crude oil extracted (excludes natural gas) (1,000 m.t.)	31,000	34,602	19,500	21,800	26,000	29,400	33,500	37,800	42,300
3. Petroleum-refined (consumption of crude oil) (1,000 m.t.)	-	32,457	-	-	-	-	-	-	-
4. Peat-extracted (1,000 m.t.)	31,800	38,779	-	-	-	-	-	-	-
5. Electric power output (mil. kw hr)	48,300	53,957.4	44,900	49,400	56,800	65,900	77,800	90,300	102,900
6. Ferrous metals (1,000 m.t.)									
a. Pig iron	15,000	18,000	8,900	10,000	11,400	13,900	16,600	19,400	22,100
b. Steel (ingots and castings)	18,300	22,400	12,200	13,300	14,500	18,600	23,300	27,300	31,400
c. Rolled steel (includes iron pipe)	13,100	15,800	8,500	9,600	11,000	14,100	17,900	20,800	23,900
7. Nonferrous metals (1,000 m.t.)	-	-	-	-	-	-	-	-	-
8. Ore mining (1,000 m.t.)									
a. Iron ore	-	34,030	-	-	-	-	-	-	-
b. Manganese ore	-	3,100	-	-	-	-	-	-	-
c. Copper ore	-	-	-	-	-	-	-	-	-
9. Chemicals (1,000 m.t.)									
a. Soda ash (1,000 m.t.)	-	673	-	-	-	-	-	-	-

[Table A (ii) continued]

	1940	1941	1945	1946	1947	1948	1949	1950	1951
b. Plastic pulp (m.t.)	-	13,500	-	-	-	-	-	-	-
c. Dry white mineral pigments (m.t.)	-	21,200	-	-	-	-	-	-	-
10. Coke (6 per cent moisture) (1,000 m.t.)	-	23,800	-	-	-	-	-	-	-
11. Grease, tallow, soap, and perfume (1,000 m.t.)	647	746	188	214	274	398	677	751	-
12. Rubber industry	-	-	-	-	-	-	-	-	-
13. Matches (1,000 cases)	9,900	11,750	1,900	2,400	3,300	5,300	-	-	-
14. Wood processing (1,000 cu. meters)									
a. Sawn lumber	35,700	28,857	9,800	10,700	13,900	21,600	-	-	-
b. Plywood	-	552.5	-	-	-	-	-	-	-
15. Paper (1,000 m.t.)	812	969.8	324	522	653	783	995	1,194	1,337
16. Cement (1,000 m.t.)	5,800	7,770	1,800	3,400	4,700	6,500	8,200	10,400	12,400
17. Building bricks (mil. units)	-	9,138	-	-	-	-	-	-	-
18. Glass									
a. Window glass (1,000 sq. meters)	44,400	59,400	28,400	46,900	55,800	66,900	79,600	84,400	-
19. Leather tanning	-	-	-	-	-	-	-	-	-
20. Textile industry									
a. Ginned cotton fiber (1,000 m.t.)	-	860	-	-	-	-	-	-	-
b. Raw silk (m.t.)	-	1,570	-	-	-	-	-	-	-

c. Cottonized fiber	-	-	-	-	-	-	-	-	-
d. Consumption of cotton (cotton cloth - meters)	4,005	4,337.8	1,674	1,959	2,605	3,230	3,682	3,976	4,851
e. Unbleached woolen cloth (mil. meters)	119.8	121.7	56.9	74.0	98.4	126.0	150.0	155.0	175.0
f. Linen (mil. sq. meters)	165	283.8	-	-	-	-	-	-	-
g. Silk woven goods (1,000 meters)	64,000	73,000	32,000	44,000	65,000	85,000	109,000	134,000	180,000
h. Knitted wear									
(1) Socks and stockings (mil. pairs)	-	583.04	-	-	-	-	-	-	-
(2) Knit underwear (mil. pieces)	-	132.36	-	-	-	-	-	-	-
(3) Knit outerwear (mil. pieces)	-	55.09	-	-	-	-	-	-	-
21. Leather footwear (factory production) (1,000 pairs)	200,000	221,600	-	-	-	-	-	-	-
22. Food industry									
a. Sugar (granulated) (1,000 cent.)	21,500	26,500	4,700	4,700	9,800	16,700	20,500	25,200	29,700
b. Macaroni products (m.t.)	-	389,500	-	-	-	-	-	-	-
c. Bread (1,000 m.t.)	-	22,100	-	-	-	-	-	-	-
d. Meat (slaughtering) (m.t.)	-	1,240,000	-	-	-	-	-	-	-
e. Butter (m.t.)	-	203,000	-	-	-	-	-	-	-
f. Vegetable oils (1,000 m.t.)	724	737	270	321	398	529	698	796	892

[Table A (ii) continued]

	1940	1941	1945	1946	1947	1948	1949	1950	1951
g. Margarine (m.t.)	118,000	125,000	27,000	-	-	-	-	192,000	-
h. Fish caught (1,000 cent.)	14,670	16,614	10,420	11,460	14,670	14,960	18,250	18,630	22,730
i-j. Canning (1,000 conv. gr. cans)	1,020	1,262	431	-	-	844	1,140	1,510	1,780
k. Confections (1,000 m.t.)	719	1,092	196	-	-	566	719	884	1,030
l. Yeast (m.t.)	-	76,000	-	-	-	-	-	-	-
m. Beer (1,000 hl)	12,000	12,860	4,160	-	-	6,750	9,380	12,480	14,480
n. Starch and syrup (m.t.)	224,000	-	-	-	-	-	-	-	-
o. Cigarettes (bil. units)	99.6	110	25	-	-	92.3	108	125	141
p. Salt (1,000 m.t.)	4,300	4,600	-	-	-	-	-	-	-
23. Machinery									
a. Electric power equipment									
(1) Steam boilers (1,000 sq. meters of area)	-	270.6	-	-	-	-	-	-	-
(2) Total prime movers (1,000 kw aggregate capacity)	-	1,325.6	-	-	-	-	-	-	-
b. Power transformers (1,000 kw)	-	4,945	-	-	-	-	-	-	-
c. Agricultural equipment and implements (units)									
(1) Tractors									
(a) Wheeled (units)	-	-	-	-	-	-	-	-	-
(b) Track laying (units)	31,100	28,000	8,400	14,500	30,300	61,900	95,900	118,000	-

(2) Agricultural machinery									
(a) Tilling implements									
Plows, tractor-drawn	-	35,450	-	-	-	-	-	-	-
Plows, horse-drawn	-	71,200	-	-	-	-	-	-	-
Harrows, horse-drawn	-	120,000	-	-	-	-	-	-	-
Gang harrows, tractor-drawn, disk type	-	-	-	-	-	-	-	-	-
Cultivators for all-round plowing									
Horse-drawn	-	43,000	-	-	-	-	-	-	-
Tractor-drawn	-	32,500	-	-	-	-	-	-	-
Ridge plows, horse-drawn	-	-	-	-	-	-	-	-	-
Weeders	-	-	-	-	-	-	-	-	-
(b) Seeding and planting machinery (units)									
Drills, tractor-drawn	-	33,500	-	-	-	-	-	-	-
Drills, horse-drawn	-	37,000	-	-	-	-	-	-	-
Combined plows and drills, horse- and tractor-drawn	-	-	-	-	-	-	-	-	-
Corn and cotton planters	-	-	-	-	-	-	-	-	-
Vegetable planters, horse-drawn	-	-	-	-	-	-	-	-	-

[Table A (ii) continued]

	1940	1941	1945	1946	1947	1948	1949	1950	1951
Fertilizer distributors	-	-	-	-	-	-	-	-	-
(c) Harvesting machinery (units)									
Grain harvesters and threshers	12,800	13,000	-	-	2,820	14,400	29,000	46,100	-
Windrowers	-	-	-	-	-	-		-	-
Reapers, self-raking	-	50,000	-	-	-	-	-	-	-
Reapers, nonraking	-	25,000	-	-	-	-	-	-	-
Potato diggers (horse- and tractor-drawn)	-	2,500	-	-	-	-	-	-	-
Corn pickers	-	-	-	-	-	-	-	-	-
Hay mowers, horse- and tractor-drawn	-	63,000	-	-	-	-	-	-	-
Rakes, horse-drawn	-	60,000	-	-	-	-	-	-	-
(d) Threshing and sorting machinery (units)									
Grain threshers, tractor- and horse-drawn	-	9,000	-	-	-	-	-	-	-
Grain-grading machines	-	23,000	-	-	-	-	-	-	-
d. Transportation equipment									
(1) Railroad equipment									
(a) Freight locomotives, series E (units)	-	0	-	-	-	-	-	-	-

(b) Freight locomotives, series FD and SO (units)	-	1,000	-	-	-	-	-	-	-
(c) Passenger locomotives, series M and SU	-	150	-	-	-	-	-	-	-
(d) Passenger locomotives, series IS	-	150	-	-	-	-	-	-	-
(e) Main line freight and flat cars in 2-axle units	50,300	104,400	-	-	-	-	-	-	-
(f) Main line passenger coaches in 2-axle units	-	1,800	-	-	-	-	-	-	-
(2) Motor vehicles									
(a) Passenger cars and trucks	147,000	131,000	83,000	115,000	150,000	215,000	280,000	364,000	-
e. Construction and roadbuilding machinery (units)									
(1) Power shovels	-	490	-	-	-	-	-	-	-
(2) Stone crushers	-	130	-	-	-	-	-	-	-
(3) Concrete mixers	-	-	-	-	-	-	-	-	-
(4) Road graders (heavy, medium and light)	-	830	-	-	-	-	-	-	-
(5) Ditch-digging machines	-	-	-	-	-	-	-	-	-
(6) Road rollers									
(a) Trailing	-	1,800	-	-	-	-	-	-	-
(b) Self-propelled	-	290	-	-	-	-	-	-	-
f. Electric light bulbs (1,000 units)	-	140,000	-	-	-	-	-	-	-

[Table A (ii) continued]

	1940	1941	1945	1946	1947	1948	1949	1950	1951
g. Telephone apparatus (for hand and automatic exchanges) (units)	-	280,000	-	-	-	-	-	-	-
h. Hoisting and handling equipment (units)									
(1) Overhead traveling cranes, electric	-	500	-	-	-	-	-	-	-
(2) Overhead traveling cranes, hand-operated	-	150	-	-	-	-	-	-	-
(3) Railway cranes, steam-operated	-	-	-	-	-	-	-	-	-
(4) Electric hoisting cranes, freight and passenger	-	610	-	-	-	-	-	-	-
i. Metal-cutting machine tools, total (units)	-	58,000	-	-	-	-	-	-	-
j. Rolling-mill equipment (m.t.)	-	20,100	-	-	-	-	-	-	-
k. Textile machinery (units)									
(1) Carding machines (cutter only)	-	1,950	-	-	-	-	-	-	-
(2) Water frames (spinners and doublers)	-	2,000	-	-	-	-	-	-	-
(3) Looms, total	-	3,150	-	-	-	-	-	-	-
(4) Knitting machines	-	1,700	-	-	-	-	-	-	-
1. Articles for home and general use(units)									
(1) Typewriters	-	7,000	-	-	-	-	-	-	-

(2) Sewing machines									
(a) Home	-	-	-	-	-	-	-	-	-
(b) Factory	-	18,000	-	-	-	-	-	-	-
(3) Bicycles	-	-	-	-	-	-	-	-	-
(4) Motorcycles	-	-	-	-	-	-	-	-	-

[a] Abbreviations used: bil., billion (10^9); cent., centner (one-tenth of a metric ton); cu., cubic; hl, hectoliter; kw, kilowatt; kw hr, kilowatt hour; lin., linear; m.t., metric ton; mil., million; sq., square; conv. gr., conventional gram.

Table A (iii)
Production Indicators for the Cotton-Goods Industry

	1927-28	1928-29	1929-30	1931	1932	1933	1934	1935	1936	1937
(1) Cotton goods (mil. rubles, 1926-27 prices)	2,742	3,088	2,631	2,649	3,047	3,186	3,496	-	-	-
Index (per cent of 1934)	78.4	88.3	75.3	75.8	87.2	91.1	100.0	-	-	-
(2) Consumption of cotton (1,000 m.t.)	354.0	380.2	325.1	349.4	407.3	405.3	444.1	442	547	721
Index (per cent of 1934)	79.7	85.6	73.2	78.7	91.7	91.3	100.0	99.5	123.2	162.4
(3) Production of cotton yarn (1,000 m.t.)	324	354	287.4	313.8	355.1	367.3	387.7	379 [a]	-	-
Index (per cent of 1934)	83.6	91.3	74.1	80.9	91.6	94.7	100.0	97.8	-	-
(4) Production of cotton woven goods (1,000 m.t.)	-	-	252	262.5	286.7	289.4	304.7	-	-	-
Index (per cent of 1934)	-	-	82.7	86.2	94.1	95.0	100.0	-	-	-
(5) Production of cotton woven goods (lin. meters, index per cent of 1934)	103.9	115.8	94.1	95.1	100.6	101.0	100.0	99.6	121.8	128.7

Sources
(1) Socialist Construction in the USSR (Moscow, 1936), p. 49.

(2) 1927-28 to 1934 from Sotsialisticheskoe stroitel'stvo SSSR (Moscow, 1936), p. 193; 1935-1937 from SSSR i kapitalisticheskie strany (ed. Ia. A. Ioffe; Moscow, 1939), p. 190.

(3) 1927-28 to 1928-29 from Ibid. p. 191; 1929-30 to 1935 from Sotsialisticheskoe stroitel'stvo SSSR, 1936, p. 195.

(4) Socialist Construction in the USSR, 1936, p. 206.

(5) 1927-28 to 1928-29 from Ioffe, p. 192; 1929-30 to 1934 from SS 1936 (R), p. 195; 1935-1936 from Plan 1937, pp. 98-99; 1937 from P. Kh., No. 5, 1939, p. 161.

[a] Preliminary data.

Table B
Derivation of Weights for Production Index

	1	2	3	4	5	6		
Industry and Commodity	Unadjusted Pay Roll (1000 rubles per month)	Employment Coverage Coefficient (per cent)	Pay Roll Tax Coefficient (per cent)	Net Value-added Weight (product of cols. 1, 2 and 3, 1000 rubles per month)	Final Adjusted Weight (1000 rubles per month)	Relative Weight (per cent to total)		
						Commodity	Group	Industry
1. Coal	80,364	103.9	114.0	95,100	95,100	9.61		9.61
2. Crude oil extracted	12,259	-	122.1	15,000	15,000	1.52		1.52
3. Petroleum refined (crude oil consumed)	3,726	94.6	123.1	4,339	4,339	0.44		0.44
4. Peat extracted	18,572	106.2	112.9	22,270	22,270	2.25		2.25
5. Electric power output	13,805	150.7	124.5	25,900	25,900	2.62		2.62
6. Ferrous metals	68,105	101.4	116.0	80,110	80,110			8.10
a. Pig iron					21,389	2.16		
b. Steel (ingots & castings)					28,759	2.91		
c. Rolled steel					29,962	3.03		
7. Nonferrous metals	10,313 [a]	102.6	114.6	12,130	12,130			1.23
a. Fireburned copper					6,125	0.62		
b. Lead					1,856	0.19		
c. Zinc					1,856	0.19		
d. Aluminum					2,293	0.23		

[Table B continued]

Industry and Commodity	1 Unadjusted Pay Roll (1000 rubles per month)	2 Employment Coverage Coefficient (per cent)	3 Pay Roll Tax Coefficient (per cent)	4 Net Value-added Weight (product of cols. 1, 2 and 3, 1000 rubles per month)	5 Final Adjusted Weight (1000 rubles per month)	6 Relative Weight (per cent to total)		
						Commodity	Group	Industry
8. Ore mining	28,775	101.6	114.1	33,360	33,360			3.37
a. Iron ore					21,611	2.18		
b. Manganese ore					5,234	0.53		
c. Copper ore					6,515	0.66		
9. Chemicals	39,018 [a]	114.4	123.6	55,170	55,170			5.58
a. Basic chemicals	8,671 [a]	121.2			22,310		2.26	
(1) Soda ash					5,573	0.56		
(2) Superphosphate					2,965	0.30		
(3) Sulphuric acid					13,772	1.39		
b. Wood chemistry	2,297	298.2						
c. Other chemicals	14,102 }							
d. Aniline dyes	9,018 }	90.6			19,140	1.94	1.94	
e. Artificial fibers (plastic pulp)	1,148 }				3,073	0.31	0.31	
f. Pharmaceutical chemicals (iodine)	2,565	116.8			6,361	0.64	0.64	
g. Paints and varnishes (dry white mineral pigments)	917	220.0			4,281	0.43	0.43	
10. Coke	5,947 [a]	102.2	118.5	7,202	7,202	0.73		0.73

11. Grease, tallow, soap and perfume (soap, hand & toilet)	2,736	131.4	128.4	4,616	4,616	0.47	0.47
12. Rubber industry (rubber produced & imported)	9,194	100.2	129.6	11,940	11,940	1.21	1.21
13. Matches	2,286	103.1	125.6	2,960	2,960	0.30	0.30
14. Wood processing	30,455	106.7	-	39,569	39,569		4.00
a. Lumber	(27,863)[b]		121.7	36,181	36,181	3.66	
b. Plywood	(2,592)[b]		122.5	3,388	3,388	0.34	
15. Paper	6,976	105.6	125.2	9,223	9,223	0.93	0.93
16. Cement	4,617	99.2	129.3	5,922	5,922	0.60	0.60
17. Building bricks	12,408	146.1	123.7	22,420	22,420	2.27	2.27
18. Glass	9,791[a]	125.4	127.9	15,700	15,700	1.59	1.59
19. Leather tanning (hides produced)	8,114	78.2	127.0	8,058	8,058	0.81	0.81
20 Textile industry	99,239		124.9	144,400	144,400		14.60
a. Ginned cotton fiber	1,971[a]	176.5		4,638	4,638	0.47	
b. Silk reeling (raw silk produced)	2,120[a]	102.7		2,902	2,902	0.29	
c. Cottonized fiber	1,139[a]	63.2		960	960	0.10	
d. Cotton goods (unbleached cotton cloth)	62,317	110.4	124.5	85,650	85,650	8.66	
e. Woolen goods (unbleached woolen cloth)	11,257	102.6	125.0	14,440	14,440	1.46	
f. Linen goods	7,592	109.5	124.6	10,360	10,360	1.05	

[Table B continued]

Industry and Commodity	1 Unadjusted Pay Roll (1000 rubles per month)	2 Employment Coverage Coefficient (per cent)	3 Pay Roll Tax Coefficient (per cent)	4 Net Value-added Weight (product of cols. 1, 2 and 3, 1000 rubles per month)	5 Final Adjusted Weight (1000 rubles per month)	6 Relative Weight (per cent to total)		
						Commodity	Group	Industry
g. Silk goods	2,514[a]	129.9	124.3	4,060	4,060	0.41		
h. Knitted wear	10,328	167.4	123.9	21,420	21,420	2.17		
21. Leather footwear (factory production	12,707	230.1	126.4	36,960	36,960	3.74		3.74
22. Food industry	-	148.5	125.9	145,930	145,900			14.75
a. Sugar (granulated and lump)	11,780	106.4	122.0	15,290	18,776	1.90		
b. Macaroni products	863[a]	120.0		1,303	1,600	0.16		
c. Baking	10,957	124.3		17,131	21,040	2.13		
d. Meat (slaughtering)	4,064[a]	184.2	125.0	9,468	11,630	1.18		
e. Dairy products (butter)	1,753[a]	440.6		9,715	11,930	1.21		
f. Vegetable oils } g. Margarine	3,204	109.7	128.6	3,888	4,774	0.48		
g. Margarine				654	803	0.08		
h. Fish curing (fish caught)	658[a]	3,128.6		25,898	31,800	3.21		
i. Processing of fruits and vegetables	2,087[a]	292.5		7,678	9,429	1.67 (i and j)		
j. Canning	4,487	99.2	128.9	5,737	7,045			
k. Confections	7,315	117.0	125.0	10,700	13,140	1.33		
l. Yeast } m. Beer	3,305[a]	100.6	127.3	4,232	520	0.05		
m. Beer					4,677	0.47		
n. Starch and syrup	1,228[a]	162.3		2,507	3,079	0.31		

o. Tobacco (cigarettes)	3,006	96.5	140.0	4,061	4,987	0.50		
p. Salt	1,031	40.8		530	651	0.07		
q. Milling	8,673	107.7		6,331	-			
r. Factory kitchens	4,860[a]	126.6		7,739	-			
s. Tea and coffee	558[a]	134.5		945	-			
t. Wines	814[a]	163.9		1,678	-			
u. Liquors, vinous and distilled	7,196[a]	115.4		10,445	-			
23. Machinery					191,101			19.32
a. Power equipment	17,200[a]	115.0	116.5	23,040	25,932		2.62	
(1) Steam boilers					2,238	0.23		
(2) Total prime movers					23,694	2.40		
b. Electric power equipment (power transformers)	12,000[a]	103.7	116.5	14,500	16,320	1.65	1.65	
c. Agricultural machinery and implements							3.77	
(1) Tractors								
(a) Wheeled	10,000[a]	107.4	116.5	12,510	13,922	1.41		
(b) Track-laying					5,966	0.60		
(c) Spare parts	6,630[a]	66.8	116.5	5,160	-			
(2) Other agricultural machinery	15,700[a]	84.4	116.5	15,440	17,378	1.76		

[Table B continued]

Industry and Commodity	1 Unadjusted Pay Roll (1000 rubles per month)	2 Employment Coverage Coefficient (per cent)	3 Pay Roll Tax Coefficient (per cent)	4 Net Value-added Weight (product of cols. 1, 2 and 3, 1000 rubles per month)	5 Final Adjusted Weight (1000 rubles per month)	6 Relative Weight (per cent to total)		
						Commodity	Group	Industry
d. Transportation equipment								
(1) Railroad equipment	20,200 [a]	117.8	116.5	27,720	31,199		3.15	
(a) Freight locomotives, series E					8,102	0.82		
(b) Freight locomotives, series FD and SO					3,632	0.37		
(c) Passenger locomotives, series M and SU					5,076	0.51		
(d) Passenger locomotives, series IS					47	0.01		
(e) Main-line freight and flat cars					9,684	0.98		
(f) Main-line passenger coaches					4,661	0.47		
(2) Motor vehicles	9,670 [a]	101.8	116.5	11,470	12,909		1.31	
(a) Passenger cars and 1 1/2 - ton trucks					7,545	0.76		
(b) Trucks from 2 1/2 to 4 tons					4,579	0.46		
(c) Trucks 5 tons and larger					785	0.08		
e. Construction and road-building machinery	3,160 [a]	122.2	116.5	4,499	5,064		0.50	

f. Electric light bulbs and appliances	3,700[a]	59.2	116.5	2,552	2,872		0.29
g. Communications equipment (telephone apparatus)	8,900[a]	81.0	116.5	8,400	9,450	0.96	0.96
h. Articles for home and general use	9,300	87.5	116.5	9,480	10,665		1.08
Miscellaneous machinery (i-q)	74,800	116.2					
i. Hoisting and handling equipment			116.5	5,163	5,811		0.59
j. Metal-cutting and pressing machinery (metal-cutting machine tools)			116.5	6,479	7,292	0.74	0.74
k. Mining, metallurgical and chemical equipment (rolling mill equipment)			116.5	18,527	20,852	2.11	2.11
l. Textile, knitting, sewing and bootmaking machinery (textile machinery)			116.5	4,859	5,469		0.55
m. Pumps and compressors			116.5	2,733	-		
n. Control and measuring instruments			116.5	6,479	-		
o. Other industrial machinery			116.5	5,568	-		
p. Other equipment			-	-	-		
q. Equipment for food industry	5,150[a]	108.9	116.5	6,543	-		
Total					989,350		100.0

[a] Based on July 1, 1934, employment data. See note on Column 1, p. 150.
[b] The combined payroll for wood processing is divided between lumber and plywood according to the relative size of their separate payrolls calculated with July 1, 1934 employment data.

Table C (i-a)
Derivation of Census Unit Values for Agricultural Equipment

Commodity		U. S. Census Data		
Soviet Terminology	U.S. Census Terminology	Quantity	Value ($1,000)	Unit Value (dollars)
A. Tilling Implements				
1. Moldboard plows	1. Moldboard plows			
a. 2-bottom, tractor	a. 2-bottom, tractor	53,365	3,479.9	65
b. 3-bottom, tractor	b. 3-bottom, tractor	14,419	1,482.7	103
c. 4-bottom, tractor	c. 4-bottom, tractor	2,322	365.7	158
2. Disk plows, tractor	2. Disk plows, tractor			
a. 4-disk	a. 4-disk	964	115.7	120
b. 6-disk and larger	b. 5-disk and larger	8,444	1,283.8	152
3. Horse-drawn plows	3. Moldboard plows, horse, walking (1-horse plus 2-horse and larger)	365,987	3,455.4	9
4. Gang harrows, tractor-drawn, disk-type	4. Disk harrows, tractor	45,816	3,747.4	82
5. Harrows, horse-drawn	5. Harrows, 1-horse, spike-tooth and spring-tooth	19,007	93.1	5
6. Cultivators for all-round plowing	6. Cultivators for all-round plowing			
a. horse-drawn	a. cultivators, horse-drawn, except disk, 1-horse	132,244	697.8	5
b. tractor-drawn	b. cultivators, tractor-drawn	10,211	1,045.8	102
7. Ridge plows, horse-drawn	7. Lister, horse, 1-bottom	23,779	510.0	21
8. Weeders	8. Weeders	15,518	309.5	20

B. Seeding and planting machinery				
1. Drills, tractor-drawn	1. Grain drills, tractor	6,123	862.4	141
2. Drills, horse-drawn	2. Grain drills, horse	52,506	5,775.9	110
3. Combined plows and drills, horse- and tractor-drawn	3. Combined listers and drills	9,231	674.4	73
4. Corn and cotton planters	4. Combination corn and cotton planters, 1-row	39,636	803.6	20
5. Vegetable planters, horse-drawn	5. Potato planters, horse	6,357	440.1	69
6. Fertilizer distributors	6. Fertilizer distributors, horse	53,427	432.7	8
C. Harvesting machinery				
1. Combines	1. Combined harvester-thresher	18,307	26,885.3	1,469
2. Windrowers	2. Windrowers and bunchers	2,380	16.7	7
3. Reapers, self-raking and nonraking	3. Reapers, self-raking	3,663	281.6	77
4. Potato diggers, tractor-drawn	4. Potato digging machines, elevator-type	12,139	939.7	77
5. Potato diggers, horse-drawn	5. Potato diggers, plow-type	3,641	63.6	17
6. Corn pickers	6. Corn pickers and huskers, field	6,193	1,591.5	257
7. Hay mowers, tractor and horse	7. Mowers	110,644	6,007.0	54
8. Rakes, horse-drawn	8. Rakes, sulky, dump	51,058	1,494.1	29
D. Threshing and sorting machinery				
1. Grain thresher, horse- and tractor-driven	1. Grain thresher, steel, width of rear 46 inches and under	12,888	11,421.2	886
2. Grain-grading machines	2. Grain cleaners and graders (for small grain only)	15,237	990.5	65

Source - Biennial Census of Manufactures, 1927 (Washington: Department of Commerce, Bureau of the Census, 1930), pp. 1039 - 1051.

Table C (i-b)

Soviet Production of Agricultural Machinery and Equipment (1000 U.S. dollars, 1927) and Production Index (per cent of 1934)

	1927-28	1928-29	1929-30	1931	1932	1933	1934	1935	1941 [a]
A. Tilling implements									
1. Plows, tractor-drawn									4,254
a. Moldboard plows									
(1) 2-bottom	33.2	234	1,280	135	0.32	6.8	19.9	0.13	-
(2) 3-bottom	0	0	6.3	2,928	1,328	327	1,846	3,853	-
(3) 4-bottom	0	0	0	6,704	5,643	8,017	8,509	6,785	-
b. Disk plows									
(1) 4-disk	0	0	0	0	0.6	31.0	35.4	0	-
(2) 13- and 16-disk	0	0	0	1,376	1,735	1,570	45.9	0	-
2. Horse-drawn plows	10,300	15,100	18,000	2,040	330	720	840	890	641
3. Gang harrows, tractor-drawn, disk-type	0	0	13.9	1,713	1,300	874	406	285	-
4. Harrows, horse-drawn	2,590	3,361	4,070	1,130	292	148	294	308	600
5. Cultivators for all-round plowing									
a. Horse-drawn	251	228	366	237	25.4	40.0	171	206	215
b. Tractor-drawn	0	0	0	1,680	1,540	1,650	870	1,400	3,315
6. Ridge plows, horse-drawn	333	1,060	4,224	3,010	238	408	509	509	-

7. Weeders	328	1,470	4,670	3,100	1,510	749	286	331	-
Total	13,835.2	21,453	32,630.2	24,053	13,942.32	14,540.8	13,832.2	14,567.13	9,025
Working total	13,840	21,450	32,630	24,050	13,940	14,540	13,830	14,570	-
B. Seeding and Planting machinery									
1. Drills, tractor-drawn	79.1	395	2,500	7,120	2,700	1,670	1,700	2,500	4,724
2. Drills, horse-drawn	6,290	10,900	16,400	4,740	2,180	2,110	2,980	3,684	4,070
3. Combined plows and drills, horse- and tractor-drawn	2,200	2,200	1,340	322	274	428	21.1	0	-
4. Corn and cotton planters	18.9	28.7	142	421	148	3.86	0.34	44.0	-
5. Vegetable planters, horse-drawn	0	310	1,178	1,280	715	179	65.2	80.1	-
6. Fertilizer distributors	0	0	0	0.13	13.8	4.4	5.9	4.7	-
Total	8,588	13,833.7	21,560	13,883.13	6,030.8	4,395.26	4,772.54	6,312.8	8,794
Working total	8,588	13,830	21,560	13,880	6,031	4,395	4,772	6,313	8,794
C. Harvesting machinery									
1. Grain harvesters and threshers	0	0	153	5,213	14,700	12,600	12,100	29,630	19,097
2. Windrowers	0	0	0	6.6	16.6	12.9	14.3	3.5	-
3. Reapers, self-raking	4,210	5,240	6,060	1,830	1,060	1,970	2,440	2,850	3,850
4. Reapers, nonraking	4,800	12,800	7,000	1,870	893	1,350	3,580	3,870	1,925
5. Potato diggers									118
a. tractor-drawn	0	0	0	0.77	38.6	25	2.4	1.8	-

[Table C (i-b) continued]

	1927-28	1928-29	1929-30	1931	1932	1933	1934	1935	1941 [a]
b. horse-drawn	0	0	0	242	246	85	12.8	6.0	-
6. Corn pickers	0	0	0	43.9	520	700	602	199	-
7. Hay mowers	3,090	4,240	7,270	5,090	2,970	3,400	3,470	4,100	3,402
8. Rakes, horse-drawn	0	31.4	556	1,613	707	1,324	1,314	1,496	1,740
Total	12,100	22,311.4	21,039	15,909.27	21,151.2	21,466.9	23,535.5	42,156.3	30,132
Working total	12,100	22,310	21,040	15,910	21,150	21,470	23,540	42,160	30,132
D. Threshing and sorting machinery									
1. Grain threshers	48,160	50,600	36,990	18,680	14,190	11,436	15,300	17,120	7,974
2. Grain-grading machines	0	457	1,750	1,090	214	0	74.9	186	1,495
Total	48,160	51,057	38,740	19,770	14,404	11,436	15,374.9	17,306	9,469
Working total	48,160	51,060	38,740	19,770	14,400	11,440	15,370	17,310	9,469
Total Agricultural Machinery	82,688	108,650	113,970	73,610	55,521	51,845	57,512	80,353	57,420
Working total	82,690	108,600	114,000	73,610	55,520	51,840	57,510	80,350	57,420
Production Index (per cent of 1934)	143.8	188.8	198.2	128.0	96.5	90.1	100.0	139.7	103.3

[a] In computing the quantity relative for 1941 an adjusted base of 55,600 has been used for 1934. This adjusted figure for 1934 excludes the items for which data are lacking for 1941.

Table C (ii-a)
Derivation of Census Unit Values for Metal-Cutting Machine Tools

Commodity		U.S. Census Data		
Soviet Terminology	U.S. Census Terminology	Quantity	Value ($1000)	Unit Value (dollars)
Metal-cutting machine tools				
1. Turning lathes	1. Engine lathes	6,660	6,407.4	962
2. Turret lathes	2. Turret lathes, including hand-screw machines	1,776	5,146.4	2,898
3. Drilling machines	3. Drilling machines, sensitive	3,533	1,518.8	430
4. Planers, vertical and horizontal	4. Planers	196	1,867.4	9,528
5. Slotters	5. Slotters	36	182.2	5,061
6. Milling machines	6. Milling machines			
a. Horizontal	a. Plain, power-feed	945	2,214.0	2,343
b. Vertical	b. Vertical, power-feed	319	779.6	2,444
c. Universal	c. Universal, power-feed	713	1,675.2	2,350
d. Bench	d. Hand-feed	252	77.4	307
7. Boring machines	7. Boring machines, horizontal and vertical	598	3,352.4	5,606
8. Threading machines	8. Pipe-cutting and threading machines	2,281	1,344.1	589
9. Grinding machines	9. Grinding machines, cylindrical, plain	1,017	2,942.5	2,893

Source - Biennial Census of Manufactures, 1927 (Washington: Department of Commerce, Bureau of the Census, 1930), pp. 1093-1100.

Table C (ii-b)

Soviet Production of Metal-Cutting Machine Tools (1000 of U.S. dollars, 1927) and Production Index (per cent of 1934)

	1927-28	1928-29	1929-30	1931	1932	1933	1934 [a]	1935 [a]	1936 [a]	1937 [a]
Metal-cutting machine tools										
1. Turning lathes	798	1,438	3,170	6,791	6,845	7,519	8,731	6,581	7,939	12,092
2. Turret lathes	0	0	0	75.3	1,484	3,040	4,860	5,561	5,541	8,897
3. Drilling machines	235	414	932	2,989	2,940	2,238	2,138	-	-	-
4. Planers, vertical and horizontal	1,725	3,780	6,031	8,499	10,180	9,842	10,940	13,835	16,730	19,630
5. Slotters	177	25	177	55.6	233	450	506	-	-	-
6. Milling machines (total) [b]	80	310	280	1,100	1,600	2,400	2,400	3,100	4,300	7,044
7. Boring machines	56	662	168	.39	376	533	869	690	970	1,402
8. Threading machines	64.8	318	307	273	507	475	501	-	-	-
9. Grinding machines	52.1	217	448	1,530	1,370	1,790	3,214	2,590	5,448	5,329
Total	3,187.9	7,164	11,513	21,352	25,535	28,287	34,159	32,357	40,928	54,394
Working total	3,188	7,164	11,510	21,350	25,540	28,290	34,160	32,360	40,930	54,390
per cent of 1934	9.33	21.0	33.7	62.5	74.8	82.8	100.0			
Selected total							31,014	32,360	40,930	54,390
per cent of 1934							100.0	104.3	132.0	175.4
Production index (per cent of 1934)	9.33	21.0	33.7	62.5	74.8	82.8	100.0	104.3	132.0	175.4

[a] The quantity relatives for 1935-1937 are computed for fewer items than for the other years, and the base figure for 1934 is correspondingly reduced. It is assumed that the production of the missing items in the years 1935-1937 moved with the index computed for the available items.

[b] A classification of milling machines even by major types was available only for the years 1932 and 1933. The weighted average price for all milling machines in 1932 is $1,448 and for 1933, $1,688. $1,500 has been taken arbitrarily as the price weight for all milling machines for all years.

Table C (iii-a)

Derivation of Census Unit Values for Hoisting and Handling Equipment

Commodity		U.S. Census Data		
Soviet Terminology	U.S. Census Terminology	Quantity	Value ($1000)	Unit Value (dollars)
1. Overhead traveling cranes, electric	1. Overhead traveling cranes, electric	2,149	27,987	13,023
2. Overhead traveling cranes, hand-operated	2. Overhead traveling cranes, hand-powered	1,042	1,258	1,207
3. Railway cranes, steam-operated	3. Cranes, locomotive, except wrecking	322	10,292	31,963
4. Electric hoisting cranes (freight and passenger)	4. Electric chain hoists	30,401	5,048	166

Source

Census of Manufactures, 1947 (Washington: Department of Commerce, Bureau of the Census, 1949), vol. II ("Statistics by Industry"); (1) overhead cranes, p. 686; (2) other cranes, p. 648.

Table C (iii-b)

Soviet Production of Hoisting and Handling Equipment (1000 U.S. dollars, 1947) and Production Index (per cent of 1934)

	1927-28	1928-29	1929-30	1931	1932	1933	1934	1935	1936	1937	1941
1. Overhead traveling cranes											
a. Electric	599	1,220	1,390	1,680	5,990	6,750	4,180	5,350	6,920	8,070	6,512
b. Hand-operated	18.1	54.3	104	257	199	229	21.7	142	186	216	181
2. Railway cranes, steam-operated[a]	0	31.9	0	384	3,900	4,830	2,650	3,640	4,700	5,470	-
3. Electric hoisting cranes, freight and passenger	25.7	27.6	36.4	40.7	64.6	61.9	42.5	41.8	46.5	41.5	101
Total	642.8	1,333.8	1,530.4	2,361.7	10,153.6	11,870.9	6,894.2	9,173.8	11,852.5	13,797.5	(6,794)
Working total	643	1,330	1,530	2,360	10,150	11,900	6,890	9,170	11,900	13,800	(6,794)
Production index	9.3	19.3	22.2	34.3	147	173	100	133	173	200	160

[a] In computing the quantity relative for 1941 "railway cranes, steam-operated" have been omitted both from the 1934 and 1941 totals.

Table C (iv-a)
Derivation of Census Unit Values for Construction and Road-Building Equipment

Commodity		U.S. Census Data		
Soviet Terminology	U.S. Census Terminology	Quantity	Value ($1000)	Unit Value (dollars)
1. Power shovels, single and multiple bucket	1. Power cranes, crawler-mounted, 1/2 - 3/4 cubic yard capacity	6,278	72,584	11,561
2. Stone crushers	2. Crushers, portable	1,435	16,985	11,836
3. Concrete mixers	3. Concrete mixers, portable, under 3 1/2 cu. ft. capacity, hand-operated	22,665	1,612	71
4. Road graders	4. Graders, pull-type and elevating	722	614	850
5. Ditch-digging machines	5. Ditchers and trenchers, ladder-type	216	2,496	11,555
6. Road rollers	6. Rollers			
a. Trailing, 4-ton	a. Pneumatic, drawn	498	528	1,060
b. Self-propelled, 9-11-ton	b. Tandem, self-propelled	1,639	4,822	2,942

Source
Census of Manufactures, 1947 (Washington: Department of Commerce, Bureau of the Census, 1949), vol. II ("Statistics by Industry"), pp. 648-649.

Table C (iv-b)

Soviet Production of Construction and Road-Building Machinery (1000 of U.S. dollars, 1947) and Production Index (per cent of 1934)

	1927-28	1928-29	1929-30	1931	1932	1933	1934 [a]	1935 [a]	1936 [a]	1937 [a]	1941 [a]
Construction and road-building machinery											
1. Power shovels (excavators) total	0	0	0	23	983	1,341	3,190	5,290	6,620	6,030	5,665
2. Stone crushers	746	4,640	9,390	15,490	19,430	15,990	14,160	11,000	7,970	8,900	1,539
3. Concrete mixers	1.8	26.4	51.1	116	78.4	34.9	30.7	45.2	60.7	60.0	-
4. Road graders, total	82	291	654	1,210	990	1,440	1,080	645	603	561	706
5. Ditch-digging machines	450	1,213	4,807	5,650	5,130	4,587	2,946	2,300	-	-	-
6. Road rollers											
a. Trailing 4-ton	0	0	535	825	261	350	476	920	-	-	1,908
b. Self-propelled 9-11-ton	0	0	0	118	203	391	659	1,030	936	1,160	853
Total	1,279.8	6,170.4	15,437.1	23,432	27,075.4	24,133.9	22,541.7	21,230.2			
Working total	1,280	6,170	15,440	23,430	27,080	24,130	22,540	21,230			
Index (per cent of 1934)	5.7	27.4	68.5	103.9	120.1	107.1	100.0	94.2			
Selective total							19,119.7 18,514		16,189.7	16,711	10,671
Working selective total							19,120 18,514		16,190	16,710	10,671
Index (per cent of 1934)							100.0		84.7	87.4	57.6
Production index	5.7	27.4	68.5	103.9	120.1	107.1	100.0	94.8	84.7	87.4	57.6

[a] The quantity relatives for 1936-1937, 1941 are computed for fewer items than for the other years, and the base figure for 1934 is correspondingly reduced. It is assumed that the production of the missing items in the years 1935-1937 moved with the index computed for the available items.

Table C (v-a)
Derivation of Census Unit Values for Articles for Home and General Use

Commodity		U. S. Census Data		
Soviet Terminology	U.S. Census Terminology	Quantity	Value ($1000)	Unit Value (dollars)
Articles for home and general use				
1. Typewriters	1. Typewriters, standard, including long-carriage types	555,021	31,770.4	57
2. Sewing machines, home	2. Sewing machines, household, foot and hand	453,990	9,093.7	20
3. Sewing machines, factory	3. Sewing machines, industrial type, electric	96,928	9,219.3	95
4. Bicycles	4. Bicycles	255,456	5,803.4	23
5. Motorcycles	5. Motorcycles	35,197	8,000.7	227

Source
Biennial Census of Manufactures, 1927 (Washington: Department of Commerce, Bureau of the Census, 1930); sewing machines, p. 1110; typewriters, p. 1117; motorcycles and bicycles, p. 1144.

Table C (v-b)

Soviet Production of Articles for Home and General Use (1000 of U. S. dollars, 1927) and Production Index (per cent of 1934)

Articles for Home and General Use	1927-28	1928-29	1929-30	1931	1932	1933	1934	1935	1936	1937
1. Typewriters	0	0	0	7.9	82.2	229	368	551	974	1,190
2. Sewing machines, home	5,710	8,500	10,800	10,000	6,380	5,320	5,220	8,060	9,390	9,770
3. Sewing machines, factory	0	0	0	234	838	1,530	1,580	1,670	1,940	2,020
4. Bicycles	249	482	814	1,860	2,950	3,050	6,310	7,410	12,800	12,400
5. Motorcycles	0	0	0	3.6	25.4	27.0	82.9	273	1,520	3,400
Total	5,959	8,982	11,614	12,105.5	10,275.6	10,156.0	13,560.9	17,964	26,624	28,780
Working total	5,959	8,982	11,610	12,100	10,280	10,160	13,560	17,960	26,620	28,780
Production index (per cent of 1934)	43.9	66.2	85.6	89.2	75.8	74.9	100.0	132.4	196.3	212.2

Table C (vi-a)
Derivation of Census Unit Values for Textile Machinery

Commodity		U. S. Census Data		
Soviet Terminology	U. S. Census Terminology	Quantity	Value ($1000)	Unit Value (dollars)
1. Carding machines	1. Carding machines	1,163	1,762.6	1,516
2. Water-spinning frames	2. Spinning machines	3,271	3,787.9	1,158
3. Water-doubling frames	3. Doubling and twisting frames, total	1,523	2,418.9	1,588
4. Looms, total	4. Loom s for weaving, except carpet and rug	28,264	15,173.5	537
5. Knitting machines, total	5. Knitting machines, total	30,370	14,344.0	472
Latch needle, total	Latch needle, total	19,933	8,356.8	419

Source - Biennial Census of Manufactures, 1925 (Washington: Department of Commerce, Bureau of the Census, 1928), pp. 1056-1057.

Table C (vi-b)

Soviet Production of Textile Machinery (1000 of U.S. dollars, 1925) and Production Index (per cent of 1934)

Textile Machinery[a]	1932	1933	1934[b]	1935[b]	1941
1. Carding machines (all types)	159	423	893	1,413	2,956
2. Water frames (total)					2,746
a. Spinners	-	193	460	492	-
b. Doublers	62	259	144	351	-
3. Looms, all kinds	161	1,035	1,137	1,980	1,692
4. Knitting machines	852	1,206	1,303	-	802
Total	1,234	3,116	3,937		8,196
Working total	1,230	3,120	3,940		8,200
Index	31.2	79.2	100		208.1
Selected total			2,634	4,236	
Working total			2,630	4,240	
Index			100	161	
Production Index	31.2	79.2	100.0	161.0	208.1

[a] No data are available for the years 1927-28 to 1931 for textile machinery by types.

[b] The quantity relative for 1935 is computed for fewer items than for the other years, and the base figure for 1934 is correspondingly reduced. It is assumed that the production of the missing items in the year 1935 moved with the index computed for the available items.

Table D

Revised Production Indices for Soviet Industry (per cent of 1934)

	1927-28	1928-29	1929-30	1931	1932	1933	1934	1935	1936	1937
A. Indices for Individual Industries										
1. Coal mining	37.8	42.6	50.9	60.4	68.8	81.1	100.0	115.9	134.5	135.3
2. Petroleum extraction	47.4	55.8	76.2	92.5	88.4	88.7	100.0	103.8	112.9	117.7
3. Petroleum refining	43.8	54.4	79.7	98.1	99.6	90.9	100.0	105.7	122.0	130.3
4. Peat extraction	29.1	37.9	44.2	67.7	81.0	75.8	100.0	101.3	122.6	130.0
5. Electric power	23.8	29.6	39.8	50.8	64.4	77.8	100.0	125.1	157.0	173.0
6. Ferrous metals	42.7	49.5	58.7	56.4	61.6	70.9	100.0	127.7	162.1	170.2
7. Nonferrous metals	31.0	38.4	49.5	55.8	62.1	65.0	100.0	151.2	207.7	230.0
8. Ore mining	30.5	43.7	52.6	49.8	54.6	64.8	100.0	128.3	143.0	150.3
9. Chemical industry	34.9	44.8	58.9	63.6	65.6	74.1	100.0	121.0	151.0	185.9
10. Coke industry	29.4	35.1	43.6	47.5	59.2	71.9	100.0	117.7	139.9	139.2
11. Grease, tallow, soap, and perfume	64.5	73.6	69.3	70.4	84.5	57.7	100.0	112.0	123.3	147.1
12. Rubber industry	24.8	21.7	27.7	47.6	60.0	56.5	100.0	107.8	163.0	218.2
13. Match industry	60.7	75.1	103.4	84.2	61.9	75.4	100.0	119.1	91.2	78.6
14. Lumber and plywood	43.9	53.8	71.3	77.9	80.3	88.9	100.0	93.5	109.8	112.6
15. Paper industry	50.3	68.0	87.5	89.3	84.6	89.5	100.0	113.3	134.9	147.0
16. Cement industry	52.4	63.2	85.1	94.4	98.5	76.7	100.0	127.0	165.6	154.5

17. Building bricks	36.0	75.8	83.9	91.4	99.0	77.6	100.0	113.6	168.1	175.4
18. Glass industry	57.2	66.9	79.6	75.8	75.2	70.7	100.0	135.6	175.6	147.2
19. Leather tanning	98.5	116.4	137.6	143.7	135.0	101.7	100.0	101.0	101.9	102.9
20. Textile industry	82.6	89.8	83.9	85.1	87.3	90.4	100.0	105.0	132.7	163.5
21. Leather footwear	39.2	64.6	99.9	114.8	112.2	106.3	100.0	119.8	128.0	217.6
22. Food industry	61.5	57.9	60.4	82.2	77.0	81.3	100.0	117.6	133.7	147.5
23. Machinery	27.5	39.1	48.3	64.6	70.9	89.5	100.0	156.7	172.4	172.0
B. Indices for Industrial Groups										
24. Large-scale industry[a]	46.9	55.1	63.1	72.5	76.2	82.8	100.0	123.6	146.4	160.5
25. Large-scale industry (adjusted for coverage)[a]	43.7	52.4	60.6	71.5	75.2	83.8	100.0	128.7	150.1	162.2
26. Fuel[b]	37.4	43.3	52.6	65.3	73.1	81.1	100.0	112.1	130.0	132.5
27. Building materials[c]	44.9	62.8	77.2	82.3	85.6	81.6	100.0	109.2	141.8	138.9

[a] Includes fisheries, excludes lumbering.
[b] Includes coal mining, crude-oil production, and peat production.
[c] Includes sawn lumber and plywood, cement, building bricks and glass.

INDEX